Best Kept
Secrets

Best Kept Secrets

From Invisible Walk-ons
to Life Champions

Charles Thomas Jr.

WESTBOW
PRESS®
A DIVISION OF THOMAS NELSON
& ZONDERVAN

WestBow Press books may be ordered through booksellers or by contacting:

WestBow Press
A Division of Thomas Nelson & Zondervan
1663 Liberty Drive
Bloomington, IN 47403
www.westbowpress.com
1 (866) 928-1240

Cover Design by Stan Webb

ISBN: 978-1-9736-7199-2 (sc)
ISBN: 978-1-9736-7201-2 (hc)
ISBN: 978-1-9736-7200-5 (e)

Library of Congress Control Number: 2019911710

Print information available on the last page.

WestBow Press rev. date: 8/28/2019

▌CONTENTS

Acknowledgments vii

Dedication ix

Public Service Announcement xi

INTRODUCTION   The Power of Language xiii

CHAPTER 1   The Walk-on Manifesto: Why We Play 1

CHAPTER 2   The Courage to Try 8

CHAPTER 3   Fear, Insecurity, and Doubt 13

CHAPTER 4   Practice as Games 23

CHAPTER 5   The Power of Coaches 29

CHAPTER 6   Healers and Creatives 39

CHAPTER 7   Life After Sports 49

CHAPTER 8   How Can I Help? 58

CHAPTER 9   From the Bench to the Boardroom 64

CHAPTER 10   The Spartan Way 72

CHAPTER 11   In Their Own Words 90

CHAPTER 12   No Longer a Secret 123

CHAPTER 13   The Walk-on Way 129

ACKNOWLEDGMENTS

Thank you to everyone who walked with me on this journey. Thank you to those who helped me. Thank you to those who chose otherwise. Thank you to my wife and kids for the constant support and reassurance. Thank you to my moms for encouraging me to carry on in my efforts to offer something of value to humanity. Thank you to my dad for once again saying, "I love you and I'm proud of you." Thank you to my youngest sister for always being in my corner.

Alex, Dani, Andrew, and Sky, thank you. Thank you a trillion times for sharing even a small piece of your journey with me. Thank you for your willingness to be vulnerable and offer a small portion of your story with others. Thank you for your pursuit of and commitment to excellence.

Thank you to Darnell, Ed, Janet, Shaun, Daryl, Susan, and Erica for providing constructive feedback to sharpen my thinking and writing. PJ and Ed, thank you for offering names for consideration as I worked to find members of my walk-on tribe who were willing to shine a light on a piece of the journey. Grandma and Aunt Yvonne, thank you. Although you are no longer with us, thank you for reinforcing the concept that I should not let the story die inside of me.

Your words transformed my life and will forever inspire, motivate, and fortify me to be better and do better. Thank you!

Thank you to my WestBow Press family for making another dream become a reality.

▰ DEDICATION

I dedicate this book to my Aunt Yvonne.

I completed this work in less than one month because I wanted Aunt Yvonne to read it before her transition. I don't share that timeline to be an exhibitionist. People have written books way quicker than that. Viktor Frankl, for example, wrote *Man's Search for Meaning* in nine days.

I offer that to inform you that I failed. When I started writing *Best Kept Secrets*, I knew that I was on a short timeline because my Aunt Yvonne was battling stage 4 pancreatic cancer. In addition to my moms, Aunt Yvonne was a consummate encourager. She inadvertently gave me the title for the book. She would get me on the phone and say, "Junior, you need to listen. I've told you stop being a secret, boi. Let your light shine. Be a champion. Be a leader worthy of following. Stop wasting time. You won't live forever."

I wanted her to read this book before it was too late. I wanted her to know that I was working to become a champion. I wanted her to know that I no longer desired to be a secret and wanted to encourage others to let their lights shine as well. I wanted her to know that I am striving to be a leader worthy of following. I wanted to hear her say, "Well done, young man" one more time.

I failed.

I started writing on 13 November 2018 and finished all chapters except chapter 11, which captures the lived experiences of some of my fellow tribe members, by 11 December 2018. By then, it was too late. Aunt Yvonne began her final walk towards the bench during the week of 3 December 2018 and checked out of the game on 15 December 2018 at 12:03 am … three minutes after my mom's, her sister's, birthday. Moms was sitting right next to Aunt Yvonne's bed when her spirit left the room and slammed the door. That was her way of saying, "Peace. I'm on my way to Heaven."

She didn't get the chance to read this before her transition, but I can still hear her saying, "Well done, young man!"

No longer am I willing to be a secret. I decided to finally listen. I will continually strive to be a champion and lift others as I climb. It's a mandate. Aunt Yvonne said so.

Thank you for the encouragement, Aunt Yvonne. Thank you for your belief in me. Thank you for walking with me every step of the way for as long as God allowed you to do so. Thank you for your gentleness. Thank you for your patience. Thank you for your kindness. Thank you for your counsel. Thank you for your courage. Thank you for being a leader worthy of following. Thank you for lifting us as you climbed. The world was definitely a better place with you in it.

Love you, Aunt Yvonne. We all do. See you when I get there.

I also dedicate this book to those who started the tribe. Thanks for allowing me to join. To those of you who recently joined or will join soon, welcome.

■ PUBLIC SERVICE ANNOUNCEMENT

If you choose to invest time in reading this book, prepare yourself for higher-level thinking, emotions, thoughtfulness, intentional energy, and focused engagement. While the context of *Best Kept Secrets* highlights the sports journey, it is not only about sports. It is also about life. The life game that we play is not for the weak. It is for the battle tested. It is for the courageous. It is for those who understand their *why*.

Transitioning from best kept secret to life champion is about more than throwing a ball through a hoop, lifting weights, running a ball into an end zone, kicking a ball into or hitting a ball over a net. The transition is about the journey from caterpillar to butterfly. In order to become a life champion, significant effort is required. Craftsmanship and personal mastery are foundational. The mandates to become artisans of our own fortunes, the best of the best, examples of human potential, and love personified are calls to action. Fear and love cannot live in the same place. To transition from best kept secret to life champion, a willingness to carry on despite the odds stacked against us is imperative. Have fun on the journey. Smile. Be a leader worthy of following.

■ INTRODUCTION

The Power of Language

"**A**re you kidding me? He's a walk-on. There is no reason that he should keep scoring on you like that!"

"She's stolen the ball from you three times today. You do realize that she isn't even a scholarship athlete, right?"

"How is it even possible that a walk-on ... a WALK-ON ... finishes every running drill first? Maybe I should put him on scholarship because he clearly wants it more."

"You can give him his gear last. He's a walk-on. He knows the pecking order." (Insert coach's laugh here.) FYI – It wasn't funny.

"Why do you care what she says? Only one of you is on scholarship."

"Shut up. You don't really even count."

"Again, *YOU* don't make any decisions here. (Insert scholarship athlete's name), what do you think?"

Can you imagine someone talking to you that way as an 18 to 22-year-old adult? Can you imagine hearing a grown person talk to one of your teammates that way? In the world of collegiate athletics, it happens more than you think. In our daily interactions with others, we have to remain aware that words can have a transformative effect on the human psyche. Don't fret, though. Everything that's said to us on the field of competition, in the locker room, or in passing isn't all bad.

Consider the more positive affirmations provided by coaches, teammates, and peers:

"I don't know why you do it, but I am surely glad that you do."

"Thank you for being here. Your presence makes us better."

"His work ethic is undeniable. Pay attention and learn from him."

"She's a leader now and she will be an even more powerful leader in the future."

"She reaffirms my faith in the pure desire that one can have about being great in something and then teaching others how to do the same."

"Man, I have to tell you that I have learned so much from you on and off the court. I don't have a genetic brother, but you are as close to a brother as I've ever had."

"Listen to me. I know that sometimes you doubt yourself because you aren't playing a lot. Stop it. You are great. You make everyone better. Know and believe that."

How great is it to have such positivity pushed into a college kid? Imagine hearing a coach, teammate, administrator, professor, or peer talking to one of your teammates that way. In the world of collegiate athletics, it happens regularly. In virtually every interpersonal interaction, the words we choose to deliver can have a transformative effect on the receiver.

Throughout this book, I am going to let you in on our secret. Who is *our*, you ask? Walk-ons, that's who. We are a select group of humans who have achieved the improbable. We are the hidden figures of collegiate athletics. We are ghosts. We are the unsung heroes that make our chosen sport better. We are the life assassins who will persist until our missions are complete. We are the counselors who help our teammates through tough times. We are the pseudo-coaches who understand the mannerisms of everyone around us and can offer insight into the varied motivations of our peers. We are the allies of the marginalized and sometimes forgotten.

We are crowd favorites. We are the ones who fall in love with the process. We are the ones who do it for a cause and not the applause (well, we love the applause too). We are the leaders of men and women before, during, and after college. We are the palm trees that aren't easily broken. We are some of the strongest links in many unbreakable chains. We are gifts. We strive to make others better. We learn to view practices as games. We smile even when we are troubled because we know that it is our choice to pivot or persevere. We live, love, and laugh. We are collegiate athletics' best kept secrets and the world's most formidable opponents.

Best Kept Secrets, at the macro level, is for people who have felt or feel marginalized and/or ostracized because they aren't the superstar in their respective space. At the micro and more personal level, *Best Kept Secrets* is a book by a walk-on, for walk-ons, about walk-ons, and the power that we possess to move from feelings of invisibility to life champions. When I say walk-on, I am talking about any non-scholarship athlete from any sport who was on the team for at least one year and didn't quit because it was *too hard* or *not worth it.* I also include in this tribe of leaders those who tried to walk-on for multiple years, but were never selected. Your desire, resilience, and pursuit of greatness during those college years have undoubtedly proven to be of value in your life post college.

From what I understand, some people now prefer the term

non-scholarship athletes because they don't want to hurt our feelings. For many years after college, I avoided the term walk-on like I was trying to avoid a life terminating event. The word made me sad. It made me angry. It made me feel inferior. For more than a decade, I tried to maneuver almost every conversation that did not occur in a weight room or on a basketball court away from sports. I didn't engage in many conversations about sports because I didn't want people to Google me only to realize that I played fewer minutes in four years than most of my teammates played in a few games.

I practiced for thousands of hours to perform at the Division I level in front of fans for only about an hour. Every time an individual would learn that I was a member of the University of Notre Dame's basketball team, I would engage in some level of self-deprecating humor or qualify my engagement. I would say something like, "It was great having front row seats at every game," or "I mean, yeah, I was a "walk-on" (I would actually use air quotes) my freshman year, but I went there on a strong academic scholarship anyway, so I wasn't trippin … plus the coaches knew me from some summer camps." I developed numerous ways to protect my weak heart. None of them felt real even when I said them, but I needed to say them to feel safe inside of my own mind. Over the years, as I reflected on the power of the walk-on journey, I have learned to better understand the world and my place in it.

I've had the idea for a book like this in my mind for several years now. Let me tell you what triggered this outpouring of emotion. Two dudes in an office were talking about whether collegiate athletes should be paid. I could hear them talking, but couldn't see them. During the conversation, one of the guys said, "Well, it's not an easy decision. It is more complex than people like to think. Some players will get paid more, some less. What about those who offer considerable value in practice, but don't play too much? What about team managers? How do you handle walk-ons?" His colleague responded, "Team managers aren't athletes and don't spend as much time as the real athletes. (His statement was highly flawed. Team managers spend significant amounts of time making sure that things go well for the team.) Also, forget a walk-on (he actually said a more inflammatory word that begins with the letter f). They don't count." I was so mad that I had to leave the area where I was sitting. The protector side of me wanted to verbally eviscerate the dude for speaking so carelessly. The pragmatic, *I want to keep my job side of me*, said deal with him later when emotions aren't as high. My head started hurting and I went to my car to relax. I was on fire. I literally had to take a nap to calm down.

When I woke up, I could tell that I cried in my sleep. Dried up tears were on my face. I neatly packaged my emotions, gathered my thoughts, and decided it was now time to address the issue. I walked back into the office, found the guy with whom I had some level of familiarity, told him I heard the comment, and asked where the other dude sat. He informed me that he didn't work at that location and was only visiting. I addressed the issue and told him to kindly notify his visitor that he and I should have a talk the next time he is here. He laughed. I didn't. I walked away. Three days later, dude and I happened to be in the same general vicinity in an office building. He experienced a verbal evisceration. The irony of the conversation was that dude was a former scholarship athlete who worked for a former walk-on. A few weeks after that conversation, I started writing.

Please do not misinterpret the essence of the words on this page or the forthcoming pages. *Best Kept Secrets* is not a comparison between scholarship athletes and walk-ons. The intent of this book is to uplift an often-forgotten tribe of people—my brothers and sisters who paid to play. My aim is to inspire future and current walk-ons to continually strive to offer value and reaffirm in former walk-ons the power, resilience, focus, supreme tenacity, and audacity to succeed against all odds. I have lived in both worlds. A walk-on who earned a scholarship, but maintained the walk-on label. You see the word *but* in the preceding sentence. I wrote it as if the word *walk-on* is less than because I used to feel that way. Not anymore. I embrace the label and challenge anyone to make me feel otherwise.

Best Kept Secrets is an outpouring of love. This is a manifesto for my forgotten tribe members. This is a clarion call for athletes and non-athletes who aspire to summit their chosen mountains. The elements of character that many walk-ons embody should be emulated by everyone to offer something of value in their specific space. The remainder of this book will illustrate stories and offer insights into how the walk-on mentality can prove to be extremely advantageous. This work will verbally illustrate how and why my experiences as a walk-on prepared me to live a life of service and transition from feelings of invisibility to undeniable forces that have allowed me and other walk-ons in the world to become life champions.

Keep an open mind and heart as you read. Don't take offense. Understand that these words are based on my lived experiences and the lived experiences of others. Nothing within these pages is law. My offered insights are based on life learned lessons, and I am obligated to share. Clear your mind. Open your heart. Everything will be alright. Let's work.

CHAPTER 1

The Walk-on Manifesto: Why We Play

The walk-on manifesto is as follows: As a member of the tribe, I will do my very best to pursue excellence as a demonstration of human potential. I will commit myself to being the best player that I can be so that I can offer value and be of service to my teammates. When I am mad, I will work harder. When I am sad, I will work harder. When I am happy, I will work harder. When new players arrive, I will share my experiences and offer insight to make them better. I am okay. I give myself permission to be great. I choose to be here. There are no limits. I disavow limited thinking and similar constructs. I will push beyond any self-imposed mental or physical barriers. As long as I breathe, I will lead. As long as I am able, I will seek feedback that will make me and, by extension, my teammates better. I trust myself to do what is right. I will be loyal to the name on the front of the jersey while creating moments of truth, beauty, and clarity for the name on the back of the jersey. I will continually commit myself to move beyond the status quo to offer something of significance. I choose to be here and will offer my best self for as long as I can. This, I pledge, from now until the day I transition from this earth.

(Note: I literally just made that up as I was typing. I read it after I wrote it and said to myself, "Hmmm. That's dope. And true.") Now the world has a walk-on manifesto. You're welcome ☺.

There are numerous reasons why we play. I can offer several based on my experiences and the experiences of the multiple dozens of walk-ons I have met and talked with over the last decade and a half. To be concise in delivery, I will offer three. First, we play to realize a dream. Second, we play to test our athletic prowess against the best in our chosen sport at our chosen level. Third, we play to show that it can be done. We play to push ourselves. We know that we are our own competition and want to win the internal battle of me versus me.

Realize a Dream

It is undeniable that many people have a desire to play sports at the Division I level in order to give themselves a chance to make it professionally. Players at the Division II and Division III levels also make it professionally. I did not include those levels in the introductory sentence because my experiences are not in that world, and I lack the knowledge to speak experientially about it. That said, I am comfortable and confident asserting that the scholarship and non-scholarship athletes at the DII level and non-scholarship athletes at the DIII level (scholarships labeled as *athletic* are not offered to DIII athletes) mirror many of the same characteristics of those individuals at the DI level.

It is equally irrefutable that those who make it to the highest levels and play professionally fly in rarefied air. Professional athletes are unique. Walk-ons are unique. Now, don't get me wrong. I am not suggesting that kids dream to be a walk-on. We don't. We dream about playing. We dream about wearing the jersey. We dream about people chanting our names. We dream about hitting our first home run, scoring our first goal, catching our first pass, making our first jump shot, and so forth. We have similar dreams as others about being on the big stage. The difference is in the path from dream to realization.

Many walk-ons were high school stars. Some were superstars who chose to decline scholarship offers because they didn't get an offer from their school of choice. Instead of listening to what everyone else wanted, they chose to listen to their hearts and traverse the walk-on road. I know that's my story. I also know that is the story of countless other individuals who opted out of the athletic scholarship route to achieve their objective at their *heart school*. Saying that you will climb a mountain, dreaming about climbing that mountain, engaging in the training regimen to climb that mountain, and summiting the peak of that mountain are beautiful things. Many of the walk-ons that I've encountered on my life journey are those metaphorical mountain climbers. A dream to achieve the improbable scares many people. Not us. We revel in the challenge of doing something that even our internal selves arguably consider far external to the norm.

At the energetic and innocent age of nine, I knew that I wanted to earn an opportunity to play professional basketball, read books, write books, and be on TV on a regular basis. (I have checked the box on the first three. The fourth will be realized at some point in the not-too-distant future.) I was unaware of the actual process to be like Isaiah Thomas, Joe Dumars, Tim Hardaway, or Kevin Johnson, but I knew and spoke that I wanted to be in the big leagues. Kid stuff, of course. Still, I learned a long time ago to speak what I seek until I see what I've said.

My DI visions didn't come into focus until tenth grade, and my visions of being an Irishman didn't materialize until the summer before my senior year. I did not have to be pushed. The vision pulled me. My dream of being a Division I level college athlete permeated my being and propelled my imagination into an alternative universe. I have talked to dozens of former walk-ons and heard the same excitement in their voices about wanting to play collegiate sports. Again, the dream wasn't necessarily about being a walk-on. It was about getting to the top of their chosen mountain. The dream was about winning against themselves. For some, it was about proving other people wrong. It's a magnificent feeling to dream about something that consumes your entire reality and then wake up to catch the dream.

A Test of Skill, Wit, and Might

Walk-on does not mean unskilled. It simply means that the individual is not on an athletic scholarship. Throughout my varied conversations with walk-ons, and based on my own experiences, it is undeniable that the tests associated with proving yourself to yourself and to others is exhilarating. To learn that you are, in fact, worthy of representing your selected college or university is soul-stirring. Challenging Goliath is one thing. Slaying him is an entirely different ball game.

Initially, the excitement carries you through grueling training sessions. The adrenaline, hope, and optimism that saturate your presence are mesmerizing. Ultimately, the youthful cheerfulness fades. You become almost obsessively focused on the pursuit of your chosen objective of making the team and showcasing your talents to the world.

In order to make it, your focus has to be singular. You have to fall in love with the process. You have to believe that you believe. You have to commit to taking a step forward each day, even if the step is only a baby step. Practically, this means engaging in the predetermined activities to hone your craft—shooting a thousand shots per day, lifting weights, running, swimming, playing pickup games, practicing varied soccer kicks, running routes, batting cage practice, etc. If you aren't willing to commit, you choose not to play at the highest of collegiate levels. Committing to the aforementioned activities does not guarantee success, but it enhances the probability of goal achievement.

Your willingness and ability to engage in short term sacrifices for long term gains confirm your resolve to compete. You will get stronger, smarter, faster, wiser, and even more focused on your quest to greatness. You will see your progress and decide to work even harder. It is a virtuous cycle in your favor.

When the opportunity to showcase your skills to future teammates and coaches presents itself, you will be ready. If you do what you are supposed to do in preparation to catch that dream, you will be afforded the opportunity, and rightly so, to do what you want to do. Knowing that you have put in the requisite hours during your pursuit of excellence will make dream realization that much sweeter when you put on that practice or game jersey for the first time.

Pursue Excellence as a Demonstration of Human Potential

Limiting beliefs cause many people to fail before they have even tried. Fear of failure, fear of success, fear of the unknown, fear of naysayers, fear of one's own potential, and so on can prove to be quite debilitating for some individuals. Not us. We ask to be thrown into the lion's den because we know that we will ultimately lead the pride. Cartesian philosophy teaches us cogito, ergo sum—I think, therefore I am. The walk-on corollary to that school of thought is I do, therefore I am. (I don't know how to Latinize that saying, and I'm not even going to leverage Google Translate to figure it out, but I am sure that it is as magnificent as cogito, ergo sum.)

Renaissance humanism teaches us to pursue excellence as confirmation of human ability. The myriad of walk-ons that I have talked to during my life journey echo that sentiment. We know that we can achieve the improbable and set out to do it. This is not a comparison with anyone else. Those who embody a comparable philosophy are legion. I'm simply talking about the walk-on tribe right now—my tribe. I also don't want it to sound like walking on to a Division I or Division II college or university is an impossibility. It's not. It's also not necessarily that easy. Only a select few have the opportunity to wear a jersey at the college level. You can search and verify the statistics online. Apologies for the digression. Back to the third reason why we play.

The idea of achieving the improbable fuels us. A lot of walk-ons who make teams are not preferred walk-ons or recruited walk-ons. They are unrecruited walk-ons and must try out with everyone else to make the team. Even as a recruited walk-on, your spot is not guaranteed. Consistent, focused, and thoughtful daily action is required to secure the honor of wearing that jersey. The privilege to wear that jersey and climb a mountain worth the time, attention, and effort is most exhilarating.

On your ascent, you will hear an orchestra of negative feedback. Some internal and some external. We learn to disregard that. The thrill of victory is more poetic than the agony of defeat. Akin to mostly everything else in life, doing something simply to show that it can be done offers sustaining value to more than just the individual who achieved the improbable. Seeing someone do something that others believed unlikely and sometimes impossible is motivating, inspiring, and can lead to emotions that defy reason and logic. This is why we play.

Every day when you look in the mirror, you can serenely or energetically say, even if internally, I can do it. Every day when you put on your armor, you know that you are not only watching yourself, but that there are also tens of thousands (maybe, many millions) of others that you can inspire. Maybe more. You engage in focused thinking. You engage in deliberate action. You have locked in on your target and understand your mission. You are a life assassin, a life champion, and will not quit until your mission is accomplished. And on that day, oh that glorious day, when your name is called and you put on that jersey, you can look into the mirror with your chest out and shoulders back because you achieved the improbable. You not only pursued excellence as validation of human capability, but you also caught it. This is why we play.

■ CHAPTER 2

The Courage to Try

In the preceding chapter, I offered a few reasons why we play. While it sounds cool to realize a dream, test your skills, and pursue excellence as a demonstration of human potential, none of that can happen without courage. We regularly look at people who have accomplished the improbable with admiration without knowing the journey. I've had the blessed fortune to interview hundreds of people on a variety of topics. The one constant that rings true for those individuals who identified a mountain to climb and subsequently summited that mountain is courage. I frequently talk about integrity, honesty, decency, and courage as foundations of character that command respect. Courage, however, is likely the most important. Dr. Maya Angelou is credited with saying that courage is the greatest of all the virtues. I agree. From my personal experiences and the stories that others have shared with me, courage is not indicative of the absence of fear. It implies that you have a heightened sense of awareness and are willing to enter the realm of the unknown.

It is easy not to try. It is easy to make excuses for lack of engagement. It is easy to run in place, but it takes heart to put yourself in a position to succeed. It takes heart to actively engage in life. It takes heart to move forward. Some people are paralyzed by fear and the thought of failure. Others choose not to take the metaphorical shot because success is a daunting prospect. Once they prove to themselves and others that their self-imposed beliefs were unwarranted, they must continue to play at a high level. That is scary for some people.

There is an adage that says, *sticks and stones may break my bones, but words will never hurt me.* False. All the way false. Wars have commenced, families have been ripped apart, and homicides, suicides, and an array of other undesirable actions have taken place because of words. It takes strong-mindedness to disregard the onslaught of negative emotions, damaging self-talk, and detrimental feedback from naysayers in order to carry on.

During the summer of 2009, I attended a high school summer league basketball game with some new acquaintances to watch their boys play. The difference in the language of the two fathers with their respective sons was remarkable. The impact on the boys was even more amazing. After the game, we were all talking and dad 1 *jokingly* says, (in his son's presence), "He's gotten some partial offers from some small to mid DI schools, but he wants to play with the big boys. He keeps talking about he will walk on, but *he doesn't have it in him.* He only had 17 (points) and nine (rebounds) tonight … you see how big that boy is! He has to do better." Yikes. The looks of dejection and rejection on his son's face were unbelievable. I was mortified that a dad would say such a thing to his son. I was even more saddened that he chose to devalue his boy in front of others. The other dad and I told him to forget what his dad said and give it his best shot wherever he decided to go if, in fact, he chose to attend a school that did not offer him a basketball scholarship. We were too late. The damage was already done. It was clear that such degrading and confidence-shattering language was consistently used and accepted.

Now, juxtapose dad 1's comments to dad 2's words to his son. In front of the group, dad 2 says, "Lil Johnny (name changed) is a fighter. He has some offers too, but I keep telling him to aim high and make it happen. We don't know what will happen if he does try out, but we definitely know what will happen if he doesn't. I believe in him, though. He for certain has what it takes to make it happen." Lil Johnny lit up like the stars in the sky. A 6' 5" kid looked at his dad with a level of admiration that was awe-inspiring. It was a cool experience.

Fast forward a few months. Boy 1 and boy 2 attend separate colleges. I don't need to let you know that boy 1 didn't make it. You already knew that. The sadder part is that he didn't even try. Fear of failure, fear of success, fear of proving people right, and fear of proving people wrong all played a role in his decision to no longer hunt his dream of playing high level Division I basketball. Boy 2 was exactly as his dad described him, a fighter. He fought and did what he had to do to make that team. His journey, however, was not without challenges. His level of engagement required colossal fortitude.

Lil Johnny's journey to representing the names on the front and back of the jersey required resolve and resilience. While he dealt with many setbacks, they did not prevent continued forward progression. During his senior season and after his high school graduation, Lil Johnny shot at least 750 shots per day. He lifted weights, ran, played pick-up games with athletes from the hometown university, practiced his ball-handling, and ate well. He was a young man on a mission.

When he arrived on campus, he increased his output. He shot 1000 shots per day, ran harder, lifted more, and studied more than he ever had. He wanted to show himself that he could make it. He knew that he had to try. There were many obstacles that he had to overcome during his quest to dream achievement—harder than anticipated classes, dudes who didn't want him to make it, NCAA rules that prevented him from talking to coaches and actually *practicing* with the team, a sprained ankle, a broken finger, and a breakup. None of that mattered. Lil Johnny had heart. Lil Johnny had the resoluteness to try. And try he did. He played pick-up games with the team, pick-up games in the city, and pick-up games with students who had no interest in *playing at the next level*, but were absolutely willing to help him get better.

During the three days of tryouts during his freshman year, Lil Johnny gave it his best shot. He ran, defended, scored, cheered for his teammates, and he was coachable. None of it was enough. He was not selected. Johnny was devastated. His father told him that everything would be alright and to try again next year. Lil Johnny believed his dad. He continued to work out every day. He ran. He shot. He lifted. He studied. He believed his dad's words even when he didn't believe in himself. He tried. Day after day, same story. During the fall of his sophomore year, he was ready to tryout again. This time, his work ethic, talent, and desire to achieve his goal were undeniable. Lil Johnny made the team. #DreamAchieved. Lil Johnny now had the opportunity to represent the names on the front and the back of the jersey.

The journey was not easy, but Lil Johnny had the resolve and patience to try. He had the will to win. Sometimes that is all it takes. Sprinkle a little bit of backbone on top of desire, focus, commitment, and determination and bingo … cake baked. The path to goal achievement has not, is not, and will never be straight. We have to be ready and willing to run as fast as we can for as long as we can and jump over as many obstacles as mandatory to achieve the desired objectives. Now, several years post college, Lil Johnny is still using the life learned lessons he acquired before and during college to be a life champion. He knows that all he needs to make it happen is the boldness to try.

■ CHAPTER 3

Fear, Insecurity, and Doubt

Fear, insecurity, and doubt impact scholarship players, non-scholarship athletes, students, government officials, academics, parents, teachers, CEOs, and every other type of human who walks this earth. We are not excluded from that less than holy triumvirate. Regardless of the words we hear, and the niceties exhibited during your tenure as a walk-on, our journey is a little different. That is okay. There will be many days prior to making the team, during your assignment as a collegiate level athlete, and in your professional life in which you will be afraid. You will exhibit some level of insecurity. You will most certainly doubt yourself.

The aforementioned are not restricted to walk-ons, but those feelings are definitely heightened prior to making it and certainly experienced during the collegiate journey. Don't fret. Keep reading. Indulge me as I offer some pragmatic recommendations regarding how to handle fear, insecurity, and doubt at each level. And yes, the levels and types of fears, insecurities, and doubts do vary at the different life stages.

Fear, Insecurity, and Doubt – Before Making the Team

Prior to making a team, many of us are anxious. We are not fearful of the process, but unsure of the outcomes. My direct experiences and indirect experiences as a result of talking with others indicate that fear of failure, fear of success, and fear of the unknown play major roles when en route to making the team.

Fear of failure can be paralyzing. It creates feelings of anxiety, apprehension, confusion, and a litany of other possibly demoralizing and progress-reducing feelings. Fear of failure has made many people quit during the earliest phases on even the shortest of journeys. The fear that you face early on will challenge your identity. You might be afraid to ask for help because you don't want to face rejection. The fear of sharing your dreams with others can be a daunting proposition. What if they project their weaknesses and dashed hopes on you? You will likely feel the fear of having someone directly express that they do not believe in your dream of making it and by extension, they don't believe in you, which will enhance your feelings of uncertainty. It's a vicious cycle. At least it can be for some. It's an unnerving prospect to fight so many external battles when you are already battling with yourself. Stay focused. Don't let it happen *to* you. Even if it does happen *to* you, use it as a learning experience and know that it is actually happening *for* you. It's all a matter of perspective.

Fear of *success* (whatever that means to you) also happens. Sometimes the expectations associated with *success* also prevent people from moving forward. Once you have proven that you have the knowledge, skills, and abilities to achieve your heart's desires, you can no longer go back to a previous version of you. Well, you can but doing so is not advisable. Success raises the bar. Success puts a bullseye on your back. Everyone wants to associate with a winner. Those who associate choose to do so for three reasons: 1) to offer their assistance in genuine ways as you climb the mountain, 2) to learn what you are doing and potentially ask for your assistance so that they can also summit their desired mountains, 3) to drag you down or push you off the mountain once you reach its apex. Pretty simple. The challenges associated with *success* are numerous and diverse. Getting what you want is hard. Keeping what you want is harder. That scares some people. Stay focused. Don't let it happen *to* you. Even if it does happen *to* you, use it as a learning experience and know that it is actually happening *for* you.

Fear of the unknown also plays a role in one's willingness to engage in pursuing a goal. Discovering new paths can be a daunting individual or team level task. Not knowing where these paths may lead prevents many people from even trying to progress. When you decide to try out for the team, a myriad of what-if scenarios will creep into your mind. You will ask many *what, who, why, and how* questions. If you choose to consult with others, you will receive a constellation of insight. Some of the counsel will be experience-based and informed. Some insight and advice will be complete nonsense, based on indirect exposure to what the counselor deems to be some version of truth. Stay focused. Don't let it happen *to* you. Even if it does happen *to* you, use it as a learning experience and know that it is actually happening *for* you.

Insecurity and doubt are tricky little monsters before making the team, regardless if you try out at as a freshman or senior. He will knock on your door when you least expect it. When you answer, he will pretend to be confidence. He will pretend to be a house made of bricks. That initial house, however, is made with straws. It takes time to build a solid foundation and a home made of bricks. Insecurity will tell you that you aren't ready. Doubt will scream that you didn't put in the demanded effort to represent the names on the front and back of the jersey on a big scale. Insecurity will ask why you deserve to get what you want. Doubt will communicate to you that many have tried and many have failed. Insecurity will make you question your past successes and heighten the impact of your past failures. Doubt will make you think that everyone is tracking your every movement and rooting for you to fail. Insecurity will make you take yourself too seriously and not allow you to laugh on those days when things don't go your way. Doubt will loudly and proudly co-sign everything insecurity says. Stay focused. Don't let it happen *to* you. Even if it does happen *to* you, use it as a learning experience and know that it is actually happening *for* you.

Fear, insecurity, and doubt have ruined the lives and careers of many people. As you prepare to climb your mountain of choice, allow me to offer you five recommendations regarding how to effectively handle fear, insecurity, and doubt when they sneak up on you.

1 – Mimic nature's wisdom. When an animal in the wild gets scared, it acts. It does not sit and ponder the various outcomes associated with inaction. A frightened gazelle knows that if it does not run, it will die. The same is true for you. Hesitation can prove fatal. If you choose not to act when you have the chance, you may not be provided with another opportunity. While hesitation or inaction might not literally kill you in this scenario, it can kill your dream. Even if you are afraid, you must act. Do it scared. Don't overthink. Run as long as required to achieve your goal. Even if you miss the

proverbial shot, at least you will be able to look at yourself in the mirror and know that you had the courage to try.

2 – Believe that you believe. You need to believe in you. If you don't, who will? More importantly, if you don't believe in you, why should anyone else? Self-belief, not egotism, is critical when embarking on any journey of consequence. Neither arrogance nor conceit are appropriate during any phase of your journey. Strive to remain free of delusions of grandeur. #BeHumble. Self-belief enhances your endurance and confidence. Knowing that you have what it takes to climb the mountain is powerful. Believing it is even more potent.

3 – Find a circle of people who are truly rooting for your success. Sticks in a bundle are stronger together. As young adults, pride can prevent us from asking for help. We think that we know everything and want to do it our way. That's silly. Don't do that. Employ humility to ask for assistance and be or become sufficiently wise to accept genuine help when offered. When playing the game of life, you are not alone. Remember that. Someone has done what you are trying to do. Seek their counsel and support. At some point, you will be in the position to return the favor.

4 – Smile in the face of fear, insecurity, and doubt. Actually, laugh. The life journey is full of unknowns and change. Other than death, change is the only constant in life. At some point, you will transition from this earthly realm. Unknowns are all around us, and change is inevitable. Embrace the fear, insecurity, and doubt. Change what you can change, fix what you can fix, and do what you can do. Play your role and God will play His. Nothing is happening *to* you, it is happening *for* you.

5 – Keep trying until you no longer have the option to do so. It will serve you well in life. Samuel Beckett said, "Try again. Fail again. Fail

better." Confucius said, "Our greatest glory is not in never falling, but in rising every time we fall." My moms says, "Nothin' is wrong with you, boy. Keep trying until you figure it out. Get some help if you need too. Either way, figure it out." Of all the great philosophers, moms is the most profound. Remember what Samuel Beckett, Confucius, and my moms said. Keep trying until you no longer have the energy and then try some more. The world needs people like you.

Fear → Anxiety, Insecurity, and Doubt – During Your Collegiate Tenure

The fear that you feel once you are on the team is different than the fear that can consume you prior to accomplishing your goal. It transitions away from fear to some level of anxiety. Not debilitating anxiety, but anxiety, nonetheless. Fear transitions to some version of anxiety because you have already looked fear in the face and laughed. Seeing the view from the top of the mountain is great.

The new challenge is staying there so that you can enjoy everything that such a view has to offer. The anxiety can kick in because of the recognition that you are now a volunteer at a company of majority paid employees. Volunteers are sometimes not treated the same. Sometimes they do not have access to the same resources to excel in the selected role. Sometimes people devalue their contributions. Sometimes you are marginalized. Every single day you go to work and realize that your best efforts may not be satisfactory.

Every single day, a decision maker can say that we no longer need volunteers for said task. The work analogy also rings true on the field of competition. Although you are offering your services for free, the coach may not deem the delivered services to be of value.

Such consciousness can prove to be anxiety producing. Stay focused. Don't let it happen *to* you. Even if it does happen *to* you, use it as a learning experience and know that it is actually happening *for* you.

One of the main reasons that anxiety can occur during your tenure as a member of the team is because you feel like an imposter. Even though you put in the work, that silly voice in your head telling you that someone made a mistake and you really aren't worthy to represent the names on the front and the back of the jersey is serious business. The voice that tells you to follow your dreams and your heart's desires usually whispers. The voice telling you that you are an imposter screams. The spoken words are unmistakable. Feeling like a fraud can very rapidly decrease your self-confidence, which in turn lessens your ability to perform on the field of competition, which causes you to lose even more self-confidence. This is another vicious cycle that does not benefit you. Stay focused. Don't let it happen *to* you. Even if it does happen *to* you, use it as a learning experience and know that it is actually happening *for* you.

Anxiety heightening situations also increase at the end of a season. The mere thought of having to try out in order to prove yourself again can induce stress, anxiety, apprehension, fear, insecurity, doubt, and a host of other feelings due the unknowns that are sure to be present throughout the process. This situation becomes more anxiety producing when there is a coaching transition. You hope that the current coach offers positive recommendations and insights to the new coach regarding your value to the team. You hope that the new coach is willing to a) talk to you and b) give current and prospective walk-ons the opportunity to be a part of the team. That's a lot to write. It is definitely a lot to think about and deal with in real time. Transitions such as the aforementioned are not easy, but they happen regularly. Not knowing is tough.

Stay focused. Don't let it happen *to* you. Even if it does happen *to* you, use it as a learning experience and know that it is actually happening *for* you.

When you are anxious, insecurity and doubt know that it is time to throw a party in your head. Insecurity will bolster the thought that you aren't really *that* good and inform you that someone really did make a mistake. Doubt will cause you to question even the smallest of slights and/or compliments. Because of your insecurity, you will doubt that the positive comments are authentic and personalize the negative comments. Insecurity will make you challenge what you know to be true about yourself in year one on the team or during year four.

Doubt will make you question your commitment to the person in the mirror. Insecurity will make you think that people are laughing at you when you get in the game instead of cheering for your success. In your head, *wooooooo hoooooooo* can sound like *boooooo*. Doubt will make you freeze when you get in the game. Insecurity will state that if you don't try out next year, you won't have to deal with such feelings anymore. Doubt will loudly and proudly co-sign everything insecurity said. Stay focused. Don't let it happen *to* you. Even if it does happen *to* you, use it as a learning experience and know that it is actually happening *for* you.

Anxiety, insecurity, and doubt have been the culprits behind many people giving up and no longer wanting to play the chosen sport. When you have reached your initial goal of making that team and start to feel the effects of anxiety, insecurity, and doubt, follow these five recommendations to stay in the game.

1 – Leverage your support network. It is normal to feel anxious, insecure, and doubtful at various moments in our lives. Talk to trusted people within your circle and let them know how you feel. It

is completely acceptable to show vulnerability to those individuals and ask for guidance. Even if they have not climbed the mountain that you have climbed, they have climbed a different one. They have surely experienced similar feelings and will be able to offer thoughtful counsel regarding how to best proceed.

2 – Talk to the person in the mirror like you would talk to someone that you are responsible for helping. When you feel anxious, insecure, or doubtful, avoid negative self-talk and negative thoughts. When you hear you talking or thinking negatively about yourself, stop it. Take the time to remember the you who fought so hard to get to where you are. Remember why you trained, practiced, and put in the effort to achieve your goal. Remember the fun you had while trying to climb your mountain. Remember the focus, desire, resilience, patience, faith, and pursuit of excellence that you exemplified early in the journey. Remember your determination. Now, go back to that mindset. Give yourself the same advice when you feel anxious, insecure, and doubtful as you would give to someone else who is in the early phase of his or her journey. Talk purposefully and positively to yourself. Don't simply remember. Act accordingly.

3 – Take comfort in knowing that you are paving the way for others. Representing the names on the front and back of the jersey should not be underestimated. People that you do and don't know are paying attention. Even if you only play one minute, people will know your name. Walking on at a Division I, Division II, or Division III school is no easy task. Many have tried and many have failed. You are one of the select few who had the skill and ability to successfully slay the dragon. People respect you for that. People envy you because of that. People want to be you. Do not take the opportunity to have front row seats at every single game for granted. And if you don't care that others are watching, know that the younger and older versions

of you are watching. Don't allow your present self to betray your past or future selves.

4 – Know that you are there for a reason, even if that reason is only for a season. Do your best while you can because the effort that you put in now will translate to future engagements. You made the team because you offered something of value. Know that. Believe that. Every day when you go to practice, understand that your engagement makes the team better. You should know that the bricks you lay are building the foundation for a beautiful city. You are necessary and appreciated for your efforts. Tell yourself that and respond properly.

5 - Smile in the face of fear, insecurity, and doubt. Actually, laugh. The life journey is full of unknowns and change. Other than death, those are the only two constants in life. At some point, you will transition from this earthly realm. Unknowns are all around us, and change is inevitable. Embrace the fear, insecurity, and doubt. Change what you can change, fix what you can fix, do what you can do. Play your role and God will play his. Nothing is happening *to* you, it is happening *for* you.

Now, I know that future walk-ons and current walk-ons are nodding their heads in agreement while reading this saying, "I'm with you. This is dope. Thanks for dropping these gems." You're welcome. Former walk-ons are reading with anticipation wondering what I will say about the journey post college when you experience heightened awareness, insecurity, and doubt. I have no idea. I am still working to figure that out. Only kidding, I will talk about that too (although I still am trying to figure it out myself). Keep reading. Those nuggets of wisdom are coming in Chapter 7.

▮ CHAPTER 4

Practice as Games

Life is quite easy when you have thoughtful perspectives. Dr. Wayne Dyer said, "When you change the way you look at things, the things you look at change." Eckhart Tolle opined, "Pain is the non-acceptance of what is." I agree with both sages. Often, the pain that we feel is self-inflicted. The anxiety, apprehension, insecurity, and doubt that we sometimes feel are manifestations of our personal perspectives, experiences, and meaning that we attach to varied life situations. Knowing how to effectively protect your heart and mind from yourself and outside influences is one of the main catalysts that will push you to becoming a life champion.

Many people will not become famous. Many people do not even have such aspirations. Some choose to remain anonymous. Even the majority of those who choose to live in the shadows want to be great at their chosen task. Those who argue that they have little to no interest in wearing the craftsman badge are lying to you, themselves, others, or a combination of all three. Those who say otherwise have lost some level of hope, excitement, determination, and zest for life somewhere along the journey.

As walk-ons, many of us are not afforded the opportunity to play big minutes during each game. Well, I will speak for myself. I wasn't afforded that opportunity. Maybe I was good enough. Maybe I wasn't. All I can speak on is the reality of my journey. An analogous story holds true for many people post college, regardless of your sports affiliation during college. Many individuals in the professional environment do not play on the biggest of stages. Everyone isn't going to be in the C-Suite. Not all academics can work at Tier 1 research institutions. The option to become a general in the military is not available for everyone. That does not mean you have the right to loiter and speak in *woulda, shoulda, couldas* all the days of your life. For many walk-ons, practices are our games. The same rule holds true post college. We may not get a chance to perform when the entire world is watching, but we do get the chance to practice our craft every day. That is a very valuable skill to learn. As walk-ons, many of us learn to embrace the gift. The best ones transfer that gift to all aspects of one's life.

When I began to embrace the *practice as games* motto (I will share how I learned of this life philosophy later) during my senior year of college, the journey became more enjoyable. I no longer felt marginalized. The insecurity associated with sitting on the bench lessened. I still hated not playing, but I was no longer as insecure. The pressure to make excuses dissipated. My *sad day* occurrences were less frequent. I think that I even became nicer. That last assertion could be all the way false because I might not be that nice now. I do, however, think I remember feeling that way during that time in my life. All jokes aside, embracing and living the motto of *practice as games* made a tremendous difference in my life journey. Before I offer ideas into how that motto will help you as a productive citizen, allow me to offer some insight into how it will affect you while on the team.

When practices become your games, you will feel less pressure. Not less pressure to perform, but less pressure to defend yourself to yourself when you don't get a chance to play in games. Even if you are a walk-on that plays in every game (even in the first half ☺), viewing practices as games can be quite liberating.

As a walk-on, you should put in extra effort. You should be more vigilant. You should be even more competitive than your counterparts. You are there to get better and make your team better. You are there to learn, teach, and offer value in every way imaginable. The same truisms hold true for your scholarship teammates. I love them, but I am talking to you right now. When you begin to view practices as games, you will notice that three things will happen psychologically even before they occur behaviorally. First, you will be less anxious because of the decrease in self-imposed pressure. Next, you will listen to your coaches and teammates differently. This transition happens because you begin to take things slightly less personally. Finally, you will see differently. Your view of the court will be clearer. You will observe your teammates differently. You will see yourself differently. The aforementioned changes occur when you engage in practice as games because you will better understand your role. You will have clearer expectations of yourself and others.

When you engage in each practice as if it is a game, you will think quicker, your focus will be heightened, and you will be willing to force yourself to move to the next level. Such commitment to excellence and intentional engagement on the court may very well translate into meaningful playing time. It might not. I am certain, however, that if you view practice as meaningless, the likelihood of you ever playing is extremely low.

Viewing practice as games will also afford you the opportunity to push yourself to levels once deemed unimaginable. You will run a little faster. You will jump a little higher. You will smile a little more. You will be in perpetual create mode. You will still experience, apprehension, anxiety, and anger, but it will be more controlled and perceived as less of an attack against you. You don't have to tell anyone that practices are your games. They will see it. They will feel it. You will own it. Your quiet confidence will be deafening. Your leadership will be emulated. Your work ethic will be applauded. You will know that you are doing your best for however long you are afforded the opportunity to do so. Upon completion of your playing career, the practice as games mentality will serve you well in the real world.

The transition from college to the real world is easy for some and harder for others. If you have let the walk-on journey discourage you, varied life situations may be harder to handle when you enter the unstructured, dynamic, loving, cruel, boring, and fun world of adult life. The unknowns, constant life-changing landscape, and internal battles that you will undoubtedly fight can be nauseating at best and paralyzing at worst. That is, of course, if you don't view each day (game) as practice. If you participated in the practice as games lifestyle during your collegiate career, you have the right ingredients to bake a magnificent life cake. You have to believe it and do it.

When you move into adult life, you can view every engagement as a self-imposed apprenticeship in which you can learn, mature, and ultimately teach others. Alternatively, you can lose faith, offer pessimistic viewpoints on varied situations, think cynically, and become beaten down by a cold and cruel world. Want my advice? Doesn't matter, here it is. Wake up. Persist. View the world through the eyes of an innocent child. As adults, regardless of your athletic orientation, if you were paid to play, if you paid to play, or if you didn't play at all, your perceptions can make or break you.

I am a seasoned adult now. Many former walk-ons that I have met are now veterans in the game of life as well. You want to know how they are currently doing in life? Sure, you do. Magnificently well, is the answer. You want to know why? Sure, you do. Prior to, during, or shortly after their collegiate sporting experiences, they decided to actively participate in life. They decided to pursue excellence as verification of human ability. They decided to enjoy the journey. They decided to leverage the self-imposed apprenticeship model in an effort to read, study, and learn about everything that was salient to them. If you are a former walk-on who is reading this book, you are currently nodding your head in agreement (I hope ☺).

Being a walk-on teaches you how to function in life, in general. The probability of effectively leveraging the lessons learned is heightened when you embrace practices as games as an adult. Every day when we wake up to the play the game of life, we see it as a skill building opportunity. Many people are in a constant state of worry. The *if-then-else* scenarios that continually infiltrate their minds and hearts are not ideal. The game of life for humanity, akin to the games we play in college as walk-ons, is fragile. As a volunteer in college, you can go to practice one day and can be asked not to return the next day. As a participant in life (active or not), the opportunity to offer value from second to second can evaporate. Those who employ the *practice is the game* mentality are keenly aware of such fragility and act accordingly.

If you can espouse and exhibit such a mindset while playing, it will be just as easy to implement post your time on the field of competition. When you know that each practice day might be your last, you live, listen, learn, and leave nonsense behind. You learn to think with a servant's mind. You learn to feel with a servant's heart. You learn to listen with a servant's focus. You learn to ask questions with servant-like curiosity. You learn to act with servant-like intentions. Servant level engagement should not be misinterpreted as being passive, feeling inferior, or not doing your very best to offer sustained value. It simply means that you understand your life role. Even if you are a superstar, you should engage as a servant. Being a walk-on and viewing your daily practices as games teaches you the importance of being and doing your best at all times so that you can help others be and do their best at all times.

Knowing and believing that each practice, each day is an opportunity for you to leave it all on the court takes away the stress associated with looking in the mirror at the end of the day knowing that you didn't give your best and hoping for another opportunity tomorrow. Putting in game time effort during practice is liberating. You know that you did your best. Your teammates or colleagues know that you did your best. There is no shame in that. You are of a blessed lot. Proceed accordingly.

CHAPTER 5

The Power of Coaches

Coaches have the power to change the trajectory of a kid's life via their words and actions. This is especially true of the walk-on tribe. Although we have silverback fearlessness, many of us are also perpetually on high alert. Many of us feel that we have to offer value every single day. And rightfully so. We do have to offer value. As volunteers, we can easily be told that our services are no longer needed. That is an alarming prospect for someone who simply wants to do something that he or she loves and be recognized for his or her talents and efforts.

Such feelings aren't reserved for walk-ons. Scholarship athletes feel the same way. When I earned a scholarship, my feelings of apprehension and desire to offer my best self every day did not change. In all fairness, that is likely because I still carried the walk-on flag and I knew that earning a scholarship didn't necessarily change anyone's perception of me. I knew that my coaches had an affinity for me because they provided the opportunity for me to represent the names on the front and the back of the jersey. I also knew that I had to continually work to prove myself. There was no denying that. I have talked to dozens of athletes who were walk-ons during their entire college tenure, athletes that were on scholarship the entire time, and athletes who walked on and were on and off scholarship during various semesters of their collegiate athletics career. The consensus remains the same. Coaches make a difference. A much bigger difference than many of them realize.

I, from what I understand, am the only walk-on in Notre Dame's storied history to play for three different basketball coaches in four years. Each of those coaches played incredible roles in my life and offered me insights that have proven to be of immense value. The words and actions directed towards me and those that I experienced indirectly as a result of their words and actions being directed towards a teammate, sometimes created clarity and chaos within my mind and heart. Since I was in no position to offer my thoughts to them in any meaningful way in person, I wrote letters to each of them several years after college. I never gave them the letters. Maybe they will read them now. Who knows? These letters were all written as I was in the process of writing my first book. It was my way of accepting the past, releasing unhealthy spirits, and positively directing my thoughts. These letters, as you will experience, demonstrate the power of a coach's words and actions. I still get chill bumps when I read them.

Coach MacLeod

Note: Coach MacLeod recently transitioned on 14 April 2019. Although he is no longer able to read the below message to him, I am hopeful that his son and my former teammate, Matt, and the entire MacLeod family know how much Coach MacLeod meant to me. Without his approval, my Notre Dame basketball journey would have never started.

Thank you. Thank you. Thank you. A trillion more times, I say thank you. There is no reason that you should have believed in me and given me such an opportunity, but you did. Thank you. Coach BT, Coach Doles, and Coach McCaffery ... thank you. When I received the call from Coach BT letting me know that I had proven myself and could return to campus to officially join the team prior to tryouts, I was overwhelmed with excitement.

I knew that I had the skill and will to make it, but I had obvious gaps in several areas. Literally, everyone on the team was taller, bigger, and stronger than me. Heart and desire were my most distinguishable attributes. You recognized that. I remember you telling me that I had a *heart of gold* and deserved to wear the Notre Dame jersey. I couldn't believe what I heard. In my heart I knew that, but to hear you say it was transformational.

I was so excited to make the team and be considered a Division I athlete that very few things bothered me. I wish we would have won more games during the season, but I knew that we would get better. I wish I could have traveled with the team, but I knew that would happen too in the near future. I was so excited to wear that jersey that it didn't even really bother me that I might not play in one single game. You even gave me that opportunity. The feelings of pure excitement, love, and thankfulness permeated every fiber of my existence. When I walked past you and the other coaches, you all said, "Go get 'em, Chuck." I couldn't do too much *gettin'* because there was only one-minute left in the game, but I did *get* a rebound. My first stat as a Division I athlete. Thank you.

I didn't talk with you a lot during the season. That's understandable.

There was no reason for you to talk with me. I was sub 6 feet tall as a freshman (I'm 6 feet now ... so hype), I weighed less than 150 pounds, and I couldn't offer value to you in any meaningful way. I was at the gym jogging on the treadmill when I learned of your departure. When I saw on TV that you were leaving ND, I thought to myself, "Ahhhhhh! This can't be!" I was scared, nervous, and angry. I knew you made the decision that was best for you and your family, but the selfish part of me was not happy. I knew that I was going to have to start over and convince another set of coaches that I was worthy of being an Irishman. I don't know if you remember, but I came to the office to ask for your help.

I asked you what I should expect in the very near future. I asked you what I should do to convince the next coach that I was willing and ready to wear the Irish uniform and do whatever I could to help my brothers win. You looked at me and said (with absolute sincerity) and I am paraphrasing here, you remind me of a smaller version of Sky. You have the heart and desire to make it happen. You and Ray [Jones] sent me so many letters that we had to pay attention to you. You are definitely not the biggest, strongest, or best player, but you are not afraid. You want this just as much as anyone else I have coached in the past. You have what it takes to play here until you graduate, you just have to know that and keep pushing. I will tell the next head coach that they should seriously consider you as a part of the Irish family. You keep working hard and *never* give up. You have come too far to slow down now. I am glad that I had the chance to get to know you, even if only for a little while. I am excited for what the future holds for you. After you shook my hand, you nodded and said, "Go Irish. Remember, you are a part of that when people say it."

Thank you for your kind words. Thank you for giving me a chance. Thank you for being gracious with me. Thanks to your coaching staff for helping this kid from Flint realize a dream. I will take the lessons learned and do what I can to help others.

With Sincerest Respect,

Charles Thomas Jr.

Coach Doherty

You have no idea how many times I have loathed even hearing the sound of your name. You have no idea how often I used to hear your voice speaking negatively or sarcastically to me. You have no idea how often I used to hear your voice speaking negatively or sarcastically to my teammates. You have no idea how many times you made me laugh. You have no idea how many times I have thanked you. You have no idea how many times I used the lessons learned to effectively deal with life situations. So, let me tell you.

Life can be unsettling for a walk-on. It's even scarier when dealing with a volatile personality. You made negative comments about my tattoos. You questioned my reasoning and offered negative prophecies about how they would impact my life journey. I didn't accept that. You made me cut my hair. I was not happy about that. My braids were dope. You knew I was on my Allen Iverson kick. Moms said you were right about the hair, so I didn't have a choice. I didn't accept that either, but I had to do it. I wanted to be on the team and I didn't want to get yelled at by her. Y'all won.

When I played extremely well in practice and gave my teammates buckets, you would try to motivate them by saying something negative about me. "Are you seriously gonna let him keep scoring on you like that? He's a walk-on. Maybe I should give him the scholarship." "You're just gonna let Chuck bully you and get to the rim that easily.

I know he is fast, but give me a break. He barely weighs 150 pounds."
"C'mon, now. How does he block your shot? He might not even be
five feet tall." Many of your comments were funny and made us all
laugh. Some of the comments were super mean. I wasn't a fan of that
motivational tactic back then, but as an adult, I understand what you
were trying to do. I can appreciate your style more as I have become
wiser and can think through the *whats, whys, and hows* a little bit
better.

As I think more about your journey, I now realize that there
were times in which you had no idea what you were doing. You were
learning and maturing at the same time. When you were a head
coach for a Big East school, you weren't even 40 years old. That's
remarkable. Your anger wasn't malicious, it was misplaced. Your
language, while sometimes not very thoughtful, wasn't intended
to pierce the soul. It was meant to light a fire in the person. Your
ego wasn't narcissism. You were on a rocket ship to the top at an
early age. Unfortunately, you flew too closely to the sun and your
wings were clipped. You were resilient, though. I was glad to see
you bounce back.

It is also essential for you to know that you forever changed my
world for the better. You sat me in your office one day and told me
that I had earned an athletic scholarship. Lil ol' me! On that cherished
day, you made me a Division I scholarship athlete. I maintained the
walk-on label and was on scholarship. You told me that I was one of
the hardest working kids you had ever met and that you were proud
of me. You said that my parents and loved ones were proud of me
because I was doing the team and the university a great service by
offering my time and talents to make others better. You said that
even though I would not play a lot, I was a leader and should act
accordingly. You told me that even on those days when you say or do

wild things, it's to push me to be a better man. You told me to *walk tall* even though I was a *lil fella* ☺.

I remember your words. Even though there were plenty of days during the remainder of that season in which I was not the happiest person in the world, I believed what you told me in that office and was able to better handle your words and actions. I believed you when you said I was a leader and that I was a doing a great service to my teammates and university. I believed you when you said that my parents were proud of me. I believed you when you said *walk tall* even though I was a *lil fella*. Every single day, even as a *lil fella*, I walk tall. Thank you. I sit in board rooms, classrooms (jail and university), and any other room knowing that I am doing a great service to others by offering my time and talents. I know that I am a leader. Thank you.

Best wishes to you and your family.

With Sincerest Respect,

Charles Thomas Jr.

Coach Brey

Man, man, man ... what can I say? From day one, even as a walk-on, you told me that I was a part of the family. You called me during the summer when you accepted the job and told me that Coach D had spoken highly of me. You told me that I was an Irishman. You expressed that I was a leader and you were very confident that I would offer value to the team. In all fairness, you did also tell me that I likely wouldn't play many minutes because a McDonald's All-American might be on the way (I completely ignored that part initially because I didn't want to hear it. You told the truth. Lord knows you told the truth). External to the, *I likely wouldn't play a lot part,* your words also gave me a false sense of security. They raised my expectations. I felt that I was no longer going to be the Big East's best kept secret. I felt that even as a walk-on, the crowd would chant my name and commentators would know me. The home crowd certainly chanted my name when I got in the game. The times when I checked into the few games that I played in were not what I envisioned, but hearing the chorus of people singing my name were sounds that I will always remember.

External to those early conversations, your power wasn't necessarily verbal. At least it wasn't for me. The power that impacted me the most was related to your actions and sometimes lack of words. Although I never played with the starters or saw action in the first half of any game, I knew that I could. For two years, I felt that I was one of our league's best kept secrets. I don't know if you really believed it, but you never said otherwise. In practice, you would give me the green light to attack. You allowed me to lead when I could and follow when necessary. You allowed me to interact with the varied personalities in ways that made me better (and hopefully my teammates). Even through the yelling, fiery competition, and sometimes pure sadness after a loss, you never talked down to me or made me feel inferior. When I had to miss practice (which was extremely rare) to study for a test, you didn't question me. You would simply say, "Get it done, Chuck."

Early in the season of my senior year after an emotionally exhausting few weeks of frustration, I came to you all hot and bothered to *get some answers*. I told you that I felt overlooked, devalued, and forgotten. I was not happy. You smiled and then explained the power of the journey. I'm paraphrasing here because I can't remember the conversation verbatim. You said that you didn't have to constantly talk to me because once you said it, I got it. You advised that you didn't need to tell me what to do and only needed to guide me. You reminded me that I led myself and my motivation was not external. You affirmed that every single day I would have the opportunity to do what I loved to do and occasionally massive crowds would yell the name Chuck. You said, and this is verbatim, "Forget the crowds, we get to see what you can do every day. Practices are your games. Your abilities to serve and play at a high level are not lost on me. I know that you can do it." From that day forward, I was okay. Not okay with not playing, but okay with knowing that I knew I could play, my teammates knew I could play, and you knew I could play.

I very rarely played on the big stage. Even on Senior Night versus Providence when you could have started me with my classmates, or at least afforded me the opportunity to play in front of my family for more than a few seconds, you chose otherwise. I was mad for a while, and some of my family members are still mad about it and don't like you AT ALL, but it's all good. When I removed the emotion, disregarded the embarrassment, and allowed reason to prevail, I was able to move forward. I remembered your proclamation and my acceptance of it. Practices were my games. I was able to serve and do my best to make my brothers better.

I'm in my early 30s now. I am not playing on the biggest of stages, but I know God has me on the stage that I need to be on and I can definitely play on that one. I practice every day so that I can make those around me better. I read. I write. I study. I wrestle with thoughts of consequence. I learn about everything that is salient to me so that I can be of value and service to others. Yes, I am internally motivated. Hearing it from you, though, had a deeper impact than you can imagine. I have chosen to forget the negatives. At the very least, I do not let the negatives bother me. I have also chosen to forget many of the positives because I refuse to live life with a false sense of security.

You told the team one day, "If you can shoot, you can play anywhere in the country." I took that as, *if you can create and produce, you can do whatever you want in life.* I choose to create. I choose to produce. I choose to play to the best of my abilities. I choose to enjoy the power and importance of practices and games. Thank you.

The night we lost to Duke in the 2nd round of the NCAA tournament, the entire team was sad. Many of us cried. I know I did. The superstars knew that they were going to play professionally. The underclassman knew that they would be back. I knew that my basketball journey at the Division I collegiate level was over. The rush of sadness was almost overwhelming. I put in monumental effort to be there and just like that … game over. When we were getting ready to leave the locker room, I guess your fatherly instincts kicked in because it seemed as if you also felt *my* sadness. You walked up to me and quietly said, "The world needs people like you. You created a way when there was no way. Never forget that." You were right. I haven't forgotten. Thank you.

With Sincerest Respect,

Charles Thomas Jr.

▌CHAPTER 6

Healers and Creatives

On my life journey, I've been fortunate to meet an ensemble of people. We have all read the lists describing the various types of people in the world – achievers, thinkers, supporters, manipulators, deviants, lovers, fighters, teachers, magistrates, power seekers, influencers, healers, creatives, saints, sinners, and the list continues. Of all the people that I have met in the various categories, two types stand above the rest—healers and creatives. Almost every walk-on with whom I have interacted over the last two decades can be categorized as either a healer or creative. Many are both.

Why do I have such an affinity for healers and creatives? In full transparency, I think it is because I feel like I can be categorized as both. Maybe I just like what healers and creatives represent. Indulge me as I illuminate the varied aspects of each category.

Healers

Healers, in my mind, are individuals who can leverage the power of their hands and words to make a valuable and sustainable difference in someone's life. Doctors, writers, philosophers, educators, parents, speakers, and poets are only a small portion of the healer population. These individuals understand how to solve multidimensional problems by speaking and doing.

Think about the healing power of a heart or brain surgeon. She has to engage as a thoughtful diagnostician to determine the multiplicity of reasons why something is attacking the person's body. She then has to isolate those varied symptoms to better understand how they work individually and collectively. She cannot presume a universal remedy for all conditions. She has to think, focus, and ask the right questions. Once she's made the decision regarding how to best proceed, she must act. The family trusts her. Her colleagues trust her. The patient trusts her. She trusts herself. Through the steadiness of her hands, voice, and God's healing power, she can bring a person back from the brink of death. She can solve some of the most complex human problems with her hands. She can ease a person's concerns with her words.

Consider the healing power of an educator. Wars have been waged due to misunderstandings of the spoken word. Relationships have transitioned to states of irreconcilability due to harsh, malintentioned, and indifferent speech. A speaker who speaks with an educator's heart is disciplined in his delivery. An educator who desires to understand as well as be understood creates a safe space for healing. He can synthesize massive amounts of information, understand dichotomous relationships, translate the varied paradoxes into actionable material, and offer something of value to the listener. Educators elicit the desired data points by actively listening. Excellent educators, as we all know, listen to learn. They do not listen to merely reply. When you talk to an educator who sees beyond your presentation and can ask the right questions, the healing power of his words can be life altering.

Educators can make you move from a state of indifference to heightened awareness. They can make you question presuppositions, preconceptions, prejudgments, and prejudices. They can make you understand the utility in righteous indignation and offer recommendations regarding how to effectively separate a person's intent from the actual impact. A thoughtful educator can clear your mind from worry, free your spirit from hate, and challenge you to move beyond what you thought to be possible. This all happens through the healing power of words.

Finally, consider the healing power of parents. The good ones stick with us even when we do not meet expectations. They counsel us, teach us, and lead by example. They stand with us long after others have left us to our own devices. Thoughtful parents water the plants that they have. They watch their children closely to better understand their abilities and aptitudes and let them try various activities to determine aptitude-ability alignment.

Parents do their very best to offer sage counsel even when they know that they are unsure of how to proceed. The good ones choose their words wisely. They know the power of the tongue. When children fall, parents tell them that they will be okay. When children are sick, parents hug them. When they are mischievous, parents still tell them that they love them. When teenagers and young adults lack confidence, parents tell them that they love them and are there for them. When young adults are disobedient, parents angrily, but patiently tell them that they would never purposely lead them down the wrong path. When adult children begin to suffer under the weight of the world, their parents advise them that they are not alone. When adult children have kids of their own, their parents speak life and love into the lives of their grandchildren. Through their words and actions, parents are healers.

Creatives

Creatives make you believe that anything is attainable. They capture the senses in almost unimaginable ways. Creatives are those that turn ideas into reality. They create something out of nothing. Creatives capture inspiration from the smallest of stimuli and offer the output of their imagination to the world for public consumption. Creatives see, think, and act differently. Creatives are sensitive and audacious. They have an almost religious like obsession with their chosen craft (or as some would submit, the craft that chose them). Put very simply, creatives create. They are the creators and producers of the world that make us laugh, cry, stomp our feet, pretend to be someone else, and believe that we can be and do whatever we want, if we have the intrepidity to try.

Consider the creative nature of storytellers. Without the creative imagination and story-telling prowess of George Lucas, Yoda we don't have. See what I did there? Now smile and please keep reading. Without Stan Lee, we don't have any *X-Men* to protect us. Heaven knows that we certainly need Professor X, Wolverine, Storm, and Magneto in our lives. Who creates *Grey's Anatomy* and *How to Get Away with Murder* without Shonda Rhimes? How would children and adults know how to play Quidditch if J.K. Rowling didn't write about it and show us? How would I know that in order to get something to levitate, all I have to say is *Wingardium Leviosa*? The only way I learn that is by attending the Hogwarts School of Witchcraft and Wizardry.

How does the world learn about the Miseducation of the Negro, the Souls of Black Folk, and why Race Matters if not for the writings and storytelling acumen of Dr. Carter G. Woodson, Dr. W.E.B. Du Bois, and Dr. Cornel West, respectively? Who teaches us that *storytelling is king* if Dr. Ed Catmull doesn't write Creativity, Inc? Storytellers are the real magicians. They think and write; therefore, they are. Through their words, they let us know that by moving beyond thought into action, we can become what we want to become, if we have the resolve to try.

Think about the electric, eclectic, and energizing abilities of musicians and entertainers. Prince, Michael Jackson, Imagine Dragons, Whitney Houston, Shania Twain, Tupac, Biggie, Jay-Z, Taylor Swift, Pink, Kurt Cobain, Adele, Beyoncé, the Wu Tang Clan, and a cacophony of others capture our senses through their musicality. The aforementioned and those like them can have a spellbinding affect over our lives. The instrumentation, dancing, and word selection make us feel alive. Think about the days when you are sad, lacking enthusiasm, and agitated. Now, remember how you sparked almost immediately when your *song* came on.

Nine-year-old kids can easily recite the verses to some Michael Jackson songs even without really knowing anything of his actual life. Why is that? Music gives wings to the soul and opens a part of us that is willing to accept the creative components that want to inhabit our being. Musicians and entertainers reaffirm the power of words. We sing their lyrics repeatedly to make us feel however we want to feel—happy, sad, melancholic, nostalgic, energized, angry, thoughtful, etc. Whatever emotion we want to feel at any given time, we can find a song that will take us to that space. The power of creatives is a game changing life force.

Finally, consider the imaginative and inventive nature of children. Their child-like innocence, wondrous enjoyment, and awe-inspiring creativity should be emulated until the day we transition. Kids aren't afraid until adults make them afraid. Kids don't think negatively until adults teach them to do so. Kids don't lose their imagination, adults take it from them. Kids aren't concerned with getting the wrong answer until adults punish them for doing so. Kids are free. They laugh. They enjoy their chosen activity. They are adventurous. Kids smile with their eyes and mouth. They want to love and be loved. Kids have an innate ability to create magical moments even when they have no idea what they are doing.

When a little boy does something that he finds entertaining, he radiates with enjoyment. When a little girl puts together her first Lego neighborhood without assistance, her vibrancy is contagious. The creativity, love, curiosity, and commitment to learning that emanates from children should be imitated by all. They reaffirm the power and necessity of creatives and demonstrate that we can have fun while doing it, if we have the pertinacity to try.

Healers and Creatives

Walk-ons are healers and creatives. We are surgeons, educators, parents, musicians, entertainers, writers, storytellers, and children. Every single day, we can diagnose a variety of problems (surgeons), teach others how to resolve the identified concerns (educators), offer measured counsel when our brothers and sisters require reassurance (parents), smile, sing, and laugh for the good of the team (entertainers), tell a story about what we can be if we stick together and choose not to give up on each other (storytellers), and believe in the realm of conceivable with wondrous amazement and contagious dynamism (children). Simultaneously functioning as a healer and creative is not an easy job, but we are wired for such undertakings.

During my tenure as a walk-on, I had myriad opportunities to function in a healer and creative capacity. I recognized the same characteristics in my counterparts on different teams. Our words mattered even when people acted as if they did not. Our actions mattered even when we didn't think that they did. This was especially true when I became a leader on the team. My lack of scholarship (or scholarship) played no role in my willingness and ability to lead from where I was. As a healer and creative, it was imperative to engage.

While I wasn't always the nicest of humans on the field of competition during my collegiate years, I put in extraordinary effort to do well. I also encouraged my teammates to do the same. For those of you who will be walk-ons and those who are currently walk-ons, your words and actions matter. If you are not afforded the opportunity to play a lot, it is critical that you bring something else of value to the table.

Each year that you are granted the honor of volunteering, learning about your teammates and coaches is foundational. You have to learn to become the counselor, teacher, brother, sister, and cousin whenever necessary. You must be ready to heal and create at a moment's notice because your teammates will rely on you for those intangibles. This is especially true if you are on the team for more than one year and gain the trust of your teammates. For those who have transitioned into the real world, you can affirm my assertions.

During my sophomore, junior, and senior seasons, I argued and competed with my teammates just like everyone else. I also accepted the role as confidant for several of them. As a volunteer, it is not easy to help manage the emotions of people who have no reason to heed your counsel other than you have gained the trust and relationship capital with them. Each person on the team needed something different from me on various occasions. The only way I was able to offer value external to the field of competition was by paying attention to them. I needed to know what they liked and disliked, what bothered them, and what stimulated them. I needed to know when to listen versus actively engage and offer counsel (albeit naïve). There was a litany of days on and off campus that I needed to be a healer. I had to talk as a big brother to some of my younger teammates and defer to the wisdom of some of my older teammates, as a younger brother should.

My healing power came from being able to effectively manage conflicts. We have an uncanny ability to step into tenuous situations and determine a mutually agreeable solution because we have learned to play so many roles in an attempt to offer value. We commonly engage as a neutral third party. Taking sides can sometimes create unwanted problems. We have to listen, analyze, synthesize, and transmit information in ways that are well-received by all parties involved.

Knowing yourself and working to know others can prove immensely valuable when having difficult conversations on a variety of topics. We learn to be patient, thoughtful, curious, assertive, creative, and trustworthy. Those elements of character that command respect are sometimes hard to acquire. The healer skill set translates phenomenally well in the real world regardless if you engage on a team as a principal architect or working level functionary. During college and post college, know that your words matter. They have healing power. People will come to you because they know that you have learned what you needed to learn to add value. That is an amazing healing component. Know that and proceed tactfully.

While serving as a healer is extremely useful, it is not always the most fun thing to do for some people. It requires intense concentration, active listening, observation, consideration, and patience. Creativity requires nothing more than assuredness and our willingness to listen to our instincts. It is liberating. Creativity is the transition from prose to poetry. It illuminates our reality and is soul-stirring. When we shift to create mode, our light allows others to see. The only thing that creativity asks of us is our willingness to believe in the kingdom of possible. Creating is risky. Living inside of an already drawn box is even riskier. Creatives have the ability to release unlimited and unrealized potential on the field of competition. It's a beautiful sight to behold when someone leverages his or her insight, instinct, experience, and exuberance to create motion, momentum, and movements worthy of emulation and adoration.

I revered being in create mode in practice. It was such a freeing feeling. On any given day, I was told to take on the mannerisms of certain players from the opposition. Naturally, I did not bury me. I added them to me in order to offer value to the team. On certain days, I would shoot a lot. Other days, I would pass a lot. Somedays, my objective was to simply break down the defense. On other days, my goal was to be an absolute pest on defense. I always had a blast on the *green light* days.

During any practice day, I could seamlessly move between characters. I could be Sherlock Holmes, investigating, watching, learning, and predicting the moves of my counterparts. An hour or so later or during a future practice, I could be Professor Moriarty, callously ignoring the needs of others, plotting, scheming, and ready to render my opponent defenseless. I could play like I was 6'7" or 6'.

On Sundays, when we didn't have practice, I studied and rested like Jesus commanded. Even then, I was ready to create and become a chameleon.

On any given day, I could choose chaos and/or order, light and/or dark, good and/or evil … even a combination of all. It was a brilliant upbringing. Every day, I was afforded various opportunities to be and become while simultaneously being 100% me. Even writing that section brought back fond memories.

For future and current walk-ons, the same holds true for you. You will have legion opportunities to create and to be creative. You will have the blessed fortune to leverage the styles of others and incorporate them into your own style to offer value in practice and hopefully during games. You will be blessed to learn how to most effectively leverage your instincts and experiences to create your own moments of beauty and clarity. The same prospects will materialize when your collegiate tenure has ended. After college, however, you don't need permission from anyone else. You give yourself approval to be creative and great. Then, you go and do. Being a creative in the real world is phenomenal. To reiterate Coach Brey's words, "If you can shoot, you can play anywhere in the country." Translation: if you can create, you can do whatever you want to do in life. This is a herculean proclamation to internalize as we grow.

Having the willingness and ability to heal, create, and produce can lead to dream manifestation. Creatives offer a glimpse into the Divine. As a former, current, or future walk-on, you have absolute permission to create and be great. Knowing and believing that you are a healer and creative will be paramount in your life after sports. Be strong. Be bold. Heal. Create. Offer useful service. Use that blank canvas to design whatever reality you desire. Liberate yourself and others.

CHAPTER 7

Life After Sports

In Chapter 4, I discussed the power of fear, insecurity, and doubt prior to making the team. I then offered insight into how fear transitions to anxiety while insecurity and doubt remain during your experience as a collegiate athlete. Life after sports is quite different. You are less afraid and anxious as you once were. Anxiety transitions to skepticism. Insecurity and doubt remain. As you become more mature and life teaches you how to better handle situations, it's easier to live with the arrows that will undoubtedly hit you. As an 18 or 19-year-old, one or two arrows can prevent forward momentum in our lives. As a 34 or 35-year-old who is battle tested and even more committed to offering value, it takes dozens (or even hundreds) of arrows to inhibit our progress. That said, skepticism, insecurity, and doubt still play almost unfathomable mind games with us as adults.

Cynicism should be avoided. Skepticism can be healthy. It forces you to think and ask Socratic questions to protect your mind and heart, or the minds and hearts of others. Skepticism can keep you alive. If effectively leveraged, it creates an opportunity for us to take a step back and engage in alternative perspectives analysis. Skepticism can allow us to transcend our thinking and acting from an emotional paradigm to one that is focused on the intelligent direction of sometimes inexplicable intensity. Skepticism encourages and sometimes forces us to ask questions. A lot of them.

Skepticism can also be quite harmful if we lack the knowledge and willingness to harness and appropriately focus its majestic power. It can steal our innocence if we aren't mindful of our thoughts and actions. When we are overly skeptical as adults, we begin to lose trust in people and processes. We mistakenly misidentify misalignment or non-alignment as malintent. Skepticism can make us suspicious of everything. At best, we question even the simplest of gestures in interactions. At worst, we begin to perceive people as devious, Machiavellian narcissists determined to bend us to their will. When we are overly skeptical, we are unable to think clearly and thrive because we are in survival mode. When we are in survival mode, we don't think as rationally as we should or could. We make basic mistakes that impact us and others in ways that we may not have intended.

Furthermore, skepticism can inadvertently create feelings of superiority or inferiority. The former occurs when we convince ourselves that we know the *game* that everyone is playing. We assure ourselves that we are fluent in the laws of power and human nature. We say or think things like, "Dude must think I'm stupid. I heard what he said, but I know what he meant. I'm way too battle tested to fall for that nonsense." In actuality, there is usually no nonsense involved. Our misjudgments, ill-conceived notions, faulty internal monologue, and inability or unwillingness to observe without judgment can create irreconcilable dissonance in our minds that is not easily resolved.

Feelings of inferiority can occur because we actually feel that we lack adequate discernment to see through the ploys and manipulative devices of others. We are worried that we can't protect ourselves or loved ones from their strategic undertakings of passion and will. Our emotions overpower our intelligence and we begin to question facets of life that we previously thought to be true. We wonder why we are unable to see what others seem to see so clearly. The voices in our head tell us that we knew that we were inferior all along. The same imposter syndrome that attacked us during our time as a walk-on rears its head and raises its voice again. This time, there are multiple heads and the voices are louder than before. We don't know what to do so we don't do anything. We stand still while time continues to move. Stay focused. Don't let it happen to you. Even if it does happen *to* you, use it as a learning experience and know that it is actually happening *for* you.

Insecurity and doubt are stronger when we become adults. Once you are playing the game of life and have real responsibilities, there is no retreat to the gym, classroom, dorm room, cafeteria, school library, or whatever safe haven you choose. Well, you can retreat to those places, but life is different as an adult. When we are in school, many problems simply go away if we don't directly deal with them because someone else handles those challenges for us—parents, friends, professors, coaches, or anyone else other than you. As responsible and accountable adults, we have to engage. A temporary respite to the *cabin in the woods* is simply that … temporary. We have to check ourselves back into the game. We have to work considerately, creatively, curiously, and calmly to resolve issues of varying complexity and magnitude.

Insecurity makes us feel unworthy and reinforces feelings of inferiority. Doubt makes us second guess every decision. Insecurity derails our willingness to try new things. Doubt creates *what do I do next* dilemmas. Insecurity lessens our intellectual powers. Doubt reduces our emotional intelligence. Insecurity challenges our social aptitude within and external to the workplace. Doubt tells us that the person in the mirror lacks the ability to leverage hard work to neutralize our shortcomings. Insecurity will tell us that our best should be better. Doubt will loudly and proudly co-sign everything insecurity says. Stay focused. Don't let it happen to you. Even if it does happen *to* you, use it as a learning experience and know that it is happening *for* you.

As we all know from our own lived experiences, skepticism, insecurity, and doubt can lead to irreparable life damage if we don't recognize when they are infiltrating our world, admit that the participation of such life forces are causing damage, and move in the appropriate direction to be a better person. When you find yourself to be overly skeptical, insecure, and/or doubtful, consider the following four recommendations.

1 – Free yourself from attachment. I am not suggesting that you stop caring. I am proposing that you observe situations from a place of internal harmony. Accept what happened. If you can fix it, fix it. If you can't, forget it. We allow our emotions to push us in directions that are non-optimal. We assign meaning to things that don't need meaning. We are unable to disentangle intent from impact. We believe that we have to stay connected to something or someone because that is how it started. We accidentally anchor ourselves to varied situations and remain unwilling to move even when evidence and history suggest that we should move in a different direction.

Freedom from attachment allows us to open our eyes and see

things and people for what they are. Skepticism, insecurity, and doubt cannot prevail if you listen to that voice in your head with a learner's mentality. If you are willing and able to hear that voice, study it, and allow it to move through you without loitering. The evaluation and subsequent decisions you make will be more rational and focused.

Freedom from attachment allows us to bask in the serenity of internal peace. We are able to observe a situation, orient ourselves, decide how to respond, and then act. It is a virtuous cycle in our favor. Freedom from attachment creates an opportunity structure for you to try new things with confidence that the outcome will be great regardless if you succeed or fail because you will learn something new. A freedom from attachment mindset is transformative. It will allow you to take risks that were once inconceivable, ask questions without feelings of inferiority, and observe situations with a scientific or explorer mindset.

2 – Don't take things personally. Skepticism, insecurity, and doubt can remain at the forefront of our minds because they attach themselves to our identity. We don't trust what others tell us. We look in the mirror and see something that isn't there. We doubt our own abilities even though we have a successful record of accomplishment. When people tell us that we are great, we believe them. When people tell us that we are terrible, we believe them. Disregard the hype. Disregard the non-constructive criticism that is offered with the intent to do you harm. If we know and believe that we aren't that good and we aren't that bad, life becomes easier. I am not suggesting that we view ourselves as being average. Quite the contrary. I am proposing that we see ourselves as the shining lights that we are while remaining humble. The world isn't out to get us. All people aren't bad. Yes, there are some bad apples, but most of us want to do well and help others as we walk our paths.

When we don't take things personally, we are free to be and become. We understand that our mistakes don't define us, as those failures only represent a moment in time. We are mindful that our successes don't define us. The wins only represent specific moments in time. If we choose not to take things personally, it becomes easier to engage with others and offer assistance because we know that our heart is in the right place regardless of their acceptance or rejection of a helping hand.

3 – Choose to lead with a servant's heart. When our focus is external, we don't have time to be skeptical, insecure, or doubtful. As leaders within and external to our communities, we have to do our very best to lift others as we climb. Our journey from *best kept secret* to *no longer a secret* is a transcendent one. As a servant, we strive to keep others first and do not linger within the sad spaces of our minds and hearts. Leading with a servant's heart doesn't mean that we have to be categorically selfless or altruistic. It simply means that we understand the bigger picture. We know that even though we are only one of approximately 7.7 billion humans on earth, we can still offer value to others, if we only put forth the effort to try.

When I was younger, my dad said that if I really wanted to be great, I had to be a servant of many. He probably stole that line from Jesus (or someone in the Bible), but his words rang true to me, so I will give him credit for his wisdom. Offering our time and talents to others can be a game changer for others. To somebody, we are somebody. If we take the time to connect with others in an authentic and personal way, the words we say and how we make them feel can be life altering.

Leading with a servant's heart is learned very early on in the walk-on journey. We know that we can make an impactful difference by climbing the mountain with others. We know that by treating others with dignity and respect, it will be returned … even if it takes a little while longer than expected. Leading with a servant's heart fans the flames of greatness as we are mindful that honing our skills and sharing them with others also prove to be advantageous to them. We can't go wrong by thinking and leading with a servant's heart. It may not always be easy, but it will be worth it.

4 – Intelligently direct your energy. Unfocused zeal is dangerous. When we allow our internal sparkle to project thoughtlessly into the world, we can cause problems for ourselves and others. When we allow skepticism, insecurity, and doubt to infiltrate our mind and heart, we create and transmit pessimism into our individual universe and to the multiverse around us. Negative spiritedness is magnetic. When we think, or even worse, speak despair into our lives, it drains our internal radiance and likely the vivacity of those around us.

I am a decently well-mannered individual. I also have a shadow side that can be quite dangerous if not tracked and managed. When I was young boy, for various reasons, I was quite angry. I had a noticeable chip on my shoulder, was easily offended, took things personally, and allowed my shadow side to lead me and negatively impact others more than I should have. Well-mannered did not always equal nice, helpful, thoughtful, or considerate. This was true for me pre-college, during college, and post-college (for a short period of time).

During college, I even had the audacity to write on my shoes, *Prove Them Wrong*. Who is *them*? *Them* were outsiders ... naysayers, coaches, teammates, opponents, family members, etc. I created imaginary enemies in my head and was focused on *showing them how I was wired*. They needed to know that I was *cut from a different cloth*. Now, there were some people who said and/or did negative things to me with the hopes of preventing my forward progression academically, athletically, and in life. As a reasoning, rational, discerning, and less sensitive adult, I realize that they couldn't really impact my upward trajectory with their words, unless I allowed them to do so. It surely did not feel like it when I was a child.

I still have my shadow side. That said, I have learned how to harness and focus my various energies better than I was able to do in my younger, more aggressive, and ignorant years. I still have imaginary enemies and am constantly laser focused on my selected tasks. Now, however, that drive is intelligently directed. If I am awake and active for 19 hours during a particular day (which happens more than it probably should), I offer 19 hours of controlled rage to the world. My *dark side* is integrated with the *bright side* and I move forward, as necessary. The effective combination of the two allows me to connect with others and create spaces for them to engage however they wish.

When we harness our eagerness, focus our attentions and efforts, and release them judiciously, our abilities to solve problems and change lives increase exponentially. The deliberate direction of our zestfulness changes skepticism, insecurity, and doubt to optimism, self-belief, and hopefulness. Our interactions with others will spark a change in their behaviors. We become more lucid, creative, crafty, free-spirited, unflinching, and curious. Our vigor becomes infectious. We can more easily speak to the hearts and minds of others. We no longer sleepwalk through life. Our visions are broadened and emboldened because the shadow of negativity can no longer steal our joy. When we wisely direct our enthusiasm, the rapturous vitality that emanates from our souls, the brightness that shines from our eyes, and the clarity of thought that proliferates from our minds are breathtaking. We simply must have the steadfastness to try.

Being a walk-on is a wonderful experience. Nerve-racking at

times, but worth the associated learning experiences. Even as determined, competent adults, we still have to catch the arrows of skepticism, insecurity, and doubt. One of the main differences as an adult is that we know how to break those arrows and find the optimism, self-belief, and hopefulness on the inside. We know how to leverage our lived experiences in ways that create moments of love, life, and laughter for ourselves and others. We know how to lend a helping hand even when we feel down. We know that our failures and success are temporary bruises, not lifetime tattoos, and we act accordingly. We know that we are leaders and do our very best to offer guidance and assistance when such occasions present themselves, and those opportunities abound.

■ CHAPTER 8

How Can I Help?

How can I help is a life altering phrase. During my freshman year in college, my calculus teacher said it all the time. He said it to his students and his colleagues. During one of our many conversations, he also advised that he used that phrase with his family. His reasoning was that the *how can I help* question moved the focus away from him to the other person. I didn't start regularly leveraging that phrase until about a decade ago, but I modified my behaviors sooner than that.

As a volunteer, our sole objective is to help. As walk-ons, our job is to help the team and everyone around us get better. I'm not suggesting that we have to be saintly. I am suggesting that we have to be servantly. Not out of fear, but out of love for and connection to our fellow brothers and sisters. We have the skill to contribute in our chosen sport, otherwise we wouldn't have made the team. The truth is that many walk-ons will not have ample opportunity to make a value-added difference during game time. Regardless of whether we play substantial minutes during the game or not is almost inconsequential. We still have to do the same thing every day. We have to help. At the very least, we have to put ourselves in position to help.

How can I help also lowers the defenses of the receiver of those words. Most people will not ask that question if they have no intention of offering assistance. Even those who leverage such phraseology to manipulate another person still have to actually help in the interim to establish some level of trust. *How can I help* is the catalyst for servant leadership. *How can I help* is alchemic. My calculus professor's observations were true. Even saying those words opens us up to an entirely new and exciting world of possibilities. Asking that question creates an opportunity to focus on something other than ourselves.

During our time as a few of Notre Dame's best kept secrets, me and my walk-on brothers lived that mantra. We might not have directly asked *how can I help*, but our active participation demonstrated our interest in doing so. On a daily basis, I watched us work tirelessly to offer value. We lifted. We ran. We passed. We shot. We did everything that we could in order to help ourselves and our brothers get better. Our existence may not have been readily talked about and praised, but it was appreciated. We knew that we could help by simply doing what we wanted and were expected to do … show up and get better every day. Although each one of us had a deep desire to compete during games, that yearning wasn't always satisfied. What did manifest in ways that we deemed of value, however, was our perpetual pursuit of progress.

We never gave up and always put ourselves in position to be of value on and off the court. We didn't settle. At all. We simply knew that offering ourselves in a way that would be more valuable to the collective than us as individuals would be better welcomed and received than focusing on our selfish individual ambitions. Maybe we assimilated and inadvertently settled. I don't think so, but it is feasible. Based on my experiences, we were intentional. Our individual and collective actions were by design, not default. We didn't practice and hone our craft due to an obligation. We actively participated because we knew that we could help. Most often, that help occurred in practice as it does for many walk-ons, but we helped, nonetheless. Without us, the team is not the same. Without the team, there is no us. It is a virtuous cycle in everyone's favor. That same *how can I help* mantra is easily transferred once college life is completed.

When I first began verbalizing that question on a regular basis in the work environment, some people were put off by it. They thought that I had some sort of agenda. "Why do you want to help me?" "What's your agenda?" "How does helping me benefit you?" These are only a few of the more civil questions that I was asked when I offered to help. As we grow, we learn that the world beats up on many people. Pessimism, cynicism, betrayal, doubt, and discord negatively impact many lives.

As my professor and dad suggested, and as my collegiate experiences demonstrated, if our intentions are pure and most things are not done out of selfish ambition, we will succeed. People will realize that we do want to help, without expectations of future assistance. They begin to accept our offers for support without feeling as if we have an external agenda that can be used against them in the future for our personal gain. They will appreciate that we practice our craft in order to help them get better when they are in the game. This is precisely how my journey has unfolded since college. That's not to suggest that my journey has been filled with all rose petals. There have been many thorns and thistles along the way. That's okay. I understand the power and importance of asking for and offering help. We can't do it alone.

I've had the pleasure to speak with, educate, and learn from thousands of people over the last decade. The life learned lessons that I acquired as a walk-on almost two decades ago are treasures that cannot be found without going on the adventure. Simply asking the *how can I help* question has opened doors that I previously didn't even know existed.

My parents, Jesus, and other sage counselors teach us to be servants of many and to do nothing out of selfish ambition if we truly want to be great. My calculus professor embodied it. I experienced the power of such truisms while in school, and intentionally decided to once again leverage that wisdom as an adult. Every day that we wake up is an opportunity to practice. Every day is a new opportunity to help. Every day, we can say yes or choose to say no. As a volunteer, when things needed to be done on the court, I said yes. Because of my propensity to say yes, I learned how to leverage varied resources (human or otherwise), to achieve my desired objectives.

As a result of offering my assistance and being able to do what I said that I was going to do, I built a positive reputation among my coaches and teammates. They knew that I was ready and willing to go deep into the trenches with them. If a brother wanted to work on his jump shot, I would help. If he wanted to work on his one-on-one moves, I would help. If he wanted to prepare for a class presentation, I would help. If he needed girl advice, I would *help* (not really, I didn't know either, but I tried.) If he needed to vent about not playing, not getting the grades he wanted, or simply wanted to talk, I would listen.

I am confident in my assertion that we should help others when we can. To have the time and talents to do so and choose otherwise is uncivilized. In order to offer such value, we must demonstrate the gallantry to ask the *how can I help* question. In 2011, I began offering my assistance to others without an expectation of reciprocation. I began saying yes without fear that saying yes meant that I had to sacrifice a piece of myself. I was able to create and incorporate a level of mind-body harmony so that I was not overwhelmed by self-induced pressures. Offering help and saying *yes* have been life changing.

Providing value-added assistance has afforded me the opportunity to integrate myself and others more deeply within the community. Volunteering has allowed me to learn by teaching. Volunteering has allowed me to lead by doing. On a weekly basis, two of my brothers and I volunteer our time on the radio to add value to others. When I asked them to join me on a journey to connect with others, it's because I knew that we could help. I asked several dozen people how I could help them resolve various life issues. Overwhelmingly, the response was to start a radio show.

For decades, I have prepared myself to create and deliver content via the spoken or written word. I was unaware of how such delivery would manifest itself, but I kept trying. Every day, every practice was my game. In August 2016, Divergent Thought was born. On a daily basis, we read, write, and study so that we can offer value to our guests and listeners on a weekly basis. Having a platform for others to share their expertise and experiences is remarkable. Having a live show and podcast to which people listen and download is even more amazing. With voluminous quantities of content in the world, having a show that has captured the minds and hearts of other individuals is nothing short of miraculous. We know that and remain humble and grateful.

It's incredible what can happen when we lead with a servant's heart and ask *how can I help*? It's even more magnificent to witness and experience the level of excitement and liveliness when a guest, caller, or listener realizes that we actually put in the requisite level of work to make them better. We know that iron sharpens iron. The imagery is iconic when it reveals itself in life. I've experienced the iron sharpens iron phenomenon for 20+ years. It's not new to me. It is still wondrous to be an active participant in its manifestation.

The same lessons that I learned as a walk-on are ever present. The same life lessons that you will learn during your time as a walk-on will prove to be most beneficial as you walk your path. If you are a former walk-on, the life learned lessons during your collegiate tenure have undoubtedly aided in your acquisition of wisdom, knowledge, and discernment. The walk-on journey teaches us that offering the best version of ourselves enhances the likelihood that others will reciprocate.

Asking how you can help is not a clichéd platitude that should be offered without considered thought. When we choose to put those words together in sequence, we should be ready to engage at whatever level mandated to get the job done. Offering your assistance can change the trajectory of your life and the lives of others. If you want to experience a meteoric ascent, give more of yourself. Next time you have the inclination to do some good in the world, simply ask someone, *how can I help?*

CHAPTER 9
From the Bench to the Boardroom

For four years, I sat on the bench and absorbed everything that I could. Some of my teammates and others that I have met had parallel experiences for one, two, three, or four years as well. Walk-ons have a unique opportunity to enhance their social skills, behavior analysis, and leadership acumen just like coaches and scholarship players. Coaches don't have to manage down. Their political dexterity only needs extension to donors, administrators, and professors. When they speak, we listen. We, equals everyone on the team. Even if we choose not to listen, we definitely hear them. Scholarship athletes, especially the superstars, have a different level of freedom. Their stress levels are accentuated due to thoughts of making it to the professional ranks and figuring out who to date because they have so many options. For the volunteers on the team, our journeys are noticeably different.

As a four-year team member, I was blessed to learn many names, personality styles, and behaviors. The laboratory was a marvelous learning environment. In my case, I had three coaches in four years, new teammates each year, new basketball team managers, new individuals within the athletics department, new teammate family members to meet, and new opponents to learn about and watch during the games (remember, I had front row seats … every game). As a walk-on, I learned to manage in all directions—coaches, teammates, and peers. I paid attention because a senior on the team during my freshman year offered such counsel. Towards the end of the season, he told me that I was a baby pup being raised by wolves and that I "better pay attention before I get chewed up." He went on to say that *paying attention* wasn't only about basketball. He told me that he was also talking about life. "Even when you become a wolf, you still have to pay attention. They fight and kill each other too." I heard him loud and clear. I also deduced that he really liked wolves.

Coaches

Okay, back to managing in all directions. I learned rather quickly that influence is sometimes more powerful than power. I didn't need to be the biggest, fastest, strongest, smartest, or the overall best player on the team. I needed to maximize my utility to stay in the good graces of the coaching staff. Not just the head coach, all coaches. On most basketball teams (I can't speak for other sports as I didn't play anything else in college), there are usually four or five coaches that have some level of power. The head coach, three or four assistants, and sometimes someone who has a basketball operations role.

You must have some influence with all of them to stay safe. It's like being the perfect courtier. This is not to suggest that I was manipulative. I am saying that it was necessary for me to have my own personal relationship with each coach. Doing so increased the likelihood that they perceived me as more than *just* a walk-on. Talking to the coaches on a more personal level humanized me. They knew Chuck the human. They knew Chuck the reader. They knew Chuck the angry kid. They knew Chuck the well-mannered kid. They knew Chuck the basketball player. They saw me in the aggregate instead of isolated pieces. That proved to be favorable for me. I didn't have any real insight into their lives, but they knew me.

In my world, their affinity towards me was pivotal. It was the difference between staying on the team the following year or being advised that my services were no longer needed. In my mind, if one of the four or five coaches didn't like me and saw no tangible or intangible reason for my presence on the team, it was game over for me. I think the same is true for any volunteer student-athlete. Coaches need to be in our corner. Again, I wasn't some saint walk-on. I was just as aggravating to them as everyone else on the team, I would imagine. I had some good days and I had some bad days. Overall, however, they knew that my intentions were good. They understood that my heart was in the right place. Despite my youthful selfishness and ignorance, they knew that I was a team player.

Although I could not have predicted the carousel of coaches between my freshman and junior years, having a majority of the coaches speak well of me played an indispensable role in me being a member of the team for four years. I don't have any real evidence to substantiate such a declaration, but my instincts don't tell me otherwise. If during any coaching transition, had even two coaches spoke ill of me, I would have no longer been presented with the honor of wearing that #5 jersey. **Side note:** Think about that jersey number for a second. For four years, I was able to wear the same number. That is a preferred number for several athletes. A scholarship athlete never tried to take it away from me (at least not that I can remember). God is good, all the time. And all the time, God is good. **Side Note #2**. The Number 5 in Biblical numerology means God's Grace. Not to get overly philosophical or theological on you, but I wasn't offered that number as a freshman by accident. God doesn't always call the already qualified. He does always qualify the called. That knowledge has reigned supreme in my journey from the bench to the boardroom. #Grace.

Back to the story. After my freshman year, Coach MacLeod gave the positive head nod to Coach Doherty. After my sophomore year, Coach D gave the positive head nod to Coach Brey. Skill was only part of it. Knowing how to communicate, behave, influence, and being willing to share the true me worked in my favor.

Teammates

Effectively managing my teammate relationships was central to my survival. Scholarship players have to do the same, but the sanctions are less harsh if they do it wrong. For us, knowing when, where, why, how, and with whom we should engage in varied situations is not a trivial task. Now don't get me wrong, we don't have to be masterminds, but effectively managing relationships is imperative. I was only partially good at it. I am sure that there are a few of my teammates who do not think fondly of me based on what I said and/ or did during our tenure as teammates. Again, youthful naïveté, ignorance, arrogance, and aggression. All life learned lessons that have proven to be immensely valuable in my adult years.

Learning how to gauge temperaments, read situations, defuse arguments, offer counsel, and remain quiet are all learned on the field of competition and in the locker room. As walk-ons, we have to align ourselves well. Offending the wrong influential teammate can prove disastrous for your desire to continually engage in your desired athletics pursuits. They may or may not try to get you removed from the team, but it is an option.

The same thing can happen in the real world. Alliance management is fundamental. Fortunately, as a volunteer, we do sometimes have the luxury to *sit back and watch*. You learn how to approach your brothers and sisters. You learn how to use words to de-escalate emotional situations. You learn how to quickly assess how other teammates will respond and then decide what you need to do in order to prevent catastrophe. In addition to being teammates, we are also counselors, psychologists, pastors, and parents. You learn how to read more than books. Most importantly, you learn who you are.

I am not a *do something halfway kind of dude*. When I commit, I commit. I am also hyper-competitive and borderline overly ambitious. Mix that with unfocused forcefulness and unbottled rage, and you have a problem. In my case, it worked out decently well in my favor because I was me. My relationships with my teammates were not fabricated. The heat that I felt from my teammates and the heat that I offered were non-discriminatory.

I evolved throughout my years, as did they. Authenticity always reigned supreme. That's why even after a heated argument, hard foul, silent treatment, or however else we ignorantly responded, we were able to apologize and move on. At least I was. I think the same for my former teammates. Earlier in this chapter, I said that some might not think fondly of me. I hope that's not the case, but it might be. If so, my apologies. If not, great. Having the willingness to remain accountable for my shortcomings has also been advantageous on my journey from the bench to the boardroom.

Peers

Playing sports and having to learn new personalities each year wasn't reserved for the court. The skills that I learned in the lab translated magnificently well to the factory floor. My day-to-day peer interactions were enhanced because of what I learned every day as a walk-on. Being a relative unknown kept me humble. Not being the smartest student prevented pretentiousness. While I am keenly aware that many students across the country would have traded places with me in a heartbeat if given the opportunity to be an Irishman, I never felt envy. I only felt encouragement, empowerment, and energized optimism regarding the realm of probable.

The levels of camaraderie, love, and companionship that I felt from my classmates were amazing. The resolution to carry on during many weakened moments was emboldened by the words of my peers in the classroom, recreation center, library, dining hall, or dorm hallway. To know that people were rooting for my success was encouraging. The peer relationships that were established during my freshman year blossomed through senior year and beyond. I was never silly enough to really believe that I was big time or isolated from others simply because of being on the team. While it is true that most of my interactions were with my teammates, I was mindful of the rest of the world.

I enjoyed hearing my roommates' stories. I appreciated studying with my intellectual superiors so that I could get better. I was grateful for the opportunities to impart knowledge on others when requested (or when I felt like doing so), and I was thankful for the genuine nature of the relationships. The knowledge, skills, and abilities that I acquired in the lab bolstered my capabilities to effectively operate outside of my own little world. The positive reinforcement and lessons learned during my daily interactions strengthened what I knew to be true.

To the Boardroom

I mentioned it before, but it bears repeating. If you can shoot, you can play anywhere in the country. If you can create, you can do anything that you want to do. I learned and practiced that as a walk-on. I teach that as a father. I encourage that as a friend. I live that as a man.

I've been able to create solid relationships with coaches, teammates, and peers. In the work environment, I've created healthy relationships with managers, peers, and those that I've had the honor of leading on various projects. I learned that in the lab. I put in focused effort. I practice my craft. I ask for help. I uplift others. I fall down seven times and get up eight. I learned that in the lab. I listen and learn. I observe, experience, and experiment. I think and respond accordingly. I shoot and I miss. I create, therefore I am. I learned that in the lab.

Absolutely every learning experience as a walk-on prepared me for the real world. The same holds true for you. As a walk-on, you learn how to leverage instinct, intelligence, education, and training. The learning experiences, naturally, are at a smaller scale while a collegiate athlete and the consequences aren't usually that dire from a big picture perspective (most things aren't), but the correlation to the real world is astounding.

To transition from the bench to the boardroom, we have to know our strengths. We have to leverage the knowledge, skills, and abilities of others to mitigate our weaknesses. We have to dream big, think systemically, act pragmatically, and evolve regularly. We have to be ready and willing to function as an architect or bricklayer. Situational understanding, action, and leadership are obligatory. We have to observe without judgment. We have to make hard decisions. We have to foster spirits of grit, autonomy, mastery, creativity, community, curiosity, and craftsmanship in others. We have to operate within the confines of integrity, honesty, decency, and bravery. We have to know what we want and believe that we can get it. Knowing is intellectual. Believing is emotional. Combine the two and what was previously considered impossible becomes reasonable.

To transition from the bench to the boardroom, we must be willing to stand on an island even if we have to stand alone. We must think and act futuristically. We have to be okay with not knowing. We need the confidence to seek counsel when we lack knowledge. We have to search for truth, love our neighbors, love ourselves, and keep moving forward until we achieve the desired objectives. We have to lift as we climb, learn as we teach, and teach as we learn. When something seems implausible, we must believe that we can make it otherwise.

The evolution from the bench to the boardroom wasn't easy for me. It wasn't easy for the countless number of people that I have encountered over the last decade and a half and the billions of others that I have not had the pleasure of meeting. It will not be easy for you. It will, however, be worth it. The worth factor comes into play when you decide what your *boardroom* is. It might not be the traditional boardroom that you see in your mind. The *boardroom* might be your dinner table. It might be your classroom. It might be your car. It might be your church. The *boardroom* is wherever you choose to go and give a piece of yourself to offer value for the betterment of others and yourself. I sit in many boardrooms. I make decisions in some and offer advisory counsel in others. I am content while I continue to strive. I learned that in the lab. You will too, if you haven't done so already.

CHAPTER 10

The Spartan Way

Being a walk-on teaches us how to be collaborative and independent. We learn how to lead and follow. We work to create new and better versions of ourselves. Our desire to be great is internal. The external pressures ultimately dissipate, and we learn how to effectively operate within order and chaos. Not many people can do what we do. Not many people want to do what we do. We are the chosen few who decide to voluntarily punish ourselves for free. This is what it means to be a Spartan. Not a Spartan from Michigan State (no disrespect), but a Spartan Warrior.

Being a Spartan means that we never quit. We only retreat when we need to plan, plot, and strategize how to overcome an obstacle. We challenge ourselves for fun. We engage to achieve what was once only a fantasy in our minds. We want to know what version 72 of us looks like. Heightened awareness of our aptitudes, abilities, intelligence, instinct, education, experience, and stamina propel us forward. Being a Spartan means that no one is left behind. We push ourselves and we push each other. We dig deep into our souls and push our minds and bodies to the brink of exhaustion. We learn that as long as we don't quit, our bodies will adapt.

Working out is one thing. Completing a Spartan Sprint, Super, or Beast is something completely different. Achieving the coveted trifecta (completion of a Sprint, Super, and Beast in one calendar year) and becoming a member of the #TrifectaTribe cements your legacy in history. Songs will be sung about your adventures and the obstacles you overcame. (Literally, there are obstacles in each race.) Your name will be mentioned with Achilles, Apollo, Artemis, Aphrodite, Poseidon, Zeus, and Athena. History books will discuss your perseverance, tenacity, determination, discipline, and focus. Non-Spartan warriors will be envious, inspired, or a combination of both. Movies will visually represent you and your achievements in such a way that the stars in the sky will shine a little brighter. You will be hailed as a king of kings or queen of queens. Horns will sound at the majesty and miracle of your conquests. #Sike. None of that will happen in real life for most of us, but you definitely got excited even imagining that it might be true. I smiled writing it.

Although no one will care about the completion of a trifecta other than you and the 171 people who click the *like* button on Facebook or Instagram (actually, they don't care either as it requires zero effort to like a picture on a social media platform), it is a phenomenal accomplishment. The internal aspiration to inflict such self-punishment simply to see if you can is the walk-on way. It is the Spartan way.

A Spartan Sprint consists of three to five miles of running, jogging, or walking up and down hills (sometimes mountains or ski slopes depending on where you are) in mud, through the woods, through water, etc. and 21-25 obstacles. A Spartan Super consists of eight to

10 miles and 25-29 obstacles. A Spartan Beast consists of 12-14 miles and 31-35 obstacles. A Spartan Ultra consists of approximately 30 miles and 60+ obstacles. I don't even know why I just wrote about a Spartan Ultra because I almost passed out thinking about doing something that crazy. A Sprint, Super, and Beast are plenty to prove your bravery and heroism to yourself ... don't be silly ☺. Unless, of course, you want to run an Ultra, then do that.

I began my Spartan Journey in the summer of 2017 and it was an extraordinary and enlightening experience. I was challenged to do something that I had never done before and the journey mirrored what I encountered prior to climbing the walk-on mountain. The adrenaline, determination, owl-like focus, and life assassin mentality were very present. I was scared, nervous, insecure, and doubtful. I was curious. I only needed a few kicks in the rear and a few less than nice names to be yelled at me in order to engage. Only kidding. I didn't need a great deal of prodding. Although my friends who challenged me to do it did say, "Stop whining like a baby and make it happen."

Once I saw how challenging it was, I wanted to do it. I had to do it. If for no other reason than as a testament of human fitness. I wanted to prove to myself that I could do it. I wanted to *jump over the fire* and then cross the finish line. The only thing I needed to do in order to *make it happen* was to get rid of the scared version of me. I told the almost 40-year-old version of me to channel the passion, power, and purpose from the 19-year-old me. I was lightweight shook, though. I hadn't run a mile straight in 16 years. I hadn't traveled three to five miles in a row on foot ever. What did I do to get ready? I trained.

I worked out 10-12 times per week for a little over three months. Five to six times during the mornings, I would do 150-200 push-ups (sets of 50), 100 pull-ups (sets of 15-20), jump rope for nine-12 minutes (one-minute intervals), run one to two miles, then go to work. In the afternoons, I would do a regular work out, and run another one to two miles. There was no way that I would let a few obstacles defeat me. I had a proven record of accomplishment as a kid. I knew that I could do it as an adult.

I was 212.7 pounds when I started training. On race day in September 2017, I was 192.4 pounds. I was excited to beat the weak version of me. That excitement vanished approximately four minutes into the race when we hit that first incline. #Yikes. I almost passed out 57 times when I ran my first Sprint, but I made it.

SPARTAN RACE - DUNK WALL

I ran two more Spartan Sprints before I made the decision to join the #TrifectaTribe. I ran faster and felt stronger in my subsequent Sprints. I put in the effort so I knew that I could do it. I didn't really care who knew. I did post on Instagram because why not? Let me be great and get my 43 likes. My practices became my games. I ran up hills and down hills. I lifted. I jumped rope. I ran stairs. I carried buckets of water and bags of rice on flat ground and elevated ground. I did more pull-ups. I did more push-ups. I practiced doing monkey bars. I put in the effort to prepare myself so when the time came, I was ready. Let me be clear, though. My process did not prepare me for the bucket carry. #YikesAgain. Every day I practiced like it was the real thing. Not to impress anyone else, but to show myself that I was capable of doing great things. I knew that the scared version of me didn't like it, but I didn't care. I had a dream. Not like Dr. King's, but a dream, nonetheless. Let me live.

SPARTAN RACE — BUCKET CARRY

SPARTAN RACE — RINGS

SPARTAN RACE — A-FRAME

I pushed myself. I pushed my brothers and sisters. My brothers and sisters pushed me. We all had a goal. We all saw the finish line in our heads. We all envisioned *jumping over the fire* in order to cross the finish line. Spartan Sprints two and three were complete.

SPARTAN RACE — FIRE JUMP

Prior to finishing the third Sprint, I told myself that was it. I had no intention of doing another race. I didn't think that I was interested in doing a Super or Beast. Towards the end of that race, that thought process seemed to be more like a reality. I felt like my right leg was going to break. My knee looked like a baby watermelon. Every part of my calf and ankle felt like they were on fire. After I completed the race (not finishing was not an option), I scheduled an appointment to see the doctor. As I suspected, it was a torn meniscus in my right knee. This was not a career ending injury, but it was surely a setback. I was not happy with myself.

As is the case more than I would like to admit, feelings of

inferiority, insecurity, and doubt crept in. Fortunately, I knew how to respond. I freed myself from attachment, didn't take it personally, and intelligently directed my energy. I've been hurt before so I knew how to respond. Near the end of my senior year in college, one of my professors told me that the reason I made it as far as I did is because I never quit. As he continued to elevate me and offer counsel about life after college, he followed the *I always tried and never quit* statement by telling me that he *gave me permission to go in any direction, but backwards.* He told me that even if I had to take baby steps or detours that I always had to keep moving forward. That counsel has remained with me through the fortunate and unfortunate times.

Coach D used to say to me, "You can't get hurt. I do not give you permission to get hurt. I need you to play certain roles so that we can be better." I accepted that. When the doctor told me that he would do the knee surgery in early June 2018, I told him that I couldn't be hurt. I advised him that I did not give myself permission to get hurt because there were certain roles that I needed to play to make myself and others around me better. He laughed and said, "You can make them better in a couple of months because right now your knee is messed up."

I began physical therapy about a week post-surgery and it ended on 15 August 2018. 20 August 2018 was a normal day. Wake up, workout, go to work, workout, read, write, eat, and then sleep. Oh yeah, I talked to the family during some part of that day, I'm sure. When I woke up on 21 August 2018, I felt like someone had stuck a bunch of needles on the right side of my neck, right shoulder, and shoulder blade and set them on fire. The pain was so potent that I couldn't think. I couldn't have sustained conversations because I was unable to focus for an extended period of time. I had to lean very deeply to one side to relieve the pressure. It was not a pretty sight.

In mid-July, I decided to complete my first Spartan Trifecta. I had already completed the Sprint and needed to finish the Super and Beast. I had a slight problem, however. I couldn't lift weights, do push-ups or pull-ups, and I was unable to push or pull anything heavier than about 25 pounds with my right arm. This setback would make it quite difficult to climb ropes, carry buckets, swing from monkey bars, climb A-frames, crawl under barbed wire, and so forth.

After several weeks of multiple neck, back, and shoulder appointments, I was informed that I had a bulging disc, degenerating discs, and a pinched nerve. #YikesTimesThree. The Super was already scheduled for September 2018 and the Beast was on deck for November 2018. My inability to walk or physical departure from this earth were the only two things that could prevent me from going mountain climbing again. The same character traits that I needed to make the team, stay on the team, and actively participate in life after college athletics were necessary to become a member of the #TrifectaTribe.

The only thing that didn't hurt was running, jumping rope, and abs exercises. So, I ran. I ran a lot. I ran hills, stairs, technical terrain, and flat surfaces. I jumped rope for multiple minutes at a time. My abs workouts were serious business. I knew that I was unable to compete against myself at top physical strength, but I knew that I could be in great cardiovascular shape. I knew what I needed to do to succeed, so I did that. I had an almost insatiable desire to climb my newly identified mountain.

I couldn't sleep the night before the Spartan Super because I was so excited. I was like a little kid preparing for his first day of school. After approximately 9.5 miles and about 30 obstacles, I *jumped over the fire* and crossed the finish line. One more race to go before becoming an official member of another tribe.

SPARTAN RACE — FINISHER MEDAL

Fast forward one and a half months. My neck was feeling a little better, but still at a pain level of about seven on a scale of 10. All good, though. No pain, no gain, right? I was running two to three times per week and doing body weight workouts since I was unable to lift heavy weights. My mid-week runs ranged from three to five miles and my weekend runs increased from seven to 13.48 miles. 3 November 2018 was scheduled to be my longest run before tackling the Spartan Beast on 17 November 2018. Instead of running alone like I normally do, I decided to do something different. Since I planned to run 12-14 miles on that Saturday anyway, I decided to complete a half marathon. My logic was if I needed to run that far anyway, I might as well run with others in case I pass out.

Without conducting ample research, I signed up on Thursday night for a Saturday morning race. On Friday night, my wife casually asked if I knew that the half was a trail run. WHAT? No, I had no idea. I simply signed up. "Oh well," I thought. There was no turning back. I should have turned back. Unfortunately, the walk-on manifesto discourages such weakness. Additionally, According to King Leonidus from the Brave 300, "Spartans never retreat. Spartans never surrender." About three miles into this trail race, I accidentally stepped into a hole that I did not see. "FFFFFFFFFFFFFFFFFF," was the sound that emerged from my mouth. I didn't have on ankle braces, only compression socks.

There was no way that I was going to quit so I decided to *jog it off.* Exactly seven minutes later, I stepped on some rocky terrain that was covered by leaves. This time, and without hesitation, the rest of the *F-word* came barreling out of my mouth. I thought my ankle was broken. It immediately swelled to the size of a baseball. For the next two hours, I could only hobble. Running wasn't an option. I wanted to, but was unable to do so. The pain was severe. I still crossed the finish line. I could barely walk, but I made it. I didn't quit, so my body adapted.

I couldn't believe what happened. Two weeks away from joining the #TrifectaTribe and I made a terrible decision. From 3 November to 10 November I could barely walk. I couldn't lift and couldn't run. So, what did I do? I drank tequila. Only kidding. Sike. Well, maybe I am serious. You don't need to know that part ☺. What I will tell you is that I visualized success. I knew the goal and was determined to make it happen.

I watched CrossFit, Spartan, and other obstacle course racing videos. I needed to visualize the outcome. I needed to see me *jumping over the fire* again. I iced my ankle, added heat, did movement exercises, and worked my core. I had to stay focused. The same life assassin and mission mindset that I employed at the age of 17 was as strong as ever. Nothing would deter me from *getting it done*. As long as I could walk, I was going to succeed. 17 November 2018 was game day. Approximately 35 obstacles, unbelievable amounts of mud, fantastic soreness, and 13.25 miles later, it was all done. Success. I joined the other eagles flying in rarefied air and became a member of the #TrifectaTribe.

SPARTAN RACE — BEAST RINGS

SPARTAN RACE — TRIFECTA MEMBER

SPARTAN RACE — TRIFECTA MEMBER

The desire to achieve an intentional objective and willingness to physically overcome a mixture of obstacles in pursuit of my Spartan journey goals, paralleled my walk-on journey. I have only completed one trifecta so far and a total of six Spartan races, but the journey has been transformational. In reality, my accomplishments in the obstacle course racing world are miniscule. I'm not a boss in that space. I've never even come close to winning a race. I've met people on my Spartan journey who have finished 15, 20, 25, 40 trifectas and finished in the top 10 in almost every race.

The great news is that I am not bothered by their success. I applaud it. My competition is me. I am not comparing myself to anyone. My workouts are my games. My races serve as my workouts. My motivation is internal. I know that no one cares other than me. I am fine with that. The goal is to achieve the goals that I set for myself. The goal is to simply show that it can be done. The goal is to look myself in the mirror and say with confidence that I fought the good fight and finished the race. Nothing more. Nothing less. It's a very simple existence. I learned that as a walk-on at the University of Notre Dame.

Once again, I was afforded the opportunity to challenge myself to do something that I had not done in the past. The imagery and actual act of running, falling, getting back up, climbing over obstacles, falling, getting back up, running some more, helping others, getting help, getting hurt, and carrying on is equivalent to the life journey. The requisite level of mental and physical strength to voluntarily push your mind and body to the point of exhaustion was learned as a teen, solidified as a walk-on, and reinforced as a Spartan. Climbing the walk-on mountain was alchemic and paved the way to becoming a Spartan Beast well before I knew it was even an option.

Everything that happened *for* me during my walk-on years

prepared me for everything that has come and will come my way. I have shoulders full of stripes. I am battle tested. We are battled tested. If we climb one mountain, we can climb many more. We simply must maintain our indomitable spirits.

CHAPTER 11

In Their Own Words

In thinking and writing about the walk-on journey, I can only talk about my personal story with any level of depth and clarity. Any other insights that I offer are peripheral accounts based on information that I have gained in diverse conversations over the years. As a result, I wanted to better capture the lived experiences of some of my walk-on brothers and sisters.

In this chapter, you will read the words of four different walk-ons. They will offer insight into their lived experiences and how the walk-on journey prepared them for life after sports. The four individuals that you will now read about penned their own sections. The following are their words, feelings, and experiences.

Alex Koehler – University of Colorado, Colorado Springs – Men's Basketball

I was recruited out of high school to be a part of the University of Colorado, Colorado Springs (UCCS) Men's Basketball team. They offered me a walk-on spot, but I did not really know if I wanted to walk on or not. I was disappointed that I was not offered a scholarship. I was being recruited by a couple of different schools, but was not offered a scholarship spot on the roster. The Sports Management Program at UCCS really intrigued me, so I decided to go to UCCS and concentrate on academics. During my freshmen year, I was working within the Athletic Department and coaching at my high school, Rampart High.

While coaching, I realized that I missed playing basketball and wanted to compete at a high level again. My focus then turned to working out and doing the things that I needed to do to become a collegiate athlete. After the UCCS basketball season was over, I went into the coach's office and asked, "What do I need to do to be on the team?" The coach responded, "You don't need to do anything, you are on the team now." I was so ecstatic and excited to be on the team. After spring break, I was officially a walk-on on the UCCS Men's Basketball team. The first couple of weeks were brutal! I had been lifting weights, but not to the extent that I needed to be. Thankfully, I was in great condition.

I prepared to walk on to the basketball team by training hard on the court, in the weight room, and talking with my father. My father was a Division I Lacrosse Coach for almost 20 years. He had seen it all and told me what I needed to do to be successful and to get on the team. He also told me that I would need to work harder than I ever had before. That is exactly what I did.

I was in the gym or in the weight room for about six hours a day. If I was not in class, sleeping, or doing homework, I was in the gym. I have always been the hardest working individual on any team. I have always had that personality to work hard and believe that good things happen when you work hard and are prepared. I was also born into a military family, so I was taught discipline and practiced being disciplined. I also learned to *roll with the punches.* Even if things are not going my way, I always fight. I brought that mentality to the basketball court. I knew I was going to have to work hard at practice every single day to get some minutes on the court. My goal was to always be the hardest working individual at practice.

The personal characteristics that I possess and used to climb the collegiate athlete ladder were determination, hard work, remaining calm, and pure excitement to be on a team. These qualities really helped me step on the floor during my career at UCCS. My goal was to consistently be the hardest worker at practice and to do the little things that not everyone wanted to do. I would dive on the floor, crash for offensive rebounds, fight for defensive rebounds with the big guys, and take charges. I did not really care if I scored 20 points or two points. I just wanted to do everything that I could to help my team win. If that meant diving on the floor to secure the ball and then have someone else score, then so be it. I just wanted to win and play the game of basketball with my teammates. During practices or games, I would get fired up when a big play happened but then would go back to my calm nature and play hard. I truly believe that my sacrifice for the team was what led to me getting into games. The coaches saw that I was always going to play hard, not take a play off, and make sacrifices for the betterment of the team.

Once I officially made the team, I was so happy and excited. I did not have a try out like most walk-ons. UCCS recruited me out of high school and knew about me from watching me play high school basketball. That feeling of incredible excitement when I was told that I had made the UCCS basketball team never really wore off during my career at UCCS. There were times when being a collegiate athlete was incredibly hard, but I could never quit. My first and second basketball seasons were very tough as my team struggled to win games. I was always so thankful and grateful that I had the opportunity to play college basketball. I was living the dream that so many high school basketball players have, but are not able to fulfill.

I was treated very well by coaches on and off the court and I believe that my work ethic on the court, as well as in the classroom, was the reason. There were times when my coaches were not very happy with me and pushed me to perform differently. They never accepted the status quo. I had to push myself to unexplored limits. I am grateful that my coaches saw my potential, even when I could not see it. My coaches were tough on me, but their words and actions helped to shape me into the player that I became. Their trust in me and belief that I could perform better at each game continues to motivate me to do well as an Assistant Athletic Director. I will always push myself to do more than what is expected.

Ultimately, I had a great relationship with my teammates. It wasn't always easy, though. At first, when I showed up to practice, the players all thought, "Who is this kid?" In the spring, Division II legislation dictates how many basketball workouts a team can have. Consequently, they only really got to see a glimpse of me and what I could bring to the team during the short spring season. I had a very short period of time to prove to them that I had something to offer to the team. Once practice officially started in the fall, they could clearly see my strong work ethic, unselfish style, and skills.

After a couple of weeks, everyone associated with the team knew

I was where I was supposed to be. My teammates always pushed each other to become better players. I was proud of the fact that they hated to guard me because I was always moving, running, setting screens, diving on the floor, or crashing for rebounds on every single play. They pushed me to take the open shots instead of passing the ball and looking for the assist. My teammates made my college experience better. They were my friends, my classmates, my roommates, and my teammates. We spent a lot of time together. We loved the great times and grew in the bad times.

Being a walk-on at UCCS really helped to prepare me for life after college. You need to work for the things that you want in life and when you put in the work, good things will happen. Going into the work force after college I knew someone was not going to give me a job just because I had a degree or because I was a college athlete. I needed to work for it just like I needed to work to get some time on the court. That is exactly what I did. I started working for the UCCS Athletic Department when I was a freshman in the Sports Management Program. Initially, I set up events and games in exchange for $1.30 an hour and a $500 yearly scholarship.

I worked hard and was at every event and game. I put in work in the office and did whatever they needed me to do. The next year, I started working with a Compliance Officer and did whatever she needed me to do. I worked for her for two years before she left in the fall of my senior year. That year, I was more involved and assisted the Athletic Director with all the compliance paperwork that needed to be done throughout the year. By then, my reputation as being a committed, hard worker was apparent to everyone in the athletic department. My hard work paid off. After my eligibility ended with the UCCS Men's Basketball team, I was offered the position as Assistant Athletic Director for Compliance. I truly believe it was because of the hard work I put into basketball, the classroom, and working in the Athletic Department that helped me secure this great job.

The best advice I can give to future walk-ons is don't give up, always work hard, and be the best teammate you can be. If you aspire to be on a collegiate basketball team and are not really getting any looks by college coaches, don't give up. Send emails to hundreds of coaches at various levels and someone will notice you. Maintain an exceptional work ethic and work hard on the court, in the weight room, and in the classroom. When you think you are doing enough, do some more. Never slack off in the classroom. If you are not doing well in the classroom, you are giving your coach an excuse to get rid of you. Be one of the first ones to the gym and one of the last ones to leave. Be the best teammate that you can be and always have a positive attitude.

If you are on the bench, make sure you get up and high five people coming off of the court. If there is a big play, celebrate with your teammates on the bench. Having a bad attitude because you are not playing considerable minutes will never help you get more playing time. I know this is hard as everyone wants to play every single minute of every single game. In reality, that is not possible. Just be a good teammate and enjoy it. Coaches would rather reward a walk-on that is being a good teammate than one that is sulking on the bench the whole game. Finally, for past walk-ons who still have some insecurities, be grateful for the time that you had at your institution playing the game you loved. Most people do not get the chance to play at the collegiate level. You did. Be grateful for it and cherish those moments with your teammates for those moments will always be with you.

What am I doing now? I am an Associate Athletic Director for Compliance at the University of Colorado, Colorado Springs and have been here for the past four years. I enjoy being around student-athletes and watching/helping them grow as an athlete and a student, but most importantly as a human being. My future aspiration is to be an Athletic Director.

My last thoughts are that playing any sport at the collegiate level is not easy. It requires an incredible commitment both on and off the court. However, the rewards of being a part of a collegiate team are huge and well worth the time and effort. Being able to juggle school and athletics will help prepare you for life. Being a responsible, committed team player is exactly what will make you successful in life.

Dani Nickle – Texas Tech and University of Texas, San Antonio (UTSA) – Women's Volleyball

I started playing competitive volleyball during the time frame when the physique of competitive athletes was changing. The era of average height, athletic players was coming to a close. Long, lanky position specific athletes were taking over. Middles were six feet or taller, outsides were 5'10" or taller, the shortest (competitive) setter that I knew was 5'7", and little liberos were few and far between. My chances of playing college volleyball began to dwindle solely based on the fact that I was 5'6" and had a very athletic build.

I specifically remember my dad approaching my club coach, asking if I had a chance to play collegiately. I was terrified that he was going to say no. As a freshman in high school and no guarantee that I would grow any taller, my coach reassured us that with commitment, hard work, and my athleticism, I could definitely play. And *if* I grew, I could play anywhere. I continued to play ball year-round and before the end of my freshman /sophomore summer, I decided to focus completely on volleyball. Going into the next competitive season was exciting because I was being recruited by a few well-known schools. I traveled the whole summer break and attended summer camps so that I could continue to pursue my dream of playing in college.

By my junior year, I hadn't grown and all those well-known schools dropped off the map. Luckily, one school, Winthrop University, continued to inquire about me and eventually brought me in for a campus visit. I was ecstatic and eager. This was going to be my shot. That weekend, I fell in love with the school's high-level academics, the campus, the coaches, and the city. I verbally committed to a walk-on spot with the understanding that I would have a scholarship my last three years, once the current defensive specialist graduated. That was it! I was going to be a college athlete. I felt special. I felt accomplished. My coach checked in often and I was invited by a current player to attend the volleyball Final Four with her and her family. I attended summer camp the next year knowing that I already had a spot. I didn't envy the girls competing to join the squad in two years. I was enjoying my week at camp and they were stressing.

I couldn't believe that I would enter my senior season with the guarantee that my journey would continue. All of my hard work and dedication to volleyball was about to pay off. Until it wasn't. After some career changes for my parents, it was evident that paying to go to an out-of-state, private school was doable, but only for a semester. Without an athletic scholarship, I wouldn't be able to stay there long term. I was devastated and panic set in. Fast forward to February of my senior year in high school. While at a tournament with my club team, luck struck again. A recruiter from Texas Tech saw me play a match. Afterwards, he approached my coach to inquire about my status for the following year. My coach knew that I had verbally committed, but also knew about the financial constraints that a private, out-of-state school was imposing on my family. The recruiter followed as I played through the weekend.

A few weeks later, I was invited to visit the school. My dad told me that the only way I could go on the visit was if I called my coach at Winthrop to let him know that I was going and why. I reluctantly called my coach to let him know that I was going to visit Tech, not because I didn't want to play at Winthrop, but because I knew that I owed it to my family and myself to explore my options. I also shared that without financial support, I couldn't guarantee that I would even be at Winthrop to get that scholarship my second year. The voice on the other end of the line was clearly upset with me and I understood why. And then he told me that if I got on that plane, my chance of being an Eagle was gone. He continued by saying I was untrustworthy and unappreciative of my opportunity. I told him that I understood, was sorry, but needed to go on the visit even if that meant I wouldn't play next year.

When I hung up, I broke down. I didn't understand. I couldn't believe that my character was brought into question. How could a coach that wasn't willing to pay for my school tell me that my chances of playing were lost? How could my character be called into question? How many 18-year-olds would have actually picked up the phone? How many people would have been honest?

Even in the midst of confusion, uncertainty, and doubt, I was determined to play. The desire to prove others wrong and prove myself right was powerful, especially when the larger schools stopped recruiting me because of my size. I'd watch many of my peers give up. I refused to let this be my story. Walk-on or scholarship athlete, it didn't matter to me. I wanted to prove that a small-town girl could play at a Division I school. Most of the girls I knew were going DII/ DIII/NAIA. Not that anything was wrong with that route, but I worked hard to compete against 5A girls in club. I wanted to play against them in college, too. In addition to being laser focused on my goals, I knew that as a player, particularly a potential walk-on, that I needed trust. I learned along the way to trust myself and my abilities. I needed to be confident so when coaches walked by, they didn't keep walking because they didn't see the size they wanted. I wanted them to stop because they saw an athlete that trusted her abilities and was confident in her game.

I went on that visit and my athletic journey changed immediately! Tech was a Big 12 school. I would have the opportunity to play against top athletes in the nation. I was only going to be five hours from home. My family was going to be able to see me play. It was a dream come true. I was going to be a Red Raider! Even as a future walk-on, I was treated like a scholarship athlete before I arrived on campus my freshman year. I was sent a letter of intent so I could have a letter signing ceremony and I also received the summer workout program. I was expected to attend preseason summer camp before two-a-days and I was expected to live with my fellow freshmen. I was the same.

I knew from observations and hearing people talk that walk-ons weren't always so fortunate. The stigma was even apparent when watching collegiate games. I would hear announcers say things like, "Oh, so and so is a walk-on athlete." I also knew from my own experiences that a negative connotation could be attached to the walk-on label. When I would tell people that I was going to play at Texas Tech, they would be surprised and then immediately ask me if I was getting a scholarship. It was almost like my accomplishment wasn't valid without a scholarship. It was like they didn't expect me to survive. Maybe it was society that made me feel different. I also felt like walk-on spots weren't guaranteed. It was like I had to be amazing and on ALL THE TIME to keep my coveted spot. I didn't think girls with scholarships had the same feelings that I did.

Even though there was a feeling of similarity, I always felt the need to work harder. I always felt the need to prove myself. I needed my coaches to know that they made the right decision. I started an additional strength and conditioning program with the coach at a local university. I practiced with my old club team on a regular basis. I was doing everything and anything to keep my competitive edge and athleticism on point. I knew that I made the right decision and I knew it was going to pay off. I wanted to play.

Being a walk-on didn't scare me. I was ready for the challenge. I knew that I had put in the time and effort. I knew that I deserved that spot on the Tech squad. But I needed everyone else to know that I was working hard. I needed everyone else to know that just because I was going to walk on didn't mean that I would settle for just being on the team. I wanted playing time. I wanted to contribute and I felt that I couldn't do that from the sideline. I didn't want to wait. As a child, my parents taught me that good things didn't come to those who waited. Good things came to those who WORKED.

Summer camp was a breeze. I was competing with the upper classmen and I was having fun. It was all happening. It wasn't until our first pre-season tournament that I knew I really made it. We were between sets of our first match when Coach asked me if I had my other jersey and asked me to put it on. I was going to start the second set against UCSB (ranked 7th in the nation at the time) as libero. Excited was an understatement. I couldn't believe I was about to play. And I was going to play over girls with scholarships. I overpassed on the first two serves of the match. As our senior setter walked up to me, I was terrified. I was waiting to be reamed and pulled out of the game. I wasn't. She patted me on the back and just told me to keep doing what I was doing. I ended up having 12 digs in that set and went on to start the rest of the weekend. I continued to be a part of the regular rotation. I was one of seven girls that played while another seven rarely saw the floor.

I was lovingly called the overachiever, I became the strength coach's little project, and made the Dean's List in my first semester. I kept trying to do anything in my power to be the best. I felt the need to prove to the coaching staff that they made the right decision in bringing me on. I also wanted to prove myself right. I was a small-town girl. I played for a club that was lesser known. I didn't play on the same club team that all of the top 5A girls played on. My club was competitive, but we didn't have the big names. I was internally motivated to show that regardless of where I was from, I could compete with any girl next to me. As a walk-on, I felt an even stronger desire to perform. I didn't want to be perceived as just a filler. I was always told that I had to work for the things I wanted. I wanted to be a leader on the team. I wanted to be a starter, or at the very least have a major role on the court.

The stress got to me, though. I ended up having an emotional breakdown. I was home sick and exhausted, I had stressed myself out to the max, and I had spread myself too thin. The coaching staff could tell. In an effort to get me back to normal, my head coach let me ride home with my family after a match at Texas A&M, but that didn't calm me down. I continued to feel the need to prove myself and showcase my abilities.

My stress began to manifest as injuries and before the end of the season, I was sidelined. Visits to multiple team doctors revealed a diagnosis that could only be treated by a surgery that couldn't guarantee improvement. Surgery wasn't an option in my opinion. I was discouraged. I was upset. I settled for not playing. I was burned out and I needed a break. For the first time in as long as I could remember, I didn't want to play volleyball, and I chose not to do so anymore. After our last match, I went to my coach's office and broke the news that I was done and that after the year I was transferring home. That overwhelming excitement of being a college athlete had peaked and had slowly dissolved. I was done. I had forgone other opportunities. I passed up majoring in art. I left home ... all to play.

When I started my second semester, I realized there was a whole side of college life that I missed. I didn't know anyone other than athletes and I didn't know any of my professors in the fall since we traveled a lot. I didn't have time to do ANYTHING other than volleyball. I didn't have a social life and I wasn't a normal college freshman. I was so excited to move back home and even more excited not to be playing competitively.

I had a life. I was going to school, I was working out every day, and I was coaching club volleyball. Any time I touched a ball, I enjoyed the experience. Nothing to prove, just fun! After almost a year and a half, while coaching at a tournament, I had a chance encounter with an old coach. She was coaching at UTSA and wanted me to come meet the rest of the coaching staff. She wanted me to play again. I was dumbfounded. I was hesitant. But I was so excited. That feeling was back and I wanted to play, regardless of if I was walking on or not. I wanted to be that person again.

After coming out for a spring practice, I was invited to join the 2006/2007 squad as a walk-on. I had done it again. I was on track and my dreams were alive and well. I was excited to be an athlete and with a renewed love for my sport. I was more active and present in my workouts. I was committed to being the best and proving that I was not just some chick that was asked to come try out. I was a competitive athlete. The universe had a different plan. The week before I was supposed to report to two-a-days, I blew my knee out. We also found out that the coach that asked me to come out was also taking a head coaching position at another school. It was the worst feeling in the world. My season was done and my advocate was leaving.

Once again, I felt the overwhelming need to prove, in spite of my injury, that I was an asset to the team. I wanted to prove that even though the coach that recruited me was gone, I belonged just the same. I did hours of rehab, attended every practice, every strength and conditioning workout, traveled to every match, and stood for all of them. I turned a six-month recovery into three. When it was all said and done, I earned a scholarship for that spring semester for my commitment and hard work. I felt accomplished. I felt that I had proven myself and my ability without even stepping foot on the floor. Now more than ever, I felt that I had achieved the ultimate dream. Not only was I on the team, but I also had a scholarship. The next year was going to be incredible.

I played sporadically through the spring season, as per our athletic trainer and my surgeon, and started getting used to playing with a brace. Boy, was life different. My abilities weren't the same. I was hesitant to do even the most basic of movements. I wasn't the player I had been and I didn't feel like I was ever going to be the same.

I stayed home that summer so I could go to summer workouts every day. I played at my team's practices. I did everything I could to keep going. The revolving door of the need to prove myself was in a never-ending spin. It was almost time for the season to start and I found out that my scholarship was going to be passed to another athlete. Talk about defeat. It was time to prove that they were wrong.

I did it all during two-a-days. Running, lifting my old numbers, full practices, keeping up with all the girls ... barely a year after a complete ACL and meniscus repair. Aside from the brace, you wouldn't have known I was hurt. And it worked! I won the starting libero position, which was something that after the past three years I never thought would happen again.

I was so excited. I knew that my coaches appreciated me. They loved my passion and my drive. Every week during team awards, the girls always voted me *hardest working*. It always struck me that a scholarship player never got it. It was like some of them knew that they didn't have anything to prove, that they didn't have to work hard. It was like we were on the same level, they just got to walk across the top and I was climbing the stairs. It's hard to say that I am right, though. That's the reality that I created. Maybe they thought they were working hard. Maybe their 100% was different than mine. Either way, I knew that I had to put in the work.

We traveled to our first tournament of the year and I started and finished every match of the day. It was the best feeling. I mean I was hurting in every place possible. My knee was so swollen that I could hardly walk. It hurt so good. I didn't feel good going into day two and I made the crazy decision to go talk to my coaches. That's when it all changed.

I told them that after our first day, I knew we were in a position to do well in the tournament and I wanted that, more than anything, for the team. And then I told them that I felt for us to do well the next day, I couldn't be the libero. I was more concerned about my team and their performance then my time on the court. They deserved the best me and I couldn't be that player. I was proud of myself and I was excited for the next day, until my coach started talking. She told me that I was giving up on the team and that I was unreliable. She said that she was going to start our other libero and that I was not showing my commitment to the team. I felt broken and beat. I felt betrayed. I felt like my injury and recovery weren't being taken as seriously as some of the other girls who were a little banged up and bruised from a long day of matches. I felt singled out. Looking back, I don't even remember how we did that weekend. I just knew I wasn't playing and that it wasn't only going to be a one game thing. At the next tournament, I was sidelined again. The next game I saw limited time and it was the same with the next and the next and the next. Then, I wasn't a libero anymore.

I became a serving specialist. At practice, I was a part of the B team, a group of girls that didn't play. When we scrimmaged the starters, we couldn't compete. It was just a letdown. It was not what I was about. Walk-on or not, it was not my idea of being a Division I athlete. When we had matches, I saw limited playing time. I remember one match where I played because I was *the only one left*. I was pushed to the side. Things really took a turn for the worst when I was made to do extra workouts. It was demanded that a group of us that didn't play much go to the rec center and burn a given number of extra calories each week. The goal was to keep us in shape during the season. On top of practice, strength and conditioning, and matches, we went to the rec two to three times a week. We jokingly called ourselves the "Fat Girls Club."

At this point, I hated volleyball. It wasn't that I was burned out or exhausted, I hated being an athlete with every bit of my soul. I continued to work hard on and off the court, but I started not caring. I know that sounds hypocritical, but that was the truth. Honestly, it kills me to say it, but quite frankly, I was more excited to get home and have a social life after matches than participate in the actual matches. I felt like our coaches didn't care if I was there or not. It seemed like all of the hard work I put in was pointless. I never let go of that terrible feeling.

Although everything that I envisioned did not go as planned and I had many sad and angry days, when it was all said and done, I was a better person. I knew what hard work meant. I knew my worth. I learned not to be walked over. I learned to stand up for myself, to stand up for what is right, and to not let others treat me unfairly. But I also lost some things along the way. After my experiences, I chose to opt out of what I thought was my dream job. I didn't want to be a college coach anymore. I didn't want to work in a college athletic department. I just kept thinking to myself that even if I did right by athletes that didn't mean that others in the athletic department would because I truly felt that no one else stood up for me. College athletics wasn't the place for me. I went on to graduate with a degree in English and continued to get a MAA in Sports Management. My time as an athlete taught me persistence, drive, and commitment.

I've been able to leverage the characteristics to help open and run a few businesses. I've been able to use what I learned while striving to thrive as a walk-on. The internal elements that allowed me to remain resilient through the tough times have helped me remain highly competitive in other athletic and life endeavors. I lead a family business, while raising two spirited little boys, and coaching fitness classes from time to time. I have learned that I need to be a level-headed individual. I have also learned that one of my greatest gifts is being others' champion. I wouldn't have figured that out if my athletic career was easy. I'm grateful for my experiences.

Every so often you hear the Cinderella stories. You learn about or experience the kid that was a walk-on for one reason or another that is now the star of the team. You hear stories about the kid that committed to going to the school they wanted without a scholarship and is now a scholarship athlete. Stories abound about the kid whose dreams came true and/or whose dreams didn't completely manifest themselves as envisioned.

At some point in my college career, I was all of those things, but I was also none of those things. Scholarship or not, being a student-athlete was one of the hardest things I have ever done, and I wouldn't change it for the world. As you consider your athletic journey or look back on it, don't let a scholarship (or lack thereof) determine who you are, your worth, or your ability. Being picked to join and being accepted to a team is all that matters. Live your truth and don't let others determine your worth. You made it, when so many others didn't!

Andrew Clavin – Football – Stanford University

I believed from an early age that a degree from an elite university would increase my chances of success in my life. Of course, there are plenty of exceptions to that line of thinking, but my goal worked for me and kept me motivated to excel in the classroom and on the football field throughout high school. Since admission to top universities is so competitive, I relied both on my grades and football ability to get noticed by recruiters and admissions officers. I was recruited by several Ivy League schools, but no Division I-A (now, FBS) schools. Thankfully, I gained admission to Stanford after sending in my application and football highlight tape. Stanford was short on offensive linemen that year, and they welcomed me to walk on to the team. I believe communicating my interest to walk on helped tip the admission scales in my favor, but I'll never know definitively.

Getting admitted to Stanford was a dream come true. I was able to remain in my home state rather than relocate cross country into a cold climate. I knew, at Stanford, that I would be outmatched by the scholarship players, but I didn't mind. I was just happy to be part of the team and such a special football program and university. It was a rare opportunity and I am thankful that I was able to partake in it.

As I prepared to walk on, I knew that it wouldn't be easy. I knew that I would have to engage in ways that I had not engaged before in order to make my dream come true. I trained as hard as I could from the moment I heard I was admitted until I showed up for freshman orientation. I had the spring and summer to prepare. That's not a lot of time, but thankfully I had a good friend and mentor who was an offensive lineman at Auburn in the 1980s to train me. The summer before college began, I also hired a trainer at Gold's Gym in Venice Beach who pushed me so hard that I vomited in several training sessions. I loved the process. Even though there were no certainties, I knew that I would have to play at a level at which I had not previously played to make it happen. Stanford's strength and conditioning coaches also mailed me a workout guide, as they did with all incoming freshman. I followed it to a T.

As I reflect on my journey and think through the personal characteristics that helped me climb this mountain, work-ethic played a prominent role. I imagine a characteristic common among walk-ons, in general, is an outstanding work ethic. I think it's fair to say I've always held a strong work ethic, along with intelligence and enough athletic skill to play football at the collegiate level. Combining those things, I pushed myself to get to the best place I could go, and thankfully I got there. Of course, nobody makes this kind of journey alone. I was blessed with a solid support system of family, teachers, and coaches. A lot has to come together to get to a place like Stanford (and any other Division I school), and even then, luck plays into it.

Even more preparation and luck have to align in order to make a team at such an elite university.

When I first made the team, I was overwhelmed. I went from being a top player on my high school team to being a scrub in college. The game was faster, and the players were bigger, stronger, and more mature. But in time, I gained my footing and developed friendships with many of my teammates. Nearly everyone was kind to me. Not everyone, but nearly everyone. As a walk-on, you feel the difference. Even if that difference is only in your mind, you know that there is a slight separation between you and your scholarship counterparts. That's not a bad thing, it is simply the nature of the game that we play. Above all, I felt proud to be part of the team, and to reach the Division I-A level. It's not something I expected to happen while I was in high school, but I was thrilled to take on the challenge.

The excitement of putting on that Stanford practice and game jersey never completely wore off. I considered it an honor to be on the football team at Stanford, every single day. However, getting thrown around like a rag doll in practice freshman year wasn't the most pleasant experience. As a true freshman playing scout-team center, I remember lining up against fifth year senior and future NFL nose tackle, Willie Howard. By the time I snapped the ball and took one step, Willie had already beat me, either by knocking me backward or blowing right by me with a swim move. But by my second year, I had added 30 pounds of muscle, and started to hold my own a little better.

My teammates and coaches were great. My good days outnumbered my bad. Being a walk-on was a hard, yet wonderful experience. Most of the coaches treated me the same as the scholarship players. Head coach Tyrone Willingham was always amicable and fair. Moreover, I could tell he looked out for me, perhaps because he was a walk-on himself at Michigan State.

I looked up to Coach Willingham like a father figure, as my own father died when I was five years old. Willingham led by example, always carrying himself with class and dignity. He was a stoic and cerebral coach who didn't mince words. He was clear and effective in delivering his speeches to the team, addressing us as fellow men. He regularly advocated for our success beyond football, both in the classroom and in life after university. He would often begin his talks with quotes from historical figures, such as Winston Churchill or Abraham Lincoln. His leadership helped me believe in myself. One of the most valuable insights I learned from Willingham's leadership was not to chatter needlessly, and only speak when I had something relevant to convey. You can learn more by observing and listening to others than pontificating. If you are calculated in how you communicate and listen to others, you have a better chance to succeed in life as well as sports.

While most of the coaches and players treated me as an equal, I would be remiss if I said that experience was an absolute. Most linemen were good to me, both offensive and defensive. Lineman usually bond well and look out for one another, so in that sense I was fortunate. There were a few players at other positions who treated me condescendingly. Their behavior spoke for itself. Most of the guys noticed it and judged them accordingly. I am not sure if it was because I was a walk-on or for other reasons, but I do know that the experiences proved to be most valuable in my life. There was no differentiation between me and scholarship players by most of my coaches and teammates, other than playing time of course. Being treated as an equal by teammates as well as coaches bolstered my confidence to give my all. As for the few players who were unkind to me, I paid little attention to it. I worked hard to make it to Stanford and play on the team, and I wasn't going to let them deter me.

Perhaps the greatest and longest-lasting benefit of walking on to the team at Stanford were the friendships I forged with several players. Since graduating, we've attended each other's weddings and watched each other become fathers. It has been great to witness my friends advance in their careers and build families. We help each other along life's journeys, when necessary. Being a college athlete at a top-tier Division I university was life altering. It was not easy, though. I spent countless hours working on my craft in order to make a positive difference for my brothers and I learned a tremendous amount during the process.

I learned more valuable life lessons through football than I did in the classroom. Don't get me wrong, Stanford academics are world class, but there are some things that can't be taught in a book or lecture hall. Some of the lessons that became ingrained in me through football include:

1. Life is difficult
2. Suffering together with teammates creates strong bonds
3. It is crucial to approach life standing tall with your shoulders reared back
4. Sometimes you have to play through pain
5. You must push yourself beyond your self-perceived limits to truly improve
6. The best players play
7. The more effort you put in, the more you get out
8. There is no substitute for hard work
9. Dedication, commitment, and optimism will steer you in the right direction
10. You learn more from failure than success

When I think about my future fellow walk-on brothers and sisters, I want them to know that dreams do come true. I want them to know that if you have the opportunity to play collegiate athletics, go for it. Only a privileged few get to play college sports, whether you're on scholarship or not. You'll create friendships and memories that will last a lifetime. If you are a current walk-on, my number one suggestion is to stick with it. I know it can be daunting, and you may ask yourself, "Why am I sacrificing almost everything for no scholarship money and little or no playing time?" You have the rest of your life to rest. Continue to push yourself now while you have the opportunity in hand. You will be glad that you did. Everyone has insecurities, whether you're on scholarship or not. The fact that you walked on to a team should bolster your confidence. Only a special few possess the temerity to do it.

My walk-on journey has been transformational. I am a happily married man, and father of one child (so far). Since graduating, I have worked in the entertainment industry, specifically audience research. I derive insights from consumer viewing habits of films and TV programs to help drive business decisions to ultimately increase revenue for my company (one of the top Hollywood studios). I enjoy my career and hope to continue in the same field. On a personal note, I would like to expand our family, and one day return to being more involved in football.

I was unable to play my entire four years as a Cardinal. Not because I wasn't good enough to stay on the team or because I quit. Injuries changed the game for me. I was injured between my sophomore and junior year and had to walk away from football early. At the time it was difficult, but I want to stress to anyone going through a similar situation that it's not the end of the world.

The medical term for the injury I suffered is a perilymphatic fistula. I experienced a rupture in my inner right ear during an overhead press, as fluid leaked out of my ear while straining heavily.

It wasn't painful, but I immediately noticed significant hearing loss. I proceeded to the training room after the workout. The trainers weren't certain what happened. They suspected I'd burst an eardrum, but sent me to see a specialist. I later discovered the severity of the injury. The hearing loss was permanent, and I was medically barred from doing heavy straining for the rest of my life, meaning no more weightlifting or football.

I was devastated by the news and fell into a depression. Football was a central component of my social identity. I felt lost without it. I also foolishly and insecurely thought my teammates would no longer accept me because I was no longer able to participate on the team. I even imagined some would doubt the validity of my injury, since it wasn't outwardly visible, and think it was just an excuse to quit. Of course, those worries didn't come to fruition. Most players still accepted me like a brother after the injury, as they did when I was on the team. As for the legitimacy of the injury, that was something anyone could verify with the team doctors, trainers, or coaches, if they cared to know.

Pulling myself out of depression was not easy. It required the same work ethic I relied on to walk on to the football team. Through therapy, journaling, and deep thought, the cloud eventually began to lift. I reshaped my perspective on life and focused on gratitude for all the blessings I had, rather than the things I'd lost. As time passed, I discovered new interests, including learning to play musical instruments, golf, and getting involved in various student organizations. As I look back on my time at Stanford, I am grateful for my time on the football team, and also grateful for the time I spent exploring other things.

For anyone whose athletic dreams were cut short, please know there is happiness afterward. Most people don't leave their sport on their terms. It ends sooner than they would like, either because of injury or not advancing to the next level. Whatever the case, there is plenty to look forward to beyond collegiate athletics. They key is to carry the valuable life lessons you learn from sports with you the rest of your life, like teamwork, sacrifice, and that life isn't fair. Hopefully you'll also maintain some friendships from your athletic days as you move through life.

Sky Owens – University of Notre Dame – Men's Basketball

Basketball has been a big part of my life since I was a young boy. My family has always been into sports, but for me basketball always held a special spot. Since I was three or four years old, I always assumed that I would play basketball. Obviously, we all dream about becoming professional athletes when we are young, but we don't completely understand everything that goes in to becoming a professional athlete.

Throughout my childhood, I came to understand all the work that went into becoming a professional basketball player. I came to understand that playing basketball was very similar to an onion from the standpoint that an onion has numerous layers. There are several layers (levels) of playing basketball. You have players who excel against competition in street ball, youth ball, middle school, high school, college, semi-pro leagues, international pro leagues, professional minor leagues, and lastly, the NBA.

For me, halfway through high school it started to dawn on me that the end of my basketball career could be coming soon. My career had been solid, but it was nothing newsworthy. I played with teammates who would go on to play at Kansas University, the Naval Academy, and the University of Minnesota, amongst others. I always thought my high school basketball career could have been better. I feel my career never fully blossomed because I was never fully committed to the sport. I was never a member of an AAU travel ball team and I truly enjoyed playing football.

Football season would often run into basketball season due to our team making the playoffs and having some success in the playoffs. As a result, my high school basketball career only consisted of 47 games. My football career yielded some scholarship offers (many questioned why I would turn down football scholarships), but I knew in my heart that I only liked playing football. I loved playing basketball. I felt that my high school basketball career was underwhelming and that I could be better as a player if I fully committed myself to the game. This is why I decided to attempt to walk on to the Notre Dame basketball team. I watched Notre Dame play some games during the 1995/1996 season and determined that the system the team ran would accentuate my strengths as a basketball player. I was also intrigued by the prospect of playing in the Big East conference.

In order to prepare for this undertaking, I began doing some individual workouts with my high school coach and put in some extra sessions with some of my former teammates who were playing in college. The plan was to diversify my game more since I was a high school center at 6'2" and definitely wouldn't be able to play the same position at the college level. For the first couple of months I was able to stick to a regular schedule, but then I ran into the rigors of life. I had to get a summer job in order to prepare for life away from home. As such, the time I was planning to dedicate to basketball fell to the wayside as a greater emphasis was placed on obtaining a quality education. With my time being dedicated mostly to making and saving money, my basketball regimen and workouts became rather sparse. I guess in the back of my mind I was thinking that it may be the end of the road for me and basketball.

In August 1996, I finally arrived on campus at the University of Notre Dame as a freshman. Within a week of classes starting, I found myself in the office of assistant coach Fran McCaffery discussing my summer and the prospects of me playing basketball. A few hours later, I was playing pickup basketball with the Notre Dame men's basketball team. It was then that I realized there was a pecking order for the basketball players.

Generally, the scholarship players played first for the sake of development and to build chemistry and camaraderie. The team captains/upper classmen would determine the teams and obviously walk-ons would get the scraps. I played with the team for a few weeks, but it required a commitment of a few hours and the number of games I played didn't match up with the time commitment, so I began to question whether or not I wanted to go through with the tryout. In addition to feeling that I wasn't getting a suitable return on my time investment, I was also thinking of delaying trying out a year because I wasn't physically in peak shape. I was about 10-15 pounds overweight. I actually decided that I wasn't going to go through with it until some family friends from my hometown flew up for a football weekend and convinced me that I had nothing to lose by going through with the tryout.

I recall there being about 40 students trying out for the team over a period of two days. I wasn't completely sure how many, if any, the coaches were planning to take as there were already three walk-ons on the team. After hearing the coaches talk about what they were looking for, I figured I would go out and play the game the only way

I knew how. Fortunately, the way I played was good enough to get the coaches' attention as well as afford me an opportunity to join the Notre Dame basketball team. I have never forgotten assistant coach Parker Laketa walking over to me and asking, "Would you like to join us this year?" As an 18-year-old, that was the absolute highlight of my life up to that point. It was the first time I had set a life goal and been able to accomplish the goal. I was on the phone all night letting my family and friends back home know I was now a member of the Notre Dame basketball team.

Little did I know at the time, but that would be the highlight of my year. Don't get me wrong being a member of the team was great, but I wasn't truly fulfilled. I wanted more. The question I kept asking myself is, "How is it that you are not completely happy?" I had finally committed myself to only one sport, I was playing college basketball, and was competing against great competition on a daily basis. The answer was pretty simple. I wanted to play and contribute more to the team. The luster of just being a member of the basketball team had worn off about midway through the season.

As a freshman, I was merely a practice player who emulated our opponent's offensive and defensive sets and tried my best to disrupt the timing of the first and second teams. I got to suit up for all home games, but I never made the traveling squad. I participated in a couple exhibition games and logged my first career game action against the University of New Hampshire. The season ended with a loss to the University of Michigan in the quarterfinals of the post-season NIT tournament. At the end of the season, I decided that the upcoming off-season was going to be a decisive one for me. I vowed to completely dedicate myself to an off-season strength and conditioning program in addition to working on the numerous holes in my game. There was no way I could handle another season like my freshman season.

I would only continue my basketball career if I contributed to the success of the team.

The summer of 1997 was an amazing summer. Despite working a summer job, I had my most productive summer, basketball wise. On a daily basis, I was able to partake in multiple workouts for strength and conditioning while also mixing in developmental basketball skills training five to six days a week. I was also able to further hone the skills I was developing in daily competition against various players throughout my hometown. During the three-month summer break, I managed to strengthen my body and drop 15 pounds. I returned to campus leaner, more agile, more seasoned, more confident, wiser, and totally understanding of the task before me. I was able to see the benefits of my summer immediately in preseason workouts and pickup games. This momentum carried over into the opening week of basketball practice, which was the first time the coaching staff was able to see me in action as walk-ons didn't take part in preseason individual workouts with the coaching staff.

As a freshman, at times I felt a bit out of sorts, but as a sophomore I felt that I was able to hold my own. Instead of only being on the third team/show team, I was sometimes finding myself on the second team and competing against the first team. I could see the fruits of my labor, but there was still more work to do. Occasionally, Coach MacLeod would give walk-ons a Saturday morning off from practice, but the first time that season walk-ons were given the Saturday morning off, I was asked to come to practice by Coach MacLeod. As I was walking over to practice that morning, I ran into my other teammates on their way to practice as well. They were curious why I was going to practice when I had been given the day off and I explained to them that I was asked to be at practice. A teammate then exclaimed, "Sky, you are no longer a walk-on!"

From that point forward, I felt that the coaching staff and my teammates looked at me differently. I wasn't just a practice player. I was a contributing member of the team. This fact was further cemented for me when I found myself on the travel squad for our first Big East road game against Pittsburgh. Ultimately, I was able to travel with the team for the entire season. I also received more playing time as a sophomore. Whereas I only played in one game as a freshman, I participated in 14 games as a sophomore. The most impressive thing for me was the fact that my playing time didn't only come during mop-up time, I was able to play in the first half of games.

The success I enjoyed as a sophomore merely whet my appetite. Going into my junior season, I wanted even more. So, I decided to spend the summer of 1998 at summer school so that I could train with the Notre Dame strength coaches as well as my teammates. The plan, once again, paid off as I was able to add 10 pounds of muscle to my frame and continue to plug the holes in my game. In my eyes, my junior year was everything I thought it could be. I played in all 30 games that season. I even made the first two starts of my career against Seton Hall and West Virginia.

During my sophomore season, I felt like I was able to win over my coaches and teammates. Confidence plays a large role in a player having a successful career. The fact that the coaching staff and my teammates trusted and believed in me only helped make me better as a player. I won't pretend that I was the most talented player on the court, but I feel like my teammates appreciated my determination, resilience, work ethic, and my understanding and acceptance of my role on the team. Never once did I feel as if I was less of a player because I was a walk-on. I was always invited to team functions and frequently hung out with my teammates when we weren't practicing, playing, or traveling. To this day, I still feel the same way. Whenever I am back on campus for a football game or a basketball reunion, I am always just treated as a former player by the coaching staff, basketball staff, and former teammates.

The coaching staff was very instrumental to my development as a college basketball player. I spent enormous amounts of time picking the brains of Fran McCaffery, Billy Taylor, and Jim Dolan. Coach McCaffery was extremely valuable in helping me understand the nuances of our offensive sets and exactly how I could utilize my strengths in the system. He helped me understand that rebounding, constant movement on the court, and filling the lanes on fast breaks were some items I did well. Coach Taylor and Coach Dolan were extremely supportive in helping me build confidence in regards to our defensive strategy and free throw shooting. As a sophomore, I was 0-8 from the free throw line. Coach Taylor spent countless hours helping me get to a good place mentally so that I could overcome my free throw line anxiety. My free throw shooting improved exponentially, although I guess it couldn't get worse. He also drilled me on defending quicker and taller wing players. Coach Dolan drilled me on guarding bigger players and understanding how to utilize leverage to my advantage.

Playing defense was a deliberate focus area of mine and a way to make a mark on the game without touching the basketball. Each coach impacted me in a different way. Coach MacLeod impacted me more from a leadership standpoint. I would have conversations with Coach MacLeod about my leadership style. It was no secret that I wasn't the most talented player on the team so we'd discuss other ways I could display leadership such as leading by example in regards to my work ethic and always putting the good of the team ahead of myself.

I didn't realize it, but being a walk-on at the University of Notre Dame greatly prepared me to transition into corporate America. Being a college student is challenging. When you add athletics to the mix, you get a volatile combination. As a walk-on, you have already chosen to take on the challenge of being a student, but you also willingly choose to take on the rigors of being a student-athlete without the added benefits of being a scholarship athlete. By choosing to become a student-athlete, you instantly add about 20 hours a week to a full class schedule for conditioning, practice, and games. In other words, you learn to go the extra mile. As a walk-on, you are given nothing. You have to earn everything, develop a work ethic second to none, and become the ultimate team player.

Reminiscent of corporate America, walk-ons start at an entry level and slowly work their way up the ladder. Corporate America requires employees to be team players, which is a very natural role for a walk-on. You learn to do what is necessary to ensure the success of whatever project you are working on. You learn to manage your time as well as learning to manage and/or lead others. It's a very seamless transition that builds on life experiences. Many times over, I called upon these experiences as I was working in the tax department of a public accounting firm for over a decade.

My advice to future walk-ons is to do extensive research when contemplating the possibility of walking on to any team. It's important to understand the task at hand and what you are signing up to do. Playing a sport in college is quite rigorous. Many underestimate how tough it is to be a student-athlete. People tend to look at walk-ons in a different light from scholarship athletes because the impact of walk-ons takes place out of the public eye. Walk-ons rarely impact the stat sheet like scholarship athletes.

As a walk-on, you should check your ego at the entrance to the gym. As high school athletes, we were probably all the stars of our teams and we were highly thought of by spectators. As a college walk-on, you can't count on history repeating itself. As a member of the team, it's your role to push the scholarship players and present them with the best look at the coming opponent's tendencies. So, although walk-ons work just as hard as scholarship players, you shouldn't expect to get congratulated like you once did in high school. This is something that I had to work through and it's not something that's easy for everyone to accept. This is why I think it's appropriate to research your walk-on opportunities.

We all want the opportunity to go out and prove that we can play the game and every individual is equipped with a different skillset. It's essential, in my opinion, to find a system that accentuates your skillset. There's nothing worse than trying to fit a square peg in a round hole. If you get within a system that plays to your strengths, there's an opportunity to rise from a walk-on to an even greater role on your team.

My advice to past walk-ons with insecurities is to be proud of who you are and what you have done. No one can ever take away what you have accomplished in your life. No matter how frequently you look back to your playing days, nothing will ever change. History cannot be rewritten. Don't let someone else's negative views of your talent taint how you view your accomplishments. I look back fondly at my days as a player at Notre Dame. I know how much I grew as a player from my freshman season to my senior season. I know how much time, hard work, sweat, and tears went into my career and there is *no way* that I am going to let anyone diminish it.

As mentioned previously, there are several levels to basketball and not everyone is meant to play at every level. I know for a fact that I played at a competition level that not many expected. I may have not have graduated as a career leader in anything, but how many players actually do? A century from now, my name will still be on the Notre Dame all-time basketball rosters and no one can take that away from me.

CHAPTER 12

No Longer a Secret

We are no longer a secret. We are life assassins. We are life champions. I've traveled across the country for various reasons and have been blessed with many opportunities to talk with a variety of walk-ons. The one constant is the collective desire to be great. Individuals who played for one year or all four years consistently reference their almost insatiable drive to be and do better. They talk about how resilience, persistence, determination, focus, and craftsmanship played vital roles in their life successes. They offer insight into how they effectively transitioned through the various stages of the journey to lead fulfilling lives. They smile fondly when they recount the lessons learned.

Moving from *best kept secret* to *no longer a secret* does not imply arrogance, conceit, egoism, narcissism, or any other fancy word that describes someone's confidence negatively. The transition simply implies that God has qualified us and we can move confidently in our chosen direction. It means that we can offer thoughtful, sage counsel without feeling like imposters. It demonstrates that we have a willingness to fail. It reveals that we are ready to succeed.

Being a secret is not advisable. Doing so forces us to remain quiet and stay in the shadows. Being a secret heightens our insecurities. Living in the dark increases the likelihood that we choose to stay disconnected from the light source. If we choose to remain a secret, we do a disservice to those who were instrumental in our development. We stay silent on things that matter. We do not lift others as we climb. We do not pursue excellence. We purposely choose to bury our talents. We decide not to wrestle with thoughts and actions of consequence. We smile with our mouth, but not with our eyes. We pretend to be engaged because we presume that's what the world wants. We lose ourselves because deep down, we know that we are designed to do better.

When we purposely, or even inadvertently (due to a lack of knowledge, wisdom, or understanding), choose to remain a secret, the life journey can lead us to places that are distressing to the soul. If we walk alone, in the dark, thoughtlessly and/or aimlessly, some days can be problematic. If we allow our tribe to keep us strong and move in the light with a resolute spirit of determination, love, hope, optimism, and power, some days can be great.

Even as a prayerful, curious, courageous, free-thinking, thankful, obsessed, impatient, undeserving, and creative person, some days are hard for me as well. One of great things about no longer being a secret is that being vulnerable is okay. It's more than okay. Showing vulnerability is expected and accepted. It doesn't mean that we are weak. When we live our secret lives, we unknowingly or sometimes with purposeful ignorance conflate weakness and vulnerability. No longer being a secret allows us to ride the *some days* wave.

When I summon the nerve to be honest with myself, I know

that some days are great. Some days are good and some days include many failures. Many of us challenge ourselves to shoot for the moon, knowing that even if we do not hit that target, we will still land amongst the stars. The internal battles that many of us face daily can make us scream, cry, and laugh simultaneously. Our individual mountains are not to be compared with another individual's mountains. Our stories are different. Our journeys are different. That does not mean we are alone.

Some days, we have what seems to be thousands of people rooting for us. Some days, it appears that we only have a select few individuals walking with us. Some days, it is just you. Some days, you do not even believe in you. I know that is my truth.

Some days, I am a great husband. Some days, I am not. I am distant. I focus on too many external things that could prove detrimental to my relationship and likely my overall well-being. I live inside of my mind, striving to make a way for family and friends. I consistently engage with others in an effort to offer value and create real moments of truth, beauty, and clarity. The sweltering fire inside of me to leave a legacy that lasts longer than I do creates partitions in my world that some days seem impossible to reconnect. The struggles, sacrifices, sleepless nights, stories I tell myself, and sad moments pull me deeper into an abyss of focus and relentless persistence to change the nature of my family tree.

The paradox of my journey is that some days it appears to do the opposite. Even when I am home, I am not there. She looks into my eyes, and some days, I would imagine, sees a focus that is borderline obsessive. She looks into my eyes and sees a man who does not know what to do, so he shifts his focus to the community and to the words that he chooses to speak and write on a regular basis. Some days, she sees a man who is trying to recreate lost moments from his childhood so that he can make his family life better. Some days, I'd imagine, she looks into my eyes and sees a faith-filled man who believes in the omnipotence and omnipresence of God, yet struggles to claim his place within his divinely inspired space. Some days, I am a great husband. Some days, I am not. Fortunately, the matriarch of our house tolerates this cause and does not allow my inadequacies, fears, and failures to decrease her support of me. I keep trying to do better. Many have cautiously warned me that I have to do better. I listen. Some days, I listen better than other days. Every day, I try.

Some days, I am a great dad. Some days, I am not. I am not home enough to proclaim *greatest dad in the world*. Some days, I push baby girl to the point of exhaustion. Some days, I do not push at all because I am not there. Some days, I do not play with baby boy because I am not there. Some days, I wonder if they will forgive me for *working so hard* and trying to make a way. Some days, I wonder if it even matters. Some days, I do a great job of teaching them life-learned lessons. Some days, I do not. Some days, I think back to my childhood and realize how hard my parents worked to provide us with opportunities that they did not have. Even knowing the complexity of their journeys, some days I can still remember my internal anger because my dad did not come to several of my events. Some days, I try to convince myself that my kids will understand. Most days, I know that to be false. Some days, I feel sad because I do not know how to solve this problem. Every day, I try.

Some days, I am a great son and brother. Some days, I am not. Some days, I feel like having the financial resources to solve some of their problems is enough. Most days, I know that such thinking is an erroneous protective mechanism to guard my fragile heart. Some days, I push myself to my mental, emotional, and spiritual limits thinking about what more I can do to make their world better. Some days, I feel like a complete failure. Some days, I know that *complete failure* is an inaccurate assessment of my efforts. Some days, my soul is weary because my sister is home alone dealing with aging parents. She has to handle things that I can't, won't or don't know how to handle. Some days, I wonder if she will forgive me for my absence. Some days, I wonder if my parents will do the same.

Some days, I work so hard to create this façade of success because I know it will make them smile. Some days, hearing the laughter and excitement that result from some new achievement of mine helps me make it through that particular day. Most days, I know that the temporary euphoria will wear off and the reality that I cannot provide in the way that I deem acceptable remains. I know that I will get there, but some days are harder than other days. Some days, I look in the mirror and worry that I am not doing the best that I can. Most days, I know that such self-criticism is vexatious to the soul. Some days, I even cry. Every day, I try.

When I plug into the light source, the frequency of those *some day* occurrences decreases. When I am plugged into the light source, I am no longer a secret. When you are connected to your light source, you are no longer a secret. When we decide to liberate ourselves from the nonsense of the world and believe in what we know to be true, the game changes. When we choose to no longer be a secret, we awaken from a slumber and stop sleepwalking. We are comfortable asking who, what, when, where, why, and how.

When we transition from best kept secrets to no longer a secret, it becomes easier to lift our brothers and sisters as we climb. The need to justify our existence to others evaporates. We only need to be comfortable with the image that stares back at us when we gaze into the eyes of the image in the mirror. We know our value proposition and can remain calm in the hottest of fires and during the darkest of nights. We know that we are intelligent. We know that we are instinctual. We know that we are educated. We know that we are experienced. We are confident in knowing that others paved the way for us and that we paved the way for others.

Keeping secrets is tough. Being a secret is even harder. We are not meant to live in the shadows. We are not meant to dampen our lights. We are not supposed to feel inferior. Living in the light is liberating. When we live and act freely, we give others permission to do the same. When we are no longer a secret, we can serve as students and enjoy learning. We can teach without feeling inadequate. We can lay bricks and know that we are instrumental in building something that will change another person's life. We can operate as an architect and know that our vision will change the world and how others see themselves in that world. Being a secret is cool, until it's not. When each one of us transitions from *best kept secret* to *life champion*, the world may never know it ... but we do.

CHAPTER 13

The Walk-on Way

I love my walk-on tribe. Others may forget about us, but we do not forget about ourselves. As free thinkers who lead with a servant's heart, we are able to change the world. I know that everyone doesn't feel the way that I do and that is okay. I also know that I didn't have to write a single word about my fellow tribe members, but I wanted to. Since the age of 18, I have caught arrows, been hit by arrows, and shot an assortment of arrows myself. I'm good with that.

My volunteer status didn't and doesn't make me inferior. My scholarship status didn't and doesn't make me superior. Being a walk-on is a privilege. It is an honor. We are the souls of our chosen teams. We laugh when others are mad. We smile when others are sad. We aren't court jesters by any stretch of the imagination, but we understand our place. We know what to do, when to do it, why it needs to be done, where to do it, and how to execute. We listen and we learn. Those qualities move far beyond the field of competition. They translate magnificently into adult life.

My walk-on brothers and sisters are outstanding. We do whatever needs to be done in order to get the job done. As athletes, we strive to make our teammates better. As adults, we strive to make our teammates better. There is no differentiation. If you are on our team, we will play at the highest level possible so that you can do the same. If you are the opposition, however, sorry for you (not really). No mercy will be extended to you. We play hard. We are loyal. We are thoughtful. We think systemically. We are competitors. We are Spartans. We are hyper-focused. We need love. We want to be appreciated. We treat others as they want to be treated. We ask questions. We provide answers. We strive to be more and do more.

For many years, I felt like I couldn't speak confidently about athletics because I walked on. Even though I was considered worthy of a scholarship and received one, the internal battles that I faced were real. All of my walk-on brothers and sisters, listen. Life will be great for you if you put in the effort to make it so. Every morning when you wake up, remember that God allows you to write your own story. The canvas is blank. You draw on it as you wish. You are the artisan of your own fortune. Dream big. Take calculated risks. Ask for help. Get back up when you are knocked down. Help others when you see them fall. The actions that we need to take in order to do well in life are rather simple. We must exhibit the boldness to try.

To those of you who plan to travel the walk-on road, be encouraged. You have what it takes. Put in the effort. Lift weights. Run. Practice. Read. Write. Lift some more weights. Run some more. Practice harder. Read more. Write more. Ask for help. If you want to make it happen, you have to put in the effort. You may not succeed, but if you want it, you are obligated to try. The only requirements are that you listen to your instincts, be curious, and be sufficiently brave.

To those of you who walked on and are long gone from the college scene, thank you. Thank you for listening to the whispers of your heart. Thank you for believing in yourself. Thank you for summiting the peak of a mountain that many people dare not climb. Thank you for protecting yourself. Thank you for protecting your brothers and sisters. Thank you for giving your parents something to brag about. Thank you for being universal men and universal women. Thank you for pursuing excellence as a demonstration of human potential. Thank you for offering sage counsel to others during college. Thank you for leading after college.

The following message from President Teddy Roosevelt applies to me, current walk-ons, past walk-ons, future walk-ons, and everyone else.

> "It is not the critic who counts; not the man who points out how the strong man stumbles, or where the doer of deeds could have done them better. The credit belongs to the man who is actually in the arena, whose face is marred by dust and sweat and blood; who strives valiantly; who errs, who comes short again and again, because there is no effort without error and shortcoming; but who does actually strive to do the deeds; who knows great enthusiasms, the great devotions; who spends himself in a worthy cause; who at the best knows in the end the triumph of high achievement, and who at the worst, if he fails, at least fails while daring greatly, so that his place shall never be with those cold and timid souls who neither know victory nor defeat."

Don't listen to people who aren't in the arena. Listen to yourself. Be valiant. Don't be a secret. Put in your very best effort to be a life champion. Keep working. Keep striving. Do better. Be better. The time to make a difference has never been greater. Boldly go. The world is waiting for you. We need you.

ABOUT THE AUTHOR

DR. CHARLES THOMAS JR. is the son of Mrs. Doris and Mr. Charles Thomas Sr. He is a member of the prestigious walk-on and Spartan trifecta tribes. Charles is the author of three additional works: *Scars, Exile, and Vindication: My Life As An Experiment*, the best-selling work *Breakthrough: Stories of Resilience, Tragedy, and Triumph*, and *Leading Through Difficulty: The Darker Side of Workplace Behavior.* He is from Flint, MI and lives in Northern Virginia with his wife and children.

For more information, please visit charlesthomasjr.com.

CPSIA information can be obtained
at www.ICGtesting.com
Printed in the USA
LVHW012300230120
644554LV00007B/184

Royal London

JANE STRUTHERS

PHOTOGRAPHY BY RICKY LEAVER

*For my dear friends Stephen Cowin and
Stephen Rooke, with much love*

This edition published in 2012 by
New Holland Publishers (UK) Ltd

London • Cape Town • Sydney • Auckland

First published in 2005

www.newhollandpublishers.com

Garfield House
86–88 Edgware Road
London W2 2EA United Kingdom

80 McKenzie Street
Cape Town 8001 South Africa

Unit 1, 66 Gibbes Street,
Chatswood,
NSW 2067 Australia

218 Lake Road, Northcote, Auckland, New Zealand

ISBN 978 1 84773 964 3

Publisher: Guy Hobbs
Editor: Clare Hubbard
Layout and Design: Isobel Gillan
Cover Design: Isobel Gillan
Cartography: William Smuts
Production: Marion Storz
Reproduction by Pica Digital Pte Ltd, Singapore
Printed and bound in China by Toppan Leefung Printing Ltd

PREVIOUS PAGE *The Tower of London.*

RIGHT *Queen Elizabeth II en route back to Buckingham Palace in
November 2004 after the State Opening of Parliament.*

Contents

Introduction	6	
Map of Royal London	8	
Key to Map	10	
The Royal Family	11	
Royal Family Tree	12	
Royal Ceremonies	18	

WESTMINSTER 22

1 Constitution Hill 23
2 Queen's Gallery 23
3 Buckingham Palace 24
4 Royal Mews 27
5 Birdcage Walk 28
6 Guards' Museum 28
7 Queen Victoria Memorial
   and Gardens 29
8 St James's Park 30
9 Green Park 32
10 Spencer House 33
11 St James's Palace 34
12 Clarence House 36
13 Statue of Queen Elizabeth
   the Queen Mother 37
14 Queen's Chapel 37
15 Pall Mall 38

16 Marlborough House 39
17 St James's Square 40
18 Waterloo Place 41
19 The Mall 42
20 Horse Guards Parade 44
21 Banqueting House 46
22 Westminster Abbey 48
23 Palace of Westminster 52
24 Jewel Tower 54
25 Bust of Charles I 54
26 St John's, Smith Square 55
27 Carlton House Terrace 56

THE CITY 57

28 St Bartholomew's
   Hospital 58
29 Church of St Bartholomew-
   the-Great 59
30 Smithfield Market 60
31 St Paul's Cathedral 61
32 Temple Bar 64
33 Ireland Yard 66
34 Queenhithe 66
35 Williamson's Tavern 67

36 St Lawrence Jewry 67
37 Church of St Mary-le-Bow 68
38 Guildhall 69
39 Clockmakers' Company
   Museum 70
40 Statue of Queen
   Alexandra 70
41 Bank of England 71
42 Royal Exchange 72
43 Tower of London 73
44 Monument 76
45 London Bridge 78

PICCADILLY TO HACKNEY 80

46 Queen Street 81
47 St Anne's Church 81
48 St James's Church 82
49 Soho Square 83
50 National Portrait Gallery 84
51 St Giles-in-the-Fields 85
52 Trafalgar Square 86
53 Statue of Charles I 87
54 St Martin-in-the-Fields 88
55 Statue of George III 89
56 Coutts & Co 89

57	Savoy Chapel	90
58	Theatre Royal, Drury Lane	91
59	Somerset House	92
60	Temple Church	95
61	St Mary le Strand	96
62	St Dunstan-in-the-West	97
63	St Bride's Church	98
64	York Watergate	99
65	Holborn Circus	100
66	Gray's Inn	100
67	Ely Place	101

MARBLE ARCH TO HIGHGATE **102**

68	Marble Arch	103
69	Regent's Park	104
70	London Zoo	106
71	St Katharine's	106
72	St George's Church	107
73	Queen Square	107
74	British Library	108
75	Lauderdale House	110

WEST LONDON **111**

76	Hyde Park	112
77	Hyde Park Corner	114
78	Mandarin Oriental Hyde Park Hotel	115
79	Rotten Row	115
80	Eaton Square	116
81	King's Road	116
82	Royal Hospital Chelsea	117
83	Harrods	118
84	Victoria and Albert Museum	119
85	Royal Albert Hall	120
86	Albert Memorial	121
87	Kensington Gardens	122
88	Kensington Palace	124
89	Diana, Princess of Wales Memorial Playground	127
90	St Mary Abbots Church	127

SOUTH LONDON **128**

91	Prince Consort Lodge	129
92	Lambeth Palace	129
93	Old Royal Naval College	130
94	Greenwich Park	132
95	Royal Observatory	133

96	Queen's House	134
97	Eltham Palace	136
98	Rotherhithe	137
99	Blackheath	138
100	Royal Botanic Gardens	139
101	Kew Palace	140
102	Richmond Park	142
103	Richmond Palace	143
104	Syon House	144
105	Marble Hill House	145
106	Orleans House Gallery	145
107	Bushy Park	146
108	Ham House	147
109	Coronation Stone	147
110	Hampton Court Palace	148

DAY TRIPS FROM LONDON **151**

111	Windsor Castle	152
112	Runnymede	154
113	Hever Castle	155
114	Hatfield House	156

Further Reading	157
Acknowledgements	157
Index	158

Introduction

London offers endless fascinations. Its buildings and streets contain layer upon layer of history that is sometimes clearly visible but more usually existing in a glorious muddle of centuries, styles and stories. You can find modern buildings with Roman foundations, streets with quirky names that are reminders of their origins and contemporary skyscrapers looming over historic churches. When you walk around London you need to keep your eyes open because you never know what you'll see next.

Cities are shaped by the people who live in them, so it's hardly surprising that London is full of royal associations – these range from world-famous palaces to sites that are less well known. There are some that are often overlooked completely. Together, they make up a rich blend that tells the story of royal London – its triumphs and tragedies, its pomp and circumstance, its drama and vivid colour.

Running through the history of royal London, and indeed this book, are the royal protagonists themselves. Despite some of them having lived centuries ago, these people have such strong personalities that they still exude an aura of power and glamour. When we visit the palaces in which they lived, and other buildings with which they are associated, these kings and queens step out of the pages of the history books and come to life. Once we know the story of how Charles I was beheaded in 1649, it is difficult to stand outside the Banqueting House without imagining that freezing cold January day when he met his fate while being watched by a hushed crowd. The elaborate staterooms in Kensington Palace, designed to instil awe and obedience in the people who paid court there, form a fascinating contrast with the intimacies of the smaller rooms in which the royal residents spent much of their time.

Many places in London have royal connections so I had to be selective when choosing them for this book. They had to still exist, even if only a fragment of the original building remained. They also had to be either open to the public on a regular basis or easily visible to onlookers.

London is a huge city so I have divided the book into six geographical chapters. I have also included a section on royal sites that are within an hour's travelling time from London. Each entry contains essential visitor information, including contact and location details, travel information, opening times and an approximate admission price guide (see right).

Among London's many attractions are the royal ceremonies that take place each year, from Trooping the Colour at Horse Guards Parade to the State Opening of Parliament. This book contains information about all of these, as well as biographies of the most senior and prominent members of the current Royal Family. I hope it is the perfect introduction to the many delights of royal London.

Jane Struthers

RIGHT *St Martin-in-the-Fields viewed from Trafalgar Square.*

Map

The sites are numbered and the numbers are used on the map on pages 8–9 to show the location of all the royal places of interest (except the sites within the Day Trips From London chapter).

Visitor information

Basic information has been given as to the opening times and admission prices to the various sites. However, many places are closed on public holidays, some close regularly for refurbishment/maintenance, etc. and prices are subject to change at any time, so always check the website or call the relevant site before visiting.

Guide to pricing bands for admission fees:

££££	£20+
£££	£15–19.99
££	£8–14.99
£	Up to £7.99
Free	Free of charge

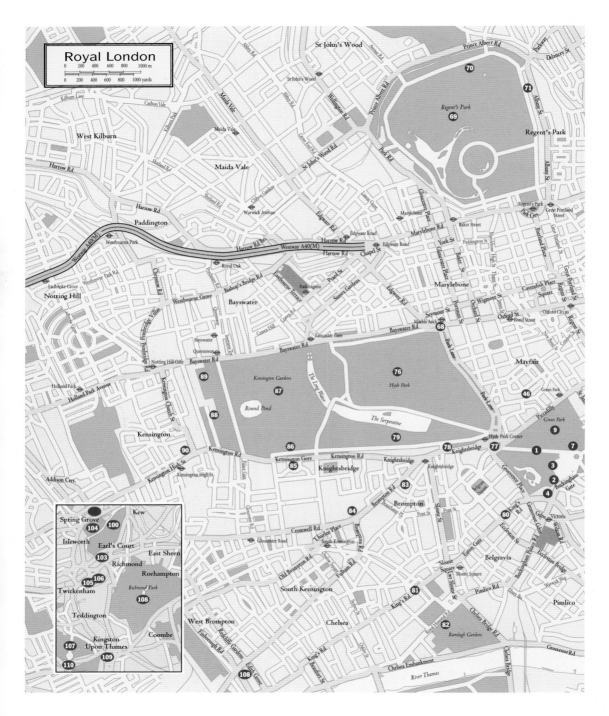

Royal London

0 200 400 600 800 1000 m
0 200 400 600 800 1000 yards

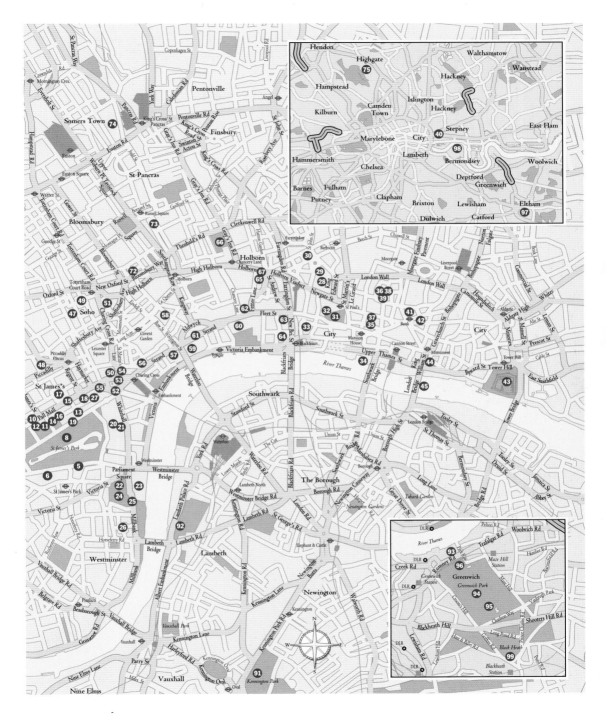

The Royal Family

Queen Elizabeth II

FULL TITLE: By the Grace of God, of the United Kingdom of Great Britain and Northern Ireland, and of Her other Realms and Territories, Queen, Head of the Commonwealth, Defender of the Faith;
BORN: 21 April 1926, 17 Bruton Street, London, W1;
SUCCEEDED TO THRONE: 6 February 1952;
CROWNED: 2 June 1953

When the Queen was born, she was third in line to the throne after her uncle, Edward, Prince of Wales (who later became Edward VIII), and her father, the Duke of York. At first, no one expected her to become queen, although her grandfather, George V, later expressed his wish that nothing would stand between her and the throne. What he meant was that he hoped his eldest son, the Prince of Wales, would somehow never become king.

She had a very happy childhood with her parents and her younger sister, Margaret Rose (as she was known at the time), until 1936, when Edward VIII abdicated and her father succeeded to the throne. This not only had a huge impact on her family life but also meant that she was now heir presumptive. The young princess was given plenty of preparation for her future role. During the Second World War, she joined the Auxiliary Territorial Service (ATS), where she trained as a mechanic. She particularly enjoyed stripping down car engines and would regale the rest of her family with all the details during meals.

Princess Elizabeth was still a teenager when she fell in love with her cousin, Prince Philip of Greece and Denmark. They were married in Westminster Abbey on 20 November 1947. Post-war rationing was still in force so, in common with every other bride of the time, the princess had to collect clothing coupons to buy the fabric for her dress.

The new Duke and Duchess of Edinburgh, as they were styled, spent part of the next few years in Malta, where Prince Philip was stationed as a serving officer of the Royal Navy. Their son, Charles, was born in 1948 and their daughter, Anne, in 1950.

Everything changed on 6 February 1952, when George VI died. The new queen was crowned in Westminster Abbey on 2 June 1953, and her coronation was the first to be televised.

In the years that followed, the Queen juggled her family life (she had two more sons: Prince Andrew in 1960 and Prince Edward in 1964) with an extremely busy schedule of royal duties. Yet it seems that, despite her innate and immutable sense of duty and responsibility to her country, at heart she is happiest when surrounded by horses and dogs. She is an expert horsewoman but had to reduce her riding in 2011 because of painful knees.

Although other members of the Royal Family have sometimes attracted headlines for the wrong reasons, the Queen remains untouched by scandal.

RIGHT *Queen Elizabeth II and Prince Philip are joined by their children at a dinner at Clarence House to mark their Diamond Wedding Anniversary in November 2007. (l–r The Prince of Wales, The Duke of York, The Princess Royal and The Earl of Wessex.)*

ROYAL FAMILY TREE

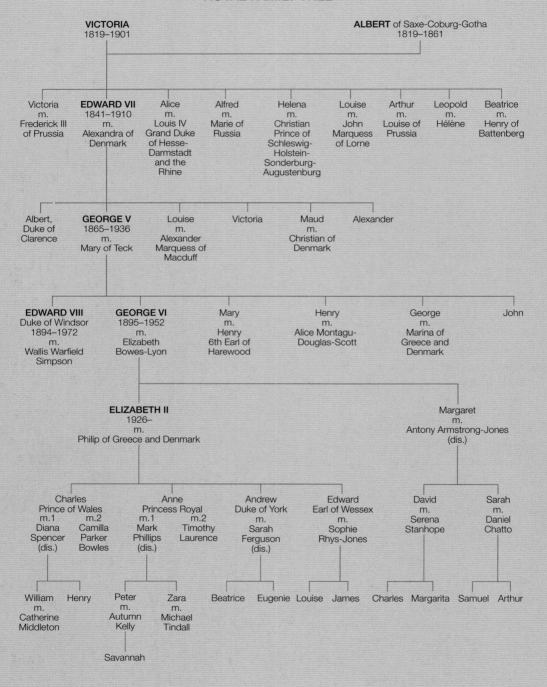

VICTORIA
1819–1901

ALBERT of Saxe-Coburg-Gotha
1819–1861

Victoria
m.
Frederick III
of Prussia

EDWARD VII
1841–1910
m.
Alexandra of
Denmark

Alice
m.
Louis IV
Grand Duke
of Hesse-
Darmstadt
and the
Rhine

Alfred
m.
Marie of
Russia

Helena
m.
Christian
Prince of
Schleswig-
Holstein-
Sonderburg-
Augustenburg

Louise
m.
John
Marquess
of Lorne

Arthur
m.
Louise of
Prussia

Leopold
m.
Hélène

Beatrice
m.
Henry of
Battenberg

Albert,
Duke of
Clarence

GEORGE V
1865–1936
m.
Mary of Teck

Louise
m.
Alexander
Marquess of
Macduff

Victoria

Maud
m.
Christian of
Denmark

Alexander

EDWARD VIII
Duke of Windsor
1894–1972
m.
Wallis Warfield
Simpson

GEORGE VI
1895–1952
m.
Elizabeth
Bowes-Lyon

Mary
m.
Henry
6th Earl of
Harewood

Henry
m.
Alice Montagu-
Douglas-Scott

George
m.
Marina of
Greece and
Denmark

John

ELIZABETH II
1926–
m.
Philip of Greece and Denmark

Margaret
m.
Antony Armstrong-Jones
(dis.)

Charles
Prince of Wales
m.1   m.2
Diana   Camilla
Spencer   Parker
(dis.)   Bowles

Anne
Princess Royal
m.1   m.2
Mark   Timothy
Phillips   Laurence
(dis.)

Andrew
Duke of York
m.
Sarah
Ferguson
(dis.)

Edward
Earl of Wessex
m.
Sophie
Rhys-Jones

David
m.
Serena
Stanhope

Sarah
m.
Daniel
Chatto

William
m.
Catherine
Middleton

Henry

Peter
m.
Autumn
Kelly

Zara
m.
Michael
Tindall

Beatrice

Eugenie

Louise

James

Charles

Margarita

Samuel

Arthur

Savannah

Prince Philip

FULL TITLE: His Royal Highness The Prince Philip, Duke of Edinburgh, Earl of Merioneth and Baron Greenwich, KG, KT, OM, GBE, AC, QSO, PC;
BORN: 10 June 1921, Villa Mon Repos, Corfu, Greece

Prince Philip is a great-great-grandson of Queen Victoria, through her daughter Princess Alice. He is the only son of Prince Andrew of Greece and Denmark and Princess Alice of Battenberg. In 1922, a revolutionary court in Greece banished his father for life, and the family was evacuated to France in a Royal Navy ship. Prince Philip was sent to England when he was seven, where he lived with his maternal grandmother (Princess Victoria of Hesse and by Rhine) at Kensington Palace and his uncle, the 2nd Marquess of Milford Haven (later his legal guardian) in Berkshire. His personal life was difficult: his mother was committed to a mental asylum; one of his sisters and her entire family were killed in an air crash; and his guardian died from cancer.

Prince Philip served in the Royal Navy and was a lieutenant when he fell in love with the young Princess Elizabeth. However, his family background presented several obstacles that had to be overcome before they could marry. He had to renounce his allegiance to the Greek crown; he had to renounce his Greek and Danish titles; he had to convert from the Greek Orthodox to the Anglican Church; and he also had to become a naturalized British subject. There was also the issue of his surname, as in 1947 'Battenberg' was considered to be far too German, so it was changed to 'Mountbatten', which was his maternal grandfather's surname.

Prince Philip's active career in the Royal Navy (he reached the rank of commander) ended on the death of George VI, when he became consort to his wife, Elizabeth II. He took on many duties by himself, in addition to those that supported the Queen. In 1956 he set up the Duke of Edinburgh's Award, designed to encourage a sense of responsibility in young people. He has been patron or president of over 800 organizations and, until recently, undertook over 300 public engagements each year, a tally that is only beaten by his daughter, Princess Anne. He is Britain's longest serving consort.

Prince of Wales

FULL TITLE: His Royal Highness Prince Charles Philip Arthur George, Prince of Wales, KG, KT, GCB, OM, AK, QSO, PC, ADC, Earl of Chester, Duke of Cornwall, Duke of Rothesay, Earl of Carrick, Baron of Renfrew, Lord of the Isles and Prince and Great Steward of Scotland; BORN: 14 November 1948, Buckingham Palace, London, SW1

Prince Charles was only three when he became heir to the throne, on the death of his grandfather, George VI. He grew up in Buckingham Palace and was the first heir to the throne to be sent to school, rather than to be tutored privately. A sensitive child, he forged an unbreakable rapport with his maternal grandmother, the Queen Mother. He also discovered a love of the countryside and nature.

Prince Charles was created Prince of Wales and Earl of Chester in 1958, but his investiture was conducted in 1969 at Caernarfon Castle (as was that of his great-uncle, Edward, in 1911). He gave his speech in Welsh and English.

In common with many previous Princes of Wales, Prince Charles has had to carve his own niche within the Royal Family. One of the most pronounced ways in which he has done this is in his charitable work, in particular with The Prince's Trust, which he founded in 1976 to help young people improve their lives and future prospects. In addition, he is patron or president of over 400 other charities. The prince also takes a keen interest in architecture, painting, ecology, gardening and complementary therapies.

Also in common with other Princes of Wales, a

great deal of media attention has often been focused on Prince Charles's private life. On 29 July 1981, he married Lady Diana Spencer at St Paul's Cathedral. That day the couple grabbed the world's headlines and were rarely out of them again. They had two sons: Prince William, born in 1982, and Prince Harry, born in 1984. However, the marriage was fraught with difficulties and the couple divorced in 1996. Princess Diana died in a car crash in 1997, and on 9 April 2005 Prince Charles married his long-term love, Camilla Parker Bowles, in a civil ceremony at Windsor Guildhall, followed by a blessing in St George's Chapel, Windsor Castle. Their London home is Clarence House, and their private home is Highgrove House in Gloucestershire.

ABOVE *Prince Charles and the Duchess of Cornwall on the first day of Royal Ascot in June 2011.*

The Princess Royal

FULL TITLE: Her Royal Highness The Princess Anne Elizabeth Alice Louise, The Princess Royal, LG, LT, GCVO, QSO, CD, GCL, TC, FRS, FRCVS;
BORN: 15 August 1950, Clarence House, London, SW1

Princess Anne began her life at Clarence House, before moving to Buckingham Palace in 1952 when her mother became Queen. At first she attended a private class held at the palace, but at the age of 13 she went to boarding school.

Like her parents, Princess Anne loves horses and her equestrian skills soon became obvious. She took part in many international events, including the 1976 Montreal Olympics. In 1983 she became president of the British Olympic Association, a post that she held for five years, and in 1988 she became one of the two British members of the International Olympic Committee.

In 1973 Princess Anne married Lieutenant (later Captain) Mark Phillips of The Queen's Dragoon Guards in Westminster Abbey. They have two children: Peter, born in 1977, and Zara, born in 1981. Zara has also become an excellent horsewoman. After divorcing in 1992, Princess Anne married Commander (now Vice Admiral) Timothy Laurence, RN, that same year, in a private ceremony at Crathie Church, near Balmoral Castle in Scotland.

In common with her father, Princess Anne is an outspoken member of the Royal Family. She is also widely seen as the most hard-working as she carries out the highest number of engagements each year, including up to three foreign tours in support of British interests abroad.

The Duke of York

FULL TITLE: His Royal Highness The Prince Andrew Albert Christian Edward, Duke of York, Earl of Inverness, Baron Killyleagh, KG, GCVO, CD, ADC(P); BORN: 19 February 1960, Buckingham Palace, London, SW1

Prince Andrew was the first child to be born to a reigning monarch for 103 years. He joined the Royal Navy in 1979 as a trainee helicopter pilot, and served in the Falklands War in 1982 where he came under direct enemy fire. Although the British government of the time was uneasy about the possible harm that the prince might suffer by being in the front line, the Queen insisted that he should not be given a desk job. He continued to serve as a Sea King helicopter pilot on HMS *Invincible*. After holding a number of positions, he formally left the Navy in 2001.

Prince Andrew married Sarah Ferguson in 1986, at which point he was created Duke of York. They have two daughters: Beatrice, born in 1988, and Eugenie, born in 1990. In 1992 it was announced that the Duke and Duchess were separating, and they were divorced in 1996.

The Duke is involved with over 100 organizations, particularly those that encourage young people to achieve their full potential. From 2001–11, he was the UK's Representative for International Trade and Investment, in addition to keeping up with his other royal duties.

The Earl of Wessex

FULL TITLE: His Royal Highness The Prince Edward Antony Richard Louis, The Earl of Wessex, Viscount Severn, KG, KCVO, SOM, ADC(P);
BORN: 10 March 1964, Buckingham Palace, London, SW1

Prince Edward's first public appearance took place after the Trooping the Colour ceremony in 1964, when his mother presented him to the waiting crowds. He studied history at Cambridge, but then spent 10 years working in theatre production. This included running his own production company.

In June 1999, the prince married Sophie Rhys-Jones at St George's Chapel, Windsor. On the day of their marriage, they became the Earl and Countess of Wessex. They have two children: Louise, born in 2003, and James, Viscount Severn, born in 2007.

In 2002, the couple announced that they were giving up their respective careers in order to help the Queen during her Golden Jubilee and to take on an increasing number of royal duties in the future.

The Duke of Cambridge

FULL TITLE: His Royal Highness Prince William Arthur Philip Louis, Duke of Cambridge, Earl of Strathearn, Baron Carrickfergus, KG; BORN: 21 June 1982, St Mary's Hospital, London, W2

Prince William is the older son of Prince Charles and the late Diana, Princess of Wales. He is related to the monarchy on his mother's side as well as his father's.

He went to Eton College and after a gap year spent working in Africa, visiting Chile and Belize and also working on British dairy farms, he studied geography at St Andrew's University in Fife. He later graduated from the Royal Military Academy Sandhurst, and in 2008 he was given his RAF wings.

This followed a royal tradition, as he is the fourth successive generation of royalty to become an RAF pilot. He then trained to become a fully operational pilot with the RAF's Search and Rescue Force.

Prince William was only 15 when his mother was killed in a car crash in Paris in 1997. He took on many of her interests, including the plight of the homeless, and in 2005 he became patron of Centrepoint (his mother was also its patron). He has worked with the staff on several occasions.

After much media speculation about his private life, it was announced in November 2010 that Prince William would marry Catherine (Kate) Middleton. Their wedding took place at Westminster Abbey on 29 April 2011.

Lesotho. On his return, he trained as an army officer at the Royal Military Academy Sandhurst. He was commissioned in 2006 and joined the Household Cavalry, with whom he served in Afghanistan in 2007–08. In 2009, he began lengthy training to become a fully operational, full-time helicopter pilot for the Army Air Corps.

Like Prince William, Prince Harry has been strongly influenced by his parents' charitable interests. In 2009, the two princes set up the Foundation of Prince William and Prince Harry to concentrate on three topics that concern them: helping young people; supporting men and women in the armed forces; and developing sustainable living.

The Duchess of Cambridge

FULL TITLE: Her Royal Highness The Duchess of Cambridge; BORN: 9 January 1982, Reading, Berkshire

The duchess grew up in Berkshire, where she attended Marlborough College. In 2001 she went to the University of St Andrews in Fife, where she met Prince William. She graduated with a degree in the History of Art. Her relationship with the prince meant that, inevitably, she attracted a lot of media interest. She was driven to complain about its intrusive nature in 2005, and both Prince Charles and Prince William voiced their concerns to various newspapers.

On 16 November 2010, Clarence House announced that Prince William and Catherine Middleton were engaged, and their wedding took place in Westminster Abbey on 29 April 2011. Their first royal tour was of Canada in July 2011.

Prince Harry

FULL TITLE: His Royal Highness Prince Henry Charles Albert David of Wales; BORN: 15 September 1984, St Mary's Hospital, London, W2

Despite being officially Prince Henry, he has always been known as Prince Harry. He is the younger son of Prince Charles and the late Diana, Princess of Wales. He is third in line to the throne and, in common with his brother, Prince William, is related to the monarchy through his mother as well as his father.

After attending the same schools as his brother, Prince Harry divided his gap year between Australia and Africa, where he worked in an orphanage in

Royal Ceremonies

The Royal Family's calendar is punctuated with ceremonies and traditions that are carried out annually – some of which are in London. A number of these ceremonies date back hundreds of years and involve spectacular pageantry, thereby shining a light on a bygone age. People come from all over the world to watch them.

Royal Maundy Service

WHEN: Maundy Thursday, Mar or Apr;
WHERE: Takes place at different cathedral or abbey each year

This is an annual ceremony held on Maundy Thursday, which is the Thursday before Easter. Until 1953 it was always held in Westminster Abbey, but the Queen decided that the service should take place in a different cathedral or abbey each year.

The ceremony dates back centuries and involves the sovereign giving specially minted money to elderly people who have contributed greatly to the life of their cathedral. The exact number of coins matches the sovereign's age, so in 2011 (on what was coincidentally her 85th birthday) the Queen gave 85 coins to 85 men and 85 women. The present form of the Maundy coins began in 1670. They are struck in sterling silver and bear the same portrait of the Queen that was used for the coins issued in 1953, her coronation year.

BELOW *The Queen and Prince Philip attended the Royal Maundy Day Service at Westminster Abbey on 21 April 2011.*

Trooping the Colour

WHEN: June, to correspond with sovereign's official birthday;
WHERE: Horse Guards Parade and then Buckingham Palace

This is a military ceremony that dates back to at least the 18th century, if not earlier. It is a reminder of the days when a regiment's colours (or flag) was trooped (or paraded) in front of the regiment so every man would be able to recognize it on the battlefield.

Trooping the Colour involves the regiments of the Household Division, which is the collective name for the Foot Guards and the Household Cavalry. They take it in turns for their regiment's colours to be paraded, so a different regiment is honoured each year. The reigning sovereign inspects the troops and takes the royal salute. After the massed bands have played, the regimental colour is escorted down the ranks of soldiers. When the ceremony is over, the sovereign leads the troops down The Mall back to Buckingham Palace.

Beating Retreat

WHEN: June; WHERE: Horse Guards Parade

The origins of this colourful musical ceremony lie in the need to notify soldiers that their day's work has come to an end and it is time to return to their camp. These days, it is a ceremonial occasion and is performed by the massed bands of the Household Division. This consists of the two regiments of the Household Cavalry (the Life Guards and the Blues and Royals), and the five regiments of the Foot Guards. These, in their order of seniority, are the Grenadier Guards, the Coldstream Guards, the Scots Guards, the Irish Guards and the Welsh Guards.

This ceremony is always performed in the evening, under floodlights, for full drama and colour.

Royal Ceremonies Held Annually in London

- Royal Maundy Service (but not always in London)
- Trooping the Colour in Horse Guards Parade, Whitehall
- Beating Retreat in Horse Guards Parade, Whitehall
- Royal Gun Salutes in Green Park, Hyde Park and the Tower of London
- Investitures at Buckingham Palace
- Garden parties at Buckingham Palace
- The Garter Ceremony at Windsor Castle
- The State Opening of Parliament at the Houses of Parliament
- Remembrance Day Service in Whitehall

Royal Gun Salutes

WHEN: To mark royal ceremonial or special occasions; WHERE: Green Park, Hyde Park, Tower of London

A traditional way of marking a royal ceremonial, annual royal anniversaries (such as the accession to the throne) or special occasions is for the King's Troop Royal Horse Artillery to fire a royal gun salute. These salutes take place in various authorized locations around the UK, but in London the gun salutes are fired in Hyde Park and the Tower of London. Green Park is used instead of Hyde Park during state visits, for the sovereign's official birthday and for the State Opening of Parliament.

A standard gun salute consists of 21 rounds, but an extra 20 are added when the royal gun salute is given in Hyde Park and Green Park because these are both royal parks.

The Garter Day Ceremony

WHEN: June, the first Mon of Ascot week;
WHERE: Windsor Castle

Each June, the members of the Order of the Garter meet at Windsor Castle for the Garter Day Procession and Ceremony. New Knights and Lady Companions of the Garter are invested into the Order in the Throne Room. After lunch in the Waterloo Chamber, they walk in procession from the State Apartments through the Upper, Middle and Lower Wards of the castle to St George's Chapel, which is the home of the Order.

Windsor Castle is closed to the public on Garter Day, and only those with official invitations are allowed to attend the Garter Day Service. Members of the public who would like to watch the procession are able to apply for tickets each year.

State Opening of Parliament

WHEN: Oct, Nov or Dec, or soon after a General Election;
WHERE: The Mall and Whitehall

The Parliamentary calendar often seems rather drab, but once a year it is brightened by a magnificent occasion. This is the State Opening of Parliament, which brings together the sovereign, the House of Commons and the House of Lords.

Some of the procedures surrounding the ceremony are reminders that the relationship between Crown and state has not always been cordial. Guy Fawkes and his cohorts plotted to blow up James I in Parliament in 1605 by placing gunpowder in the cellars. So a detachment of The Queen's Bodyguard of the Yeoman of the Guard still searches the cellars, in conjunction with the police.

Charles I came into such conflict with his MPs that it led to the English Civil War, and as a result no monarch has been allowed to set foot inside the House of Commons since 1642 when Charles tried to arrest five MPs. At the State Opening of Parliament, the MPs wait in their chamber in the House of Commons. The Queen's messenger, known as Black Rod, bangs on the door of the Commons. The door is slammed in his face, as a reminder of Parliament's independence from the Crown. He then knocks on the door three times with his staff of office and summons the MPs to attend the Queen in the House of Lords, where she reads an outline of the government's plans for the next Parliament. Being a constitutional monarch, she has no say in what these plans might be and has to announce them regardless of what she might privately think about them.

Members of the public are not allowed inside the Houses of Parliament during the State Opening of Parliament, but they can watch the sovereign's procession to and from Buckingham Palace in The Mall and Whitehall. This is a magnificent spectacle. The Imperial State Crown, the Sword of State and the Cap of Maintenance travel in their own state coach, guarded by two Sergeants at Arms. The Queen follows in the Irish State Coach. Traditionally, the sovereign's coach is always drawn by Windsor Grey horses. The procession is escorted by members of the Royal Household.

Remembrance Day

WHEN: Second Sun in Nov; WHERE: The Cenotaph, Whitehall

Each November, the nation remembers all those who have died in the two world wars and other conflicts. Although ceremonies are held in towns and villages throughout the country, the national focus is on Whitehall. The Royal Family, members of the government, High Commissioners from the Commonwealth, members of the armed services and the public gather for a short service. First, there is a two-minute silence at 11 o'clock, which begins and ends with a two-gun salute fired from Horse Guards Parade, and then the Last Post is sounded. The Queen and other members of the Royal Family lay wreaths of poppies at the foot of the Cenotaph (designed by Sir Edwin Lutyens in Portland stone and unveiled in 1920). Britain's political leaders then lay their wreaths. There is a short service, followed by Reveille and the National Anthem, and then the Queen leaves. The war veterans march past the Cenotaph and the royal salute is taken by a member of the Royal Family.

LEFT *MPs and Peers gather in the House of Lords to hear the Queen's Speech at the State Opening of Parliament.*

WESTMINSTER

From the sumptuous interiors of Buckingham Palace to the site of James I's aviary in Birdcage Walk, Westminster is an area of London that is rich in places with royal connections. Some of these sites are world-famous, while others are treasures that are waiting to be discovered.

1 Constitution Hill

SW1; TUBE: Green Park, Hyde Park Corner, St James's Park, Victoria; RAIL: Victoria

2 Queen's Gallery

Buckingham Gate, SW1A 1AA; ☎ 020 7766 7301; www.royalcollection.org.uk; open mid-Apr–early Dec; ADMISSION: adults ££, concessions ££, under-17s ££, under-5s free; TUBE: Green Park, Hyde Park Corner, St James's Park, Victoria; RAIL: Victoria

To paraphrase Lady Bracknell in Oscar Wilde's play, *The Importance of Being Earnest* (1895), to experience one assassination attempt along Constitution Hill may be regarded as a misfortune but to experience three looks like carelessness. However, this is exactly what happened to Queen Victoria (r.1837–1901), whose life was threatened here in 1840, 1842 and 1849.

Strangely enough, she was not the only monarch whose life was thought to be in danger on Constitution Hill. Charles II (r.1660–85) enjoyed taking his constitutional walks along the road, which, it is believed, is how it got its name. One day his younger brother, James, Duke of York (1633–1701), was unnerved to see Charles strolling along the route with a very modest retinue of servants. He chastised his brother for taking such risks with his personal safety, to which Charles replied, 'I am sure no man in England will take away my life to make you king.' In the event, Charles was probably right. The Duke of York succeeded to the throne as James II in 1685, but his reign lasted just three years before he became so unpopular that he had to flee to France and a life in exile.

If you stand little chance of securing a private invitation to Buckingham Palace (see pages 24–5) or Windsor Castle (see pages 152–3), the Queen's Gallery is the place to visit if you want to see a display of some of the many items that belong in the Royal Collection.

The gallery was created at the suggestion of Queen Elizabeth II (b.1926) and her husband, Prince Philip (b.1921), and it opened on 25 July 1962. It has interesting architectural connections, as it stands on the site of a pavilion that was built on the south-west side of Buckingham Palace in 1831. This was designed by John Nash as an Ionic temple, but was converted into a private chapel for Queen Victoria in 1843. During the Second World War, the chapel was completely destroyed in a German bombing raid on 13 September 1940, much to the regret of George VI (r.1936–52).

In the late 1990s, it was decided that the Queen's Gallery needed to be redeveloped. John Simpson carried out the work, at a cost of over £20 million, which was provided by the Royal Collection Trust, and the gallery reopened on 21 May 2002. Interestingly, there is still a private chapel within the Queen's Gallery, which is not open to the public.

LEFT *The east front of Buckingham Palace (see pages 24–6), showing the famous balcony on which the Royal Family appear during special occasions.*

Buckingham Palace

SW1A 1AA; ☎ 020 7766 7300; www.royal.gov.uk; open for part of summer and autumn, see website for details; ADMISSION: adults £££, concessions £££, under-17s ££; TUBE: Green Park, Hyde Park Corner, St James's Park, Victoria; RAIL: Victoria

An aged mulberry tree grows in the grounds of Buckingham Palace, the solitary remnant of the vast walled garden of 10,000 black mulberry trees planted here in the early 17th century by James I (r.1603–25). He had high hopes of establishing a profitable silk industry, but he was obviously given bad advice, as the mulberry trees he chose were unpalatable to silkworms. The worms may not have cared for the trees but the splendours of the garden were extremely popular with Londoners, who used it for courtship among other pursuits.

In 1702, John Sheffield, the 1st Duke of Buckingham and Normanby (1647–1721), leased the land and commissioned William Winde to build him a house. Buckingham House was considered 'one of the great beauties of London' and, when the duke died in 1721, his widow offered it to the Prince of Wales (later George II, r.1727–60). Negotiations came to nothing but, in 1761, George III (r.1760–1820) bought the house for £28,000 from Buckingham's illegitimate son. He intended it to be a family house and, soon after, he gave it to Queen Charlotte (1744–1818) in exchange for Somerset House (see pages 92–4), in which she had considered living. Buckingham House then became known as the Queen's House, and was extended in a manner fitting for the private residence of the monarch's consort. When Queen Charlotte died in 1818, her son, George, the Prince Regent (1762–1830), inherited the house. The building also had another change of name, becoming the King's House, Pimlico, in preparation for the prince's inevitable elevation to sovereign upon his father's death.

Nash and Blore

The builders moved in, but the renovations and improvements to the house failed to satisfy the Prince Regent who had begun to consider what to do with the royal palaces when he inherited them. By the time he became George IV in 1820 he had already decided that the King's House was far too small for him, and, after much wrangling with Parliament over the cost, he commissioned the architect John Nash (1752–1835) to build him a larger, more lavish palace. Naturally, this being the flamboyant George IV, the budget spiralled out of control and the palace became increasingly grandiose. It was still unfinished when he died in 1830, and his brother, William IV (r.1830–37), succeeded to the throne. Nash was sacked in 1831 for allowing the cost of the building to soar, which seems rather unfair, as preventing George IV from spending money was as impossible as making water flow uphill – both acts defy the laws of nature. However, the palace had to be completed, and the architect Edward Blore was given the task.

Here were two very different personalities from their respective predecessors. William IV was much more down-to-earth than George IV and had little interest in architecture. He had even less interest in Buckingham Palace, and suggested that it should be used as a barracks. However, the prime minister of the day, Charles Grey (1764–1845), persuaded William that this would be throwing good money after bad and that it made more sense to continue the original plan of turning Buckingham Palace into a royal residence. As for Edward Blore, he was seen as a

safe – not to say pedestrian – pair of hands after the flights of fancy conjured up by John Nash; there was no danger of Blore spending hundreds of pounds on intricate plaster ceilings and marble columns. Instead, he was the man to get the job done and to do it as cheaply and unimaginatively as possible.

Victoria's Family Home

Despite Blore's best efforts, the palace was still in need of considerable work when Queen Victoria moved into it shortly after her succession in 1837.

She and Prince Albert (1819–61), whom she married in 1840, lived with the builders for years while the palace was enlarged to make it into a family home. The palace flourished until Albert's death, at which point Victoria retreated into mourning and the building was neglected.

By the time Victoria's son, Edward VII (r.1901–10), became king in 1901, the palace was a fusty relic of a bygone age and in need of considerable renovation. Since then, work has been carried out as necessary. In 1913 the east front of the palace was refaced in Portland stone, using money left over from the funds raised to build the Queen Victoria Memorial (see page 29).

Public View

For decades, the only way the public could visit Buckingham Palace was if they worked here, received a special invitation or were presented at court, as, for example, young debutantes were during the coming-out season. However, in 1993 the palace was opened to the general public for the very first time. This arrangement, which occurs while the Royal Family are on holiday at Balmoral in Scotland during August and September, has continued ever since. A total of 19 staterooms are now open to the public, including the Music Room, in which members of the current Royal Family, including Charles, Prince of Wales (b.1948), Anne,

ABOVE *The balcony on the East Front of Buckingham Palace.*

the Princess Royal (b.1950), Andrew, Duke of York (b.1960) and William, Duke of Cambridge (b.1982) were all christened.

Twenty investitures take place in the ballroom of the palace each year, during which ordinary people and celebrities alike receive the honours that have been conferred on them by the Queen. There are also at least three garden parties within the palace grounds each year, following a tradition that began in the 1860s. Attendance is strictly by invitation only, with about 8,000 guests at each occasion looked after by about 400 staff. At each of these parties the staff provides about 27,000 cups of tea, 20,000 sandwiches and 20,000 slices of cake.

Buckingham Palace continues to be the pivot around which the British Royal Family is seen to revolve. It is their official London residence and a working palace, containing offices for all their staff. Every day tourists cluster around the railings of the building to watch the Changing of the Guard, in which one set of Foot Guards, from the Queen's Guard, comes off duty and is replaced by another. The proper name for this ceremony is Guard Mounting, but it is universally known by its more informal term, and it continues to be one of the most popular, traditional and evocative sights London has to offer.

4

Royal Mews

Buckingham Palace Road, SW1A 1AA; ☎ 020 7766 7302;
www.royalcollection.org.uk; open for most of year, see website
for details; ADMISSION: adults ££, concessions £, under-17s £,
under-5s free; TUBE: Green Park, Hyde Park Corner, St James's Park,
Victoria; RAIL: Victoria

The word 'mews' comes from the distinctive noise that was made by the falcons and hawks in the royal stables in what is now Trafalgar Square (see page 86). The mews moved from its original site to its present position in 1760. George III had bought what is now Buckingham Palace (see pages 24–6), and it made sense to locate his carriages and horses nearby. He added an indoor riding school in 1764 and renamed the stables the Royal Mews, Pimlico.

When George IV inherited both the crown and Buckingham Palace in 1820, he was gripped by his habitual complaint of building fever. He commissioned John Nash to work not only on the palace, but also the stables, which were drastically remodelled and expanded. The mews needed further improvements during the reign of Queen Victoria to cope with its increased workload, as she was the first monarch to use the palace as her official residence as well as her private home. So many servants were employed by the mews that, in 1855, Victoria set up the Buckingham Palace Royal Mews School, at her own expense, for the children of her employees. This was followed by new accommodation for the families in 1859.

The Royal Mews continues to adapt to its changing needs and is still a very busy and important part of the Royal Household. It supplies all the road transport for the Queen and other members of the Royal Family. A carriage from the Royal Mews conveys each newly appointed foreign ambassador from their official residence to Buckingham Palace to kiss the Queen's hands, returning to their quarters after the ceremony.

The Royal Mews is open to the public, who can view whichever modes of transport are not in use that day. Each of the state coaches, which are among the highlights on show, was built for a special purpose. The Gold State Coach was made for George III in 1762, and it is only used for coronations and jubilees. Riding in it made Queen Victoria feel sick, and George VI described the trip to his coronation as 'one of the most uncomfortable rides I have ever had in my life'. Let us hope that the Irish State Coach – so-called because it was made in Dublin – which Queen Victoria bought in 1852 and is used annually for the State Opening of Parliament, is more comfortable. Another carriage was added in 1910 when George V bought the Glass State Coach for use at royal weddings.

In addition to the carriages, the Royal Mews is home to the 30 or more working horses that help the Royal Family to carry out their official and ceremonial duties. These animals consist mostly of Cleveland Bays, which are the only British breed of carriage horses, and Windsor Greys, which traditionally pull the monarch's carriages. Motorized transport is also in evidence, including a fleet of Rolls-Royce Phantoms, which do not carry number plates.

Birdcage Walk

SW1; TUBE: Green Park, Hyde Park Corner, St James's Park, Victoria; RAIL: Victoria

Guards' Museum

Wellington Barracks, Birdcage Walk, SW1E 6HQ; ☎ 020 7930 4466; www.theguardsmuseum.com; open daily; ADMISSION: adults £, concessions £, serving military personnel £, under-16s free; TUBE: Green Park, Hyde Park Corner, St James's Park, Victoria; RAIL: Victoria

Although we often take them for granted, London street names can tell us a great deal about the local history of an area. Birdcage Walk is a classic example of this, as it derives its name from James I's aviary, which once stood here. Charles II shared his grandfather's love of birds and expanded the aviary after he came to the throne in 1660. It was during this time that St James's Park (see pages 30–31) was remodelled and Birdcage Walk created. It forms the southern border of the park, running from Buckingham Gate to Horse Guards Road.

Although the public was allowed into St James's Park during Charles II's reign, only the Hereditary Grand Falconer (the Duke of St Albans) and the Royal Family were permitted to travel along Birdcage Walk. In later years, houses were built along the road and it was opened to the public.

As its name suggests, this museum commemorates the five regiments of Foot Guards of the British army, and is housed in their headquarters at Wellington Barracks. The five regiments are the Coldstream Guards, the Grenadier Guards, the Irish Guards, the Scots Guards and the Welsh Guards. The Foot Guards, plus the two regiments of Household Cavalry, make up Her Majesty's Household Division. The museum was opened in 1988 and has displays of uniforms and medals, as well as dioramas showing some of the battles in which the Guards have fought.

The Coldstream, Grenadier and Scots Guards were formed after Charles II's restoration to the throne in 1660. They comprised two regiments from the King's Body Guard and one from Oliver Cromwell's New Model Army, which was formed during the Civil War. The Irish Guards were formed during the reign of Queen Victoria and the Welsh Guards during the First World War.

Queen Victoria Memorial and Gardens

SW1A 1AA; TUBE: Green Park, Hyde Park Corner, St James's Park, Victoria; RAIL: Victoria

When Queen Victoria died in 1901 she had been on the throne for nearly 64 years. The Queen Victoria Memorial Committee was set up in the year of her death to create some suitable monuments in her memory. One of the plans was to give The Mall (see pages 42–3) a radical facelift and make Buckingham Palace the focal point of this long stretch of avenue. It seemed fitting to erect a massive memorial to the late queen outside the east front of the palace, and Thomas Brock was commissioned to create it.

The memorial was finally unveiled in 1911. It had taken so long to complete that Victoria's son, Edward VII, was also dead and the task of unveiling the memorial fell to her grandson, who was by now George V (r.1910–36). In a crowd-pleasing moment, he knighted Brock during the ceremony.

If the late queen had been able to scrutinize the monument, she would undoubtedly have been pleased. In typical Victorian style, it is heavy with allegory, including marble carvings that represent Charity, Truth and Justice. The seated figure of Victoria at the centre of the memorial gazes down The Mall.

Aston Webb (1849–1930) was commissioned to transform the area around the memorial into the Queen Victoria Memorial Gardens. The original plan was for simple grass in the gardens, but elaborate flowerbeds were created at the request of Edward VII.

ABOVE *A gilded figure of Victory stands atop the memorial.*
BELOW *The memorial is opposite Buckingham Palace.*

8

St James's Park

SW1A 2BJ; ☎ 020 7930 1793; www.royalparks.gov.uk;
TUBE: Charing Cross, Embankment, St James's Park, Westminster;
RAIL: Charing Cross

This is the oldest royal park in London and it has the added distinction of being surrounded by three royal palaces: Buckingham Palace (see pages 24–6), the Palace of Westminster (see pages 52–3) and St James's Palace (see pages 34–5). Although it is now part of one of the most prestigious areas in London, it began life as a boggy field next to a leper hospital for women. The site of the hospital has also come up in the world, as it is now occupied by St James's Palace.

Henry VIII (r.1509–47), who always had such a canny eye for property, saw the potential of this area when he acquired it in 1532. He knocked down the hospital in order to build a palace, and drained the field to create a tiltyard and bowling alley, as well as a nursery for his collection of deer. Succeeding monarchs enjoyed the park and altered it to suit their needs: Elizabeth I (r.1558–1603) staged pageants and fêtes here, while James I improved the drainage so he could create a formal garden complete with a menagerie that included two crocodiles. Along with many royal properties, St James's Park suffered during the Interregnum (1649–60), the period between the end of the English Civil War and the Restoration, during which Charles II was in exile, and Londoners cut down many of the trees and burnt them for fuel.

Charles II rescued the park from neglect after the Restoration. He acquired a further 14.5 hectares (36 acres) of land and had the grounds landscaped in what was then the highly fashionable, formal French style typified by the designs of André Le Nôtre (1613–1700). One of Charles's lasting legacies is the park's canal, which was formed by merging some small ponds into one long stretch of water. Charles was particularly fond of the waterway, and used to parade around it with his mistresses – he was even known to swim in it on occasion. Such activities took place in full view of the public, who were admitted into the park for the first time during Charles's reign.

By the time Queen Anne (r.1702–14) came to the throne, the park had lost its grandeur and been colonized by prostitutes. However, it was gradually reclaimed by polite society and, in 1814, the Prince Regent held a spectacular gala here to celebrate the 16th anniversary of the Battle of the Nile and the centenary of the House of Hanover's British rule. A Chinese pagoda was built for the occasion, but tragically it caught fire during the fireworks display, killing one man and injuring five others.

Pelican Park

Many renovations and alterations have been carried out to St James's Park since then. However, some things have not changed. The park is home to several pelicans, which were first introduced when a Russian ambassador gave a pair of the birds to Charles II.

ABOVE *A view through the park to Buckingham Palace.*
RIGHT *The park in springtime.*

Green Park

SW1; ☎ 020 7930 1793; www.royalparks.gov.uk; TUBE: Green Park, Hyde Park Corner, St James's Park, Victoria; RAIL: Victoria

When Henry VIII acquired the leper hospital of St James's, which he knocked down so he could build St James's Palace (see pages 34–5), the adjoining graveyard came with it. Henry enclosed it, but it was not made into a royal park until Charles II laid out some pleasant walks in it. Charles also built an ice house in which cold drinks were kept in the summer; the mound that covered this ice house is still visible opposite No. 119 Piccadilly.

Having started life as the burial ground of a leper hospital, Green Park continued to have a rather insalubrious reputation well into the 18th century. It became a prime location for men to fight duels, and when Londoners were not dodging flying bullets they also had to cope with the unwelcome attention of highwaymen, who were particularly fond of this park.

Green Park is roughly triangular in shape, bounded to the north-west by Piccadilly, to the south by Constitution Hill (see page 23) and to the north-east by Queen's Walk. This latter walk was laid out for Queen Caroline (1683–1737), who was the wife of George II. A small pavilion was built here for her, in which she enjoyed sitting. She was considered to be much more intelligent than her husband, and a popular rhyme of the time ran: 'You may strut, dapper George, but 'twill all be in vain, We all know 'tis Caroline, not you, that reign.'

ABOVE *Deckchairs can be hired from March to October.*
BELOW *Late evening sunshine in the park.*

Spencer House

27 St James's Place, SW1A 1NR; ☎ 020 7514 1958;
www.spencerhouse.co.uk; open Sun, except in Jan and Aug;
ADMISSION: adults ££, concessions and children £ (no children
under 10 admitted); TUBE: Green Park, Piccadilly Circus

Spencer House is the ancestral London home of the late Diana, Princess of Wales (1961–97), and, as its name suggests, it was once owned by her family. The 1st Earl Spencer bought a lease on the site and commissioned the architect John Vardy (1718–65) to build a house for him. The work was carried out between 1756 and 1766, with James 'Athenian' Stuart (1713–88) superseding Vardy as architect in 1758.

The finished house was at the forefront of neo-classical design and was considered to be one of the finest homes in 18th-century London. It was important for the Spencer family that it should be as grand as possible, as they occupied an elevated social position and needed a house to reflect this. They had many links with the monarchy, and both the 4th and 6th Earls served as Lord Chamberlain of the Royal Household. In July 1981, the Spencers'

most dazzling association with royalty occurred when Lady Diana Spencer married Prince Charles.

Spencer House continued as the London home of the Spencer family until 1895, when they leased it out. During the Second World War, many valuable objects within the house were moved to Althorp, the Spencers' house in Northamptonshire. Today, the house has been restored to its original 18th-century splendour, complete with artefacts borrowed from the Royal Collection.

ABOVE *Looking through Green Park to Spencer House.*

St James's Palace

Cleveland Row, SW1A 1DH; www.royal.gov.uk; not open to public;
TUBE: Green Park, Piccadilly Circus, St James's Park, Victoria;
RAIL: Victoria

It is one of life's ironies that the palace from which the Court of St James – to give the British court its official title – operates was built on the site of a leper hospital. St James's Hospital was believed to date from before the Norman Conquest of 1066, although the earliest record of it comes from the 12th century. Henry VIII, who certainly had a marvellous ability to spot promising areas of land, bought the hospital in 1532, with the intention of building a palace here. The surrounding land was marshy but it was drained and became St James's Park (see pages 30–31).

The palace was completed for Henry in 1540. All that remains from his era is the gatehouse to Colour Court. His daughter, Mary I (r.1553–8), died in the palace, and Henry's other daughter, Elizabeth I, took refuge here during the threatened invasion by the Spanish Armada in July 1588.

Births and Deaths

In January 1649, after the English Civil War had ended, the unthinkable happened. Charles I (r.1625–49) was found guilty of treason against his people and sentenced to death. He spent his last night at St James's Palace rather than at Whitehall Palace, the primary royal residence of the time, because he did not want to be kept awake by the sound of workmen assembling his scaffold. On the morning of his execution, Charles took Holy Communion in the Chapel Royal within St James's Palace and walked through St James's Park to the Banqueting House (see pages 46–7), outside which he was executed.

Whitehall Palace had survived a number of fires (a universal hazard at the time), but it did not withstand a blaze that broke out in 1698, and so St James's Palace became the official London residence of the Royal Family. It was already popular with royalty, as many royal babies had been born here, including the future Charles II in 1630 and his brother James II in 1633, as well as James's daughters, Mary II in 1662 and Queen Anne in 1665.

In 1795, George, Prince of Wales (later George IV), who had been born at the palace in 1762, was married to Caroline of Brunswick in the Chapel Royal of the palace. This wedding had all the elements of a farce, as the prince could not bring himself to look at his bride (he found her extremely unprepossessing, not least because of her aversion to soap and hot water) and instead gazed at his mistress, Lady Jersey. The prince was also drunk; he had to be helped up the aisle, and at one point it looked as though he would have dearly loved to make a run for it.

A Working Palace

The palace is still the official residence of the sovereign, which is why the British court is known as the Court of St James. However, reigning monarchs have lived at Buckingham Palace since the accession of Queen Victoria. Nevertheless, St James's Palace remains a working palace and contains several royal departments, including the Central Chancery of the Orders of Knighthood. It also continues to be the home of several members of the Royal Family.

RIGHT *The Tudor gatehouse leading to Colour Court.*

Clarence House

St James's Palace, SW1 1BA; ☎ 020 7766 7303;
www.royalcollection.org.uk; open daily early Aug–early Sept;
ADMISSION: adults ££, concessions ££, under-17s £, under-5s free;
TUBE: Green Park, Piccadilly Circus, St James's Park

For almost 50 years, from 1953 to 2002, Clarence House was synonymous with one woman – Queen Elizabeth the Queen Mother (1900–2002). It became her London home after the death of her husband, George VI, in February 1952. In fact, she swapped homes with her daughter, who succeeded to the throne as Elizabeth II and who had been living at Clarence House with her husband, Prince Philip, since 1949.

Clarence House is one of the many buildings within the precincts of St James's Palace, and was built by John Nash between 1825 and 1827 for the Duke of Clarence, for whom it was named and who became William IV in 1830. The interior design was deliberately kept plain because the duke, in almost comical contrast to his brother George IV, disliked anything that was ornate or gilded. Such was his loathing of elaborate decorative schemes that, even when he succeeded to the throne, he continued to live at Clarence House, as he heartily disliked the fussy interiors at Buckingham Palace. Once, when shown one of the Old Masters collected by his brother, William IV commented, 'Aye, it seems pretty – I dare say it is. My brother was fond of this sort of nick-nackery.' The cramped living quarters meant that William and his queen, Adelaide (1792–1849), had to tidy away their belongings before holding levées in their apartments.

After William IV died in 1837 and his widow, Adelaide, moved to Bushy Park (see page 146) and Marlborough House (see page 39), Clarence House became the home of a series of royal residents. Queen Victoria's mother, the Duchess of Kent, lived here from 1841 to 1861, enabling her to keep an eye on her daughter. From 1866 to 1900, Victoria's second son, Alfred, Duke of Edinburgh (1844–1900), lived here with his wife, Marie, who was the daughter of Tsar Alexander II. A Russian Orthodox chapel was built for her on the first floor. The next inhabitants were Arthur, Duke of Connaught and Strathearn (1850–1942), and his wife, Louise (1860–1917). The duke was Queen Victoria's favourite son; he lived here from 1900 until his death, after which Clarence House was given to the War Organization of the British Red Cross and Order of St John of Jerusalem for the remainder of the Second World War.

Having been turned into offices during the war, it took a long time to convert Clarence House back into a home when it was needed for the newlywed Duke and Duchess of Edinburgh in November 1947; they did not move in for a further 18 months. Their daughter, Princess Anne, was born here in August 1950. The couple moved out soon after the duchess became Elizabeth II, and Clarence House was once again overrun with decorators, who were now preparing for the arrival of the widowed Queen Mother and her younger daughter, Princess Margaret (1930–2002). From 1970, on 4 August each year crowds gathered outside the house to celebrate the Queen Mother's birthday.

After her mother's death in March 2002, the Queen decided that Prince Charles and his two sons, the Princes William and Harry, should move into Clarence House. The following year, parts of the refurbished Clarence House were opened to the public for the first time.

13
Statue of Queen Elizabeth the Queen Mother

The Mall, SW1; TUBE: Charing Cross, Green Park, St James's Park, Victoria; RAIL: Charing Cross, Victoria

14
Queen's Chapel

Marlborough Gate, SW1Y 5HX; open to public during Sun services only; TUBE: Charing Cross, Green Park, Piccadilly Circus; RAIL: Charing Cross

The statue of the Queen Mother by Philip Jackson (b.1944), and the two bronze relief panels by Paul Day (b.1967) that flank it, refer to significant moments in her life. The statue itself shows the Queen Mother in 1952, when she was widowed at the relatively early age of 51. She is wearing the robes of the Order of the Garter, and the statue of her late husband stands nearby. One of the bronze relief panels depicts the King and Queen on a morale-boosting visit to the East End of London during the Second World War, and the other shows her in later years with her corgis, attending a race meeting and meeting war veterans. The statue was unveiled by the Queen on 24 February 2009.

BELOW *The statues of the Queen Mother and George VI stand close together in The Mall.*

In 1623, Inigo Jones (1573–1652) was commissioned to build the church for the Infanta of Spain, who was going to be the child bride of Charles I until wedding negotiations between Spain and England ran into trouble and the entire event was cancelled. The building work also ground to a halt, but it began again when Charles married Henrietta Maria (1609–69) in 1625.

When Charles II married Catherine of Braganza (1638–1705), the church was refurbished to cater for her Roman Catholicism. A variety of different religious services has been held here for English monarchs. Dutch Reformed services were held for William III (r.1689–1702) and his wife Mary II (r.1689–94); the Hanoverians attended German Lutheran services; and Queen Alexandra (1844–1925) attended services in her native Danish. Today, the services are Anglican once more.

Pall Mall

SW1; TUBE: Charing Cross, Green Park, Piccadilly Circus;
RAIL: Charing Cross

We owe the name of this street to the 16th-century delight in a game called *pallo a maglio*, which, roughly translated, means 'ball to mallet'. It became popular during the reign of Charles II, who was often seen playing it with one or more of his many mistresses in St James's Park. The original alley for pell mell, as the game was called in Britain, was dressed with a layer of powdered cockleshells and ran just inside the wall of the park. However, the alley was almost unusable in summer because passing carriages would send up choking clouds of dust. A new alley was built to the north of the first one, away from passing traffic. It was called Catherine Street in honour of Charles's wife, but was popularly called Pall Mall and has kept that name ever since.

Royal Favours

All of Pall Mall, with one notable exception, belongs to the Crown. The exception is No. 79, which was once the home of Nell Gwyn (1650–87), one of Charles II's most famous mistresses. (Sadly, this house was demolished and replaced by the present one in the 1860s.) Nell complained to Charles when she was only granted a lease on the property and insisted on being given the freehold, rather cheekily saying that she 'had always conveyed free under the Crown and always would'. When she died in 1687 the house passed to her son, the Duke of St Albans (1670–1726), but he was forced to hand it over to his creditors six years later.

Another royal alliance took place in the same house in 1766 when George III's brother, William, Duke of Gloucester (1743–1805), secretly married the Dowager Countess of Waldegrave; unfortunately they managed to make each other miserable. George's youngest brother, Henry, Duke of Cumberland (1745–90) also chose No. 79 Pall Mall in which to marry secretly in 1771. His bride was Mrs Anne Horton, a widow, but this marriage was a success. Both marriages were a threat to the royal succession, and Parliament passed the Royal Marriages Act in 1772, ruling that any royal marriage that took place without the consent of the sovereign was automatically rendered illegal.

The existence of the Royal Marriages Act – which is still in place today – did not deter George III's son, the Prince of Wales, who also married in secret. His bride, Mrs Fitzherbert, lived at No. 105 between 1789 and 1796, when her relationship with the prince was going through a low point. Their marriage was never valid in law, which was just as well as the prince later married Princess Caroline of Brunswick (1768–1821) without first ridding himself of Mrs Fitzherbert.

Pall Mall Princesses

Some official members of the Royal Family have also lived in Pall Mall. Princess Helena (1846–1923), a daughter of Queen Victoria, lived at Nos 77–8 from 1902–23, and her daughters, Princess Helena Victoria and Princess Marie Louise, remained in their family home until 1947. Princess Helena died at Schomberg House, Nos 80–82, in 1923; it has retained its original façade although the rest of the house was reconstructed in the late 1950s.

ABOVE *View down Pall Mall.*

Marlborough House

Pall Mall, SW1Y 5HX; not open to public; TUBE: Charing Cross, Green Park, Piccadilly Circus; RAIL: Charing Cross

In the early 18th century, Queen Anne granted a 50-year lease to her great friend, Sarah, Duchess of Marlborough (1660–1744) on a parcel of land adjoining St James's Palace so she could build a house. The duchess laid the foundation stone herself in 1709 and, always impatient with architects and builders, played a large role in supervising the work. The house was completed in 1711 and the duchess lived here until she died in 1744.

The lease returned to the Crown in 1817 and the house was prepared for the next residents, who were the Prince Regent's daughter, Princess Charlotte (1796–1817), and her husband, Prince Leopold of Saxe-Coburg-Saalfeld (1790–1865). However, Charlotte died in childbirth in November, and her son was stillborn, so the prince lived here by himself until he left in 1831 to become King of the Belgians. When William IV died in 1837, his widow, Queen Adelaide, moved into the house, remaining here until her death in 1849.

Bright Young Things

If the first half of the 19th century at Marlborough House was characterized by sadness, the atmosphere changed dramatically in the early 1860s when the Prince of Wales, later Edward VII, moved in. This was the start of what became known as the 'Marlborough House Set': a group of fashionable and well-connected young people whose lives revolved around the Prince and Princess of Wales. It was all rather racy and daring, contrasting with the high moral tone of Queen Victoria's reign.

Dower House

When Edward VII died in 1910, Queen Alexandra lived here until her death in 1925. Queen Mary (1867–1953) became a widow on the death of George V in 1936, and so once again another dowager queen lived at Marlborough House until her death. There are plaques in Marlborough Road in memory of both Queen Alexandra and Queen Mary.

Crisis

In the autumn of 1936, Marlborough House was the scene of much soul-searching, as the abdication crisis reached a climax. Edward VIII (r.1936), who had yet to be crowned after the death of his father, George V, was conducting a love affair with a divorced American woman, Mrs Wallis Simpson, much to the horror of both his family and the government. It was becoming increasingly apparent that he had to choose between the throne and his lover, and he eventually chose the latter. His brother, the Duke of York, was at Marlborough House when he heard the shattering news that Edward VIII had decided to abdicate, and that he would now have to become George VI. He wept on his mother's shoulder when he was told this.

Marlborough House was given to the government in 1959 and became the headquarters of the Commonwealth Secretariat.

ABOVE *The house was renovated between 1989 and 1993.*

St James's Square

SW1; TUBE: Charing Cross, Green Park, Piccadilly Circus;
RAIL: Charing Cross

It is 21 June 1815 – the height of the Napoleonic Wars. Mrs Edward Boehm, a society hostess, is giving a glittering ball at her house, 16 St James's Square. The Prince Regent is her honoured guest and everything is going splendidly until there is a commotion at the front door. A bloodstained, grubby man, his army uniform in tatters, rushes up the staircase and grabs the prince. Mrs Boehm is anxious – who is this impostor? He reveals himself to be Major the Honourable Henry Percy, bearing the astonishing news of England's victory at the Battle of Waterloo three days before. To prove his story, he lays the eagles of the French army at the prince's feet. Consternation! Delighted, the prince makes Percy a colonel right there and then, but Mrs Boehm is furious because her party is ruined, forgotten in the succeeding jubilation.

This is not the only royal event to have taken place in the square, which is one of the most prestigious addresses in Westminster. Today, it is home to businesses and various institutions, but in the past the buildings were the private homes of many important people. The original Norfolk House, at No. 3, was the

TOP The statue depicts William III as a Roman general on horseback. ABOVE View across the square.

birthplace of George III in 1738. His daughter-in-law, Queen Caroline, stayed at No. 17 in 1820, during the investigations into her alleged adultery. The hearing took place at the House of Lords, to which she travelled in a state carriage. Cheering crowds collected around her house each morning and evening, calling for her to appear at the windows, and she was always delighted to grant their wishes.

No. 21 was once the home of two other notorious women connected with royalty: Arabella Churchill and Catherine Sedley, who were both mistresses of the Duke of York, later James II. His brother, Charles II, had such a low opinion of the women that he once said they must have been inflicted on the duke by his priests as a penance.

There is a bronze statue of William III in the garden at the centre of the square. A molehill lies under the horse's hooves, as a reminder of the animal that tripped up William's horse in 1702 and caused his death from the subsequent fall.

Waterloo Place

SW1; TUBE: **Charing Cross, Piccadilly Circus;** RAIL: **Charing Cross**

Waterloo Place was built to link the southern end of Regent Street with what was then Carlton House, the Prince Regent's private residence. It was begun in 1816 and named in honour of Britain's triumph at the Battle of Waterloo.

Although Carlton House was pulled down in 1826 and Carlton House Terrace built on the land, Waterloo Place continues to have strong royal associations. A bronze equestrian statue of Edward VII, by Sir Bertram Mackennal (1863–1931) and erected in the 1920s, stands to the south of Pall Mall. It is an appropriate position for this king as he enjoyed belonging to the many gentlemen's clubs of St James's and Pall Mall, and patronized them most assiduously.

The Grand Old Duke of York

Nevertheless, the most imposing feature of Waterloo Place is the Duke of York Column, which stands above the Duke of York Steps that lead down to The Mall (see pages 42–3). There have been many Dukes of York over the centuries but the one celebrated here is Frederick (1763–1827), who was the second son of George III and the brother of George IV. The memorial was erected in the 1830s and consists of a very tall column designed by Benjamin Wyatt, topped by a square balcony, drum and dome on which stands a bronze statue of the duke by Sir Richard Westmacott (1775–1856). The joke at the time was that the statue had been placed so high in order to keep the duke away from his creditors – he had debts of about £2 million at the time of his death. The money

TOP *The Duke of York Column.* ABOVE *The statue of Edward VII silhouetted against the Athenaeum Club.*

to build the column was mostly raised by stopping one day's pay from every soldier in the army, which doubtless diminished what had been until then the duke's popularity with his men.

19

The Mall

SW1; TUBE: Charing Cross, Green Park; RAIL: Charing Cross

The Mall always comes into its own during royal celebrations, when it is thronged with the thousands of people who cannot get any closer to Buckingham Palace (see pages 24–6). During Elizabeth II's Golden Jubilee in June 2002, The Mall was the scene of a lengthy carnival procession presided over by the Royal Family and television cameras from around the world.

As with so many other streets around this area, The Mall was created during the improvements to St James's Park (see pages 30–31) that followed the Restoration of Charles II in 1660. The street replaced Pall Mall (see page 38) as the venue for the then popular game of pell mell, and became a busy avenue along which fashionable society strolled.

The Mall was transformed in 1903–04, as part of the national memorial to Queen Victoria who had died in 1901, although it was not completed until 1911. The original Mall was renamed Horse Ride, and its name was transferred to the new royal processional route leading from Buckingham Palace to Admiralty Arch.

A network of underground tunnels runs beneath The Mall, connecting Buckingham Palace with many major government departments and buildings, including 10 Downing Street.

TOP *Looking down The Mall towards Buckingham Palace.* BELOW *Admiralty Arch.* RIGHT *Union Flags hanging in The Mall to celebrate the Royal Wedding in 2011.*

ANNO·DECIMO·EDWARDI·SEPTIMI·REGIS· VICTORIÆ·REGINÆ·CIVES·GRATISSIMI·MDCCCCX·

Horse Guards Parade

Horse Guards Road, SW1A 1DH; TUBE: Charing Cross,
St James's Park; RAIL: Charing Cross

This is one of the few reminders of the long-vanished Whitehall Palace, which once sprawled over this area of London. The parade ground stands on the site of the tiltyard of the Tudor palace. It was a favourite place of Henry VIII, an accomplished rider who enjoyed jousts before his increasing girth and ill-health forced him to adopt a more sedentary way of life.

Each year, Horse Guards Parade is the scene of one of the great royal ceremonies, Trooping the Colour (see page 19). This dates back to the 18th century, and it has also been part of the official birthday celebrations of the sovereign since 1748. Tradition dictates that this official birthday always falls in the summer months, as there is then a better chance of the public ceremonials taking place on a sunny day.

Trooping the Colour commemorates the ancient military practice of parading (or trooping) the flags (or colours) of a battalion in front of its soldiers so they could easily recognize them on the battlefield. It is performed by troops from the Household Division – the Household Cavalry and the Foot Guards (which consists of the Coldstream, Grenadier, Irish, Scots and Welsh Guards). The Queen took the royal salute for the first time in 1951, when she was still a princess, because her father George VI was unable to attend. Elizabeth II always took the salute on horseback, riding side-saddle in the uniform of whichever Guards regiment was trooping, but since 1987 she has attended the ceremony in her own clothes and in her own carriage.

The Horse Guards building is guarded daily by four members of the Household Cavalry: two on horseback and two on foot. Those on horseback are relieved every hour, but the others stand motionless for two hours at a stretch. Changing of the Guard (see page 26) also takes place here daily, during which the Old Guard is relieved by the New Guard.

The building itself was designed by William Kent (c.1685–1748) and completed by John Vardy in the 1750s. The clock in the tower has a black dot over the two, to commemorate the time of Charles I's execution on the other side of the road, outside the Banqueting House (see pages 46–7) on 30 January 1649.

TOP AND RIGHT *Horse Guards Parade.* LEFT *Household Cavalry (Blues and Royals) ride away from Horse Guards Parade.*

Banqueting House

Whitehall, SW1A 2ER; ☎ 0844 482 7777 (from UK), +44 (0)20
3166 6000 (from outside UK); www.hrp.org.uk/banquetinghouse;
open Mon–Sat; closed Sun, bank holidays and from 24 Dec–1 Jan incl.;
ADMISSION: adults £, concessions £, under-16s free; TUBE: Charing
Cross, Embankment, Westminster; RAIL: Charing Cross

Just before two o'clock on the afternoon of 30 January 1649, Charles I stepped out of one of the first-floor windows of the Banqueting House on to a specially made scaffold to face his executioner. Throngs of people on the street below jostled one another for a better view of what was to come: the beheading of the reigning monarch for treason. His crime was to have allowed the Stuart belief in the Divine Right of Kings to clash with the increasing power of Parliament, triggering the English Civil War; he was therefore charged with making war on his subjects.

To Kill a King

It was a chilly day and Charles had taken the precaution of wearing two shirts, in case any shivers from the cold might be mistaken for those of fear. He was dignified to the last, saying to Dr Juxon, the Bishop of London, who was attending him: 'I go from a corruptible to an incorruptible Crown, where no disturbance can be. Remember.' He could not address the people directly, as he was kept so far away from them – Parliament wanted to prevent him making a speech. As the watching crowd saw the axe fall, an onlooker recorded: 'There was such a dismal universal groan amongst the thousands of people who were in sight of it, as it were with one consent, as I never heard before and desire I may not hear again.'

The choice of the Banqueting House as the place of execution was no accident: it was part of Whitehall Palace, which had been a royal residence since Henry VIII's reign, and the ceiling of the main room was decorated with Rubens paintings that celebrated the Stuart dynasty. The entire event was a conclusive statement of the Parliamentarian repudiation of monarchy and all it stood for.

The daring experiment of a republican Britain lasted until 1660, when Charles II was restored to the throne (having succeeded to it in theory on the day of his father's death). Once again, the Banqueting House was the focus because the formal restoration ceremony took place here on 29 May 1660.

'A Foul Protestant Wind'

A third major event in British history took place here on 13 February 1689, when the crown was offered to the Prince and Princess of Orange, who accepted it to become William III and Mary II. They took over the crown from Mary's father, James II, whose pro-Catholic stance made him too unpopular to remain king. The weathervane on top of the Banqueting House is said to have been placed here by James so he could watch for the 'foul Protestant wind' that would bring William and Mary to Britain. It duly blew them to Devon in November 1688, at which point James felt it was prudent to hotfoot it to France.

Although the rest of Whitehall Palace was destroyed in a fire in 1698, the Banqueting House was left unscathed. It was turned into a Chapel Royal, then later a museum, but is now once again a venue for important public occasions.

RIGHT *The Banqueting House is all that remains of Whitehall Palace. Its ceiling is decorated with Rubens canvases.*

Westminster Abbey

20 Dean's Yard, SW1P 3PA; ☎ 020 7222 5152; www.westminster-abbey.org; open Mon–Sat, Sun for worship only; ADMISSION: adults £££, concessions ££, under-18s £, under-11s free; TUBE: Charing Cross, Embankment, St James's Park, Westminster; RAIL: Charing Cross

As a seemingly endless succession of buses and taxis hurtle around Parliament Square, their exhaust fumes adding further accretions of dirt to those that have already collected on the English Gothic stone façade of Westminster Abbey, it takes a monumental effort to imagine how the building might have looked in a less hectic age.

In the 11th century, this was a marshy stretch of land (known as Thorney Island) outside the city walls, on which Edward the Confessor (r.1042–66) built a cruciform church to accompany his new palace. The church was consecrated on 28 December 1065 and Edward died early in January 1066. He was buried before the high altar. On Christmas Day that same year, William the Conqueror was crowned here, setting the precedent that all future coronations should take place in Westminster Abbey. There have only been three exceptions to this: Edward V (1483), who was murdered before he could be crowned; Lady Jane Grey (1553), who only reigned for nine days before being deposed and sent to the Tower of London and subsequently executed (see page 75); and Edward VIII, who abdicated in 1936 before his coronation.

A massive construction project began in 1245, when Henry III (r.1216–72) started to rebuild the abbey. He had already added a Lady Chapel in 1220, but now he wanted to create a building that was suitable for the coronations and burials of sovereigns, and he looked to European cathedrals for inspiration. This is when the abbey that we see today first began to take shape, with the central crossing between the Quire and the Sanctuary Steps large enough to be the focus of coronations. Henry also created a special shrine to St Edward the Confessor, who had been canonized in 1161 and is the only British king to have ever received such an honour.

Many monarchs have added to the history of the abbey in their own way. In March 1413, Henry IV (r.1399–1413) was making plans to visit the Holy Land and was praying before St Edward's Shrine when he was taken ill. He was carried into the Jerusalem Chamber, which was then part of the medieval lodgings of the abbey's abbot, at which point he regained consciousness and asked where he was. When told that he was in Jerusalem, he realized he was going to die; it had long been prophesied that he would die in Jerusalem.

One of the most bizarre events in the abbey's history took place on 19 July 1821, when George IV came here to be crowned. His flamboyant and dramatic coronation garments, which he had designed himself, were astonishing enough, to say nothing of the make-up that was caked on his face and that melted in the summer heat, but these paled into insignificance as events unfolded. George's marriage to Caroline of Brunswick had long been over in all but name. Nevertheless, Caroline fully expected to be crowned queen at the same time as her estranged husband was made king. Crowds lining the streets cheered as her carriage drove from her house in South Audley Street to the abbey, but when she arrived every door she tried to enter was shut in her

ABOVE *The north front of the abbey.* RIGHT *The west front, probably the most familiar view of the abbey.*

face. She finally managed to get through a door at Poets' Corner but was told that there was no place for her in the abbey and she would have to leave. Reluctantly, she did so. On her way back to South Audley Street the crowd turned against her, with boos and catcalls. Three weeks later, she was dead.

A Modern Coronation

On 2 June 1953, history was made when the coronation of Elizabeth II at Westminster Abbey was televised. This was the first time that television cameras had been allowed to record such a sacred service, and virtually none of the Queen's advisers was in favour of it. However, she ignored their protests and, as a result, many of her subjects bought their first television sets expressly so they could watch the crowning of their new queen. The Coronation Chair on which Elizabeth II sat is on view in the abbey. It was created for Edward I (r.1272–1307) in 1296, after he stole the Stone of Scone on which many Scots kings had been crowned, and triumphantly brought it back to England. The chair was first used at the coronation of Edward II (r.1307–27) in 1308 and has been an integral part of every coronation since then. Today, the Stone of Scone is back in Scotland, having been returned to Edinburgh Castle in 1996.

Royal Resting Place

In common with St George's Chapel, Windsor, Westminster Abbey is the burial place of many kings and queens, and several of them lie in the Henry VII chapel. The bodies of Henry VII (r.1485–1509) himself and his queen, Elizabeth of York (1466–1503), are behind the altar. Enemies in life are near neighbours in death: Elizabeth I lies next to her half-sister, Mary I (r.1553–8), and close by is the marble tomb of her cousin, Mary, Queen of Scots (r.1542–67), whose death Elizabeth ordered. The abbey also contains the remains of Edward I, Richard II (r.1377–99), Henry V (r.1413–22), Anne of Cleves (1515–57), James I and his consort Anne of Denmark (1574–1619), Charles II, William III and his wife Mary II, Queen Anne and her consort George of Denmark, and George II and his consort Caroline. There is also a burial urn containing what are believed to be the bones of the murdered Princes in the Tower, Edward V and his brother, Richard, Duke of York, who both vanished in 1483, thereby conveniently allowing their uncle, Richard III (r.1483–5), to take over the throne.

Westminster Abbey continues to be one of the focal points of national life and many important events have taken place here in recent years. There have been royal weddings, including those of Princess Elizabeth and Prince Philip in 1947, Princess Margaret and Antony Armstrong-Jones in 1960, Princess Anne and Captain Mark Phillips in 1973, and Prince Andrew and Sarah Ferguson in 1986. On 6 September 1997, the funeral of Diana, Princess of Wales took place in the abbey, followed by that of Queen Elizabeth the Queen Mother on 9 April 2002 and a memorial service for Princess Margaret on 19 April that same year. In a happier vein, the abbey was the venue for a service to celebrate the Queen's Golden Jubilee on 2 June 2003, 50 years to the day since she was crowned here. On 29 April 2011, Prince William married Catherine Middleton in the abbey.

Palace of Westminster

SW1A 2TT; ☎ 0844 847 1672; www.parliament.uk/visiting/visiting-and-tours; guided tours every Sat and open Aug–Sept; you can contact your MP to request a free guided tour; ADMISSION: adults £££, concessions ££, children £; TUBE: St James's Park, Westminster; RAIL: Charing Cross

Today, 'the Palace of Westminster' is another name for the Houses of Parliament, but despite this it is still a royal palace and has been ever since the reign of Edward the Confessor in the 11th century. The original fortified building created by Edward was taken over by William the Conqueror (r.1066–87) in 1066, and in due course by his son, William Rufus (r.1087–1100), who built Westminster Hall in 1099. William Rufus had big plans for the hall but these were curtailed by his death – and possible murder on the orders of his brother, Henry (r.1100–35), who then became king. Subsequent kings improved the hall, and it now has the widest unsupported hammerbeam roof in Europe. Westminster Hall is still in use as a vestibule for the House of Commons, but it comes into its own for important state occasions. For instance, the lying-in-state of Edward VII in 1910, and that of Queen Elizabeth the Queen Mother in 2002, both took place here. On 25 May 2011, the US president Barack Obama addressed both houses of Parliament in the hall.

From the 13th century until 1882, Westminster Hall was the home of the Law Courts and therefore was witness to some notable trials. In 1536, when Henry VIII had to find a way of ridding himself of his second wife, Anne Boleyn (c.1501–36), she was accused of adultery with five men (including her brother, Lord Rochford) and of conspiring to kill the king. These were undoubtedly trumped-up charges and the outcome of the trial was a foregone conclusion. Anne and her brother were tried at the Great Hall in the Tower of London (see page 75). The other four men were tried at Westminster Hall,

found guilty and sentenced to death. Anne and her brother were also found guilty and received the same sentence, which was swiftly carried out.

Remember, Remember

In 1606, Guy Fawkes (1570–1606) was tried in Westminster Hall after a failed attempt to blow up James I and Parliament; Fawkes was executed just around the corner in Old Palace Yard. However, the legacy of his actions lives on; each year the Yeomen of the Guard search the cellars, where the gunpowder was found, before the State Opening of Parliament. In 1649, in one of the most sensational trials in British history, Charles I was tried in the hall

OPPOSITE *The Clock Tower housing Big Ben, which is a bell.*
RIGHT *The Gothic splendour of the buildings.*
BELOW *The Palace of Westminster stretches along the north bank of the Thames.*

and found guilty of treason against his people and duly sentenced to death. At his trial he refused to remove his hat because he did not recognize the legitimacy of the court. The law courts moved out of Westminster Hall in 1882, but between the 1660s and this date they had shared the space with stallholders selling such wares as books, toys and clothes. It is strange to think of important trials being conducted while commerce raged all around.

Gothic Redevelopment

Over the centuries, many parts of the original medieval palace were destroyed by fire. Following a blaze in 1512, Henry VIII moved out of the Palace of Westminster into Whitehall Palace. He was the last sovereign to live at Westminster and the royal apartments were taken over by parliamentary officials. Nevertheless, the building continued to be called a royal palace. In October 1834, fire swept through the medieval palace again, but this time it was virtually destroyed; only the crypt of St Stephen's Chapel, the Jewel Tower (see page 54) and Westminster Hall survived. It was a catastrophe, but it was also an opportunity for some imaginative redevelopment. Charles Barry (1795–1860) and Augustus Pugin (1812–52) were commissioned as the architects for the new building, creating the Gothic structure that we know today.

Jewel Tower

Abingdon Street, SW1P 3JX; ☎ 020 7222 2219; www.english-heritage.org.uk/daysout/properties/jewel-tower; open daily; ADMISSION: adults £, concessions £, children £, free to members of English Heritage; TUBE: St James's Park, Westminster; RAIL: Charing Cross

Bust of Charles I

St Margaret's Church, St Margaret Street, SW1P 3JX; ☎ 020 7654 4840; www.westminster-abbey.org/st-margarets; open Mon–Sat, Sun for worship only; ADMISSION: free; TUBE: St James's Park, Westminster; RAIL: Charing Cross

After the disastrous fire of 1834, very little of the original Palace of Westminster (see pages 52–3) was left standing. Happily, however, the Jewel Tower, built in Kentish rag stone, is one of the buildings that survived. It was built by Henry Yevele in 1365–6 for Edward III (r.1327–77) and, as its name suggests, was probably intended as a safe repository of his jewels, clothes and personal belongings. The defensive moat, which is still visible outside the tower, certainly suggests this, and succeeding monarchs used the tower for their wardrobe and jewels, although there is also a theory that the Jewel Tower was originally built as a monastic prison.

The Jewel Tower continued to be the home of the royal wardrobe until the reign of Henry VII. Parliamentary records were held here from 1621 to 1864, after which it was used by the Weights and Measures Office until 1938. It is now owned by English Heritage and is open to the public.

It seems to be adding insult to injury to place a commemorative bust of Charles I in such close proximity to a statue of his old adversary, Oliver Cromwell (1599–1658), but that is what has happened at Westminster. The statue of Cromwell stands outside Westminster Hall, where Charles was tried and condemned for treason in January 1649, before being executed a few days later. Cromwell was installed as Lord Protector (while sitting in the Coronation Chair) in Westminster Hall in 1653.

The lead bust of Charles I was placed above the east door of St Margaret's Church in 1950. It is one of three that were found in a builder's yard in Fulham that same year by Hedley Hope-Nicholson, who at the time was the secretary of the Society of King Charles the Martyr. Another of the busts sits in a niche above the main door of the Banqueting House, while the third is in private hands.

St Margaret's Church has been the parish church of the House of Commons since 1614, and is where Members of Parliament are allowed to marry and be buried. Charles I clashed with Parliament in the 1630s over who had the most power, but he lost the argument and his head with it. However, after the Restoration in 1660, the bodies of several Parliamentarians, including John Pym, which had already been buried were exhumed and ignominiously reburied in a pit in the churchyard here.

St John's, Smith Square

Smith Square, SW1P 3HA; ☎ 020 7222 1061 (box office);
www.sjss.org.uk; bar and restaurant open weekday lunchtimes and
before evening concerts; church open for concerts; ADMISSION: contact
box office; TUBE: St James's Park, Victoria, Westminster; RAIL: Victoria

This building is now celebrated for the concerts that are held here, but it was once the church of St John the Evangelist and renowned for its Baroque architecture. The church was designed and built between 1714 and 1728 by Thomas Archer (c.1668–1743), who was a tremendous fan of Italian architecture. St John's had the distinction of being the most expensive of the 'Fifty New Churches' that were planned for London in 1711, and was built at a cost of over £40,000.

It is popularly known as 'Queen Anne's footstool' because, so the story goes, the queen was so irritated at being asked yet again to give her approval of a church design that she kicked over the nearest footstool and said 'build it like that'. As a result, St John's was given four lofty towers that attracted a great deal of criticism. In his novel *Our Mutual Friend* (1865), Charles Dickens described the building as 'some petrified monster, frightful and gigantic, on its back with its legs in the air'.

St John's has had an eventful history, as it was badly damaged by fire in 1742 and bombed during the Second World War, after which it was rebuilt as a concert hall.

BELOW *The imposing front of St John's.*

Carlton House Terrace

SW1; TUBE: Charing Cross, Piccadilly Circus, Westminster;
RAIL: Charing Cross

This beautiful terrace of late Georgian houses was built between 1827 and 1832 by John Nash, who was George IV's favourite architect. Nash was very familiar with this area of London as he had previously worked on Carlton House, the royal palace that was pulled down to make way for the terrace.

Carlton House first came into royal hands in 1732 when Frederick, Prince of Wales, bought it. After he died it passed to his widow, Augusta, who was the mother of George III. In due course, George III gave it to his eldest son, the Prince of Wales (later George IV), who set about turning it into one of the architectural extravaganzas for which he is still renowned.

The Prince of Wales lavished what even he described as an 'enormous' amount of money on the house. His daughter, Princess Charlotte, was born here on 7 January 1796 and her marriage to the man who later became Leopold I, King of the Belgians, also took place here on 2 May 1816.

When the prince, who was by now Prince Regent, succeeded to the throne in 1820 he knew that Carlton House was not big enough for his needs. It was pulled down, the land sold to pay for the cost of renovating Buckingham Palace, and various architectural features were used in other buildings; several of the doors went to Buckingham Palace. Carlton House Terrace was built on the site of the old house and its garden. Although little remains of the Prince Regent's ornate palace, it is still easy to imagine its grandeur and to appreciate its dominant position in such a fashionable part of London.

ABOVE *A detail of the terrace.* BELOW *The terrace adjoins St James's Park.*

THE CITY

Some of the greatest architectural and historic royal treasures of London, such as St Paul's Cathedral and the Guildhall, belong to its ancient City. The Tower of London feels as though it is part of the City of London, yet it stands outside the walls of what has long been known as 'the square mile'.

St Bartholomew's Hospital

West Smithfield, EC1A 7BE; ☎ 020 7377 7000; www.bartsandthelondon.
nhs.uk; museum open Tue–Fri; ADMISSION: free, but donations welcome;
TUBE: Barbican, Blackfriars, Farringdon, St Paul's; RAIL: Blackfriars,
Cannon Street, City Thameslink, Farringdon

Perhaps better known by its nickname, Barts, this is the oldest hospital in London. The institution was founded in 1123 by an Augustinian monk named Rahere, who had formerly held the position of court jester to Henry I. Rahere caught malaria while on a pilgrimage to Rome, and vowed to build a hospital for the poor in London if he survived the illness, which he did. He found a suitable site in Smithfield and called the hospital after St Bartholomew, who had appeared to him in a vision while he was sick.

Initially, the hospital was run by members of the priory of St Bartholomew, but it gradually became independent. This was just as well, as the priory was closed by Henry VIII in 1539, during the Dissolution of the Monasteries, although the hospital was allowed to continue. Nevertheless, its situation was very uncertain. In 1546, Henry VIII granted the hospital to the City of London, which permitted Barts to continue to tend London's poor. Henry also granted the hospital money and property. The first physician, Dr Roderigo Lopez, was appointed in 1562, but he was later hanged at Tyburn, having wrongly been found guilty of trying to poison Elizabeth I.

All that is left of the medieval complex of buildings is the tower of St Bartholomew-the-Less, which is the hospital's parish church. The rest of the church was rebuilt in 1789 by George Dance the Younger (1741–1825). However, this building rotted and was rebuilt again in 1825. The hospital itself was rebuilt to designs by James Gibbs (1682–1754), the architect of St Martin-in-the-Fields (see page 88), from 1730 to 1759. The gateway, over which presides a statue of Henry VIII by Francis Bird (1667–1731), was built in 1702.

Barts continued to be run under the charter granted by Henry VIII until 1948, when it became part of the new National Health Service. That charter is now on display in the hospital museum, in its north wing.

PREVIOUS PAGE *St Paul's Cathedral (see pages 61–3).*
LEFT *Barts stands in the heart of Smithfield. Its school of medicine and dentistry is the oldest in the UK.*

Church of St Bartholomew-the-Great

6–9 Kinghorn Street, EC1A 7HW; ☎ 020 7606 5171;
www.greatstbarts.com; open daily; ADMISSION: free for first hour,
after this adults £, concessions £; TUBE: Barbican, Farringdon,
St Paul's; RAIL: Blackfriars, Cannon Street, City Thameslink, Farringdon

London's oldest parish church, it was founded by Rahere in 1123. At that time, the church was part of the priory and hospital of St Bartholomew (see page 58), and Rahere was its first prior.

Bartholomew Fair

In 1133, Henry I gave permission for Rahere to hold a fair at the site. From that point onward, a cloth fair was held each summer around St Bartholomew's Day (24 August). Over the years this became a rowdy event, but it made money for the hospital, and continued until the 19th century.

Trouble arrived in 1539, when Henry VIII dissolved the priory in the course of his English Reformation.

TOP *The medieval gatehouse entrance to St Bartholomew-the-Great.* ABOVE *The church itself.*

The nave was demolished and only the choir was left standing for the parishioners to use. The fortunes of the church then followed the religious persuasion of the reigning monarch: in 1556, some Dominican monks were allowed to return by Mary I, who was a Roman Catholic, before being expelled in 1559 by the Protestant Elizabeth I.

The church is still a thriving parish church and has been the setting for several successful films, including *Four Weddings and a Funeral* (1994), *Elizabeth: The Golden Age* (2007) and *The Other Boleyn Girl* (2008).

Smithfield Market

Long Lane, EC1A 9PS; www.smithfieldmarket.com;
☎ 020 7332 3092; open Mon–Fri from 3am; closed on bank holidays;
ADMISSION: free; TUBE: Barbican, Farringdon; RAIL: Farringdon

Since 1855, Smithfield has been famous as London's largest meat market. Its current name is a corruption of 'Smooth Field', as the area was known in the Middle Ages when it played host to a horse fair every Friday. Long before then, it was a marshy swamp outside the city walls, which the Romans used as a general dumping ground.

Rebels and Religious Persecution

For centuries, Smithfield was a large open space near the city, and was therefore perfect for jousting. In 1357, it was the venue for a spectacular tournament attended by the English and French monarchs. In 1381, Smithfield was the scene of a much more serious event when the 14-year-old king, Richard II, met Wat Tyler and the poll-tax rebels. Tyler was deemed to have shown such scant respect for his monarch that he was pulled off his horse by the Lord Mayor, William Walworth, before being stabbed by another of the king's party, taken to St Bartholomew's Hospital (see page 58) for treatment, and then executed outside it.

Until the gallows were moved to Tyburn in the 1400s, Smithfield was a popular place for public executions. The Scottish rebel, William Wallace (c.1272–1305), who was such a thorn in the side of Edward I, endured a hideous death here, enjoying the dubious privilege of being the first person to be hanged, drawn and quartered.

Smithfield was particularly busy during the religious persecutions of the Tudor monarchs. Mary I ordered more than 40 executions here, in which Protestant martyrs were burned at the stake. However, Mary's half-sister, Elizabeth I, preferred to dispatch Catholic martyrs at Tyburn. In the 1840s, archaeological excavations around the entrance of St Bartholomew-the-Great (see page 59) revealed burnt stones and charred bones – powerful evidence of these 16th-century Marian burnings.

BELOW *The view of Smithfield Market from Little Britain.*

St Paul's Cathedral

St Paul's Churchyard, EC4M 8AD; ☎ 020 7246 8357;
www.stpauls.co.uk; open Mon–Sat, Sun for worship only;
ADMISSION: adults ££, concessions ££, children £; TUBE: Blackfriars,
Cannon Street, Mansion House, St Paul's; RAIL: Blackfriars,
Cannon Street

St Paul's dominates the summit of Ludgate Hill, which is the more westerly of the two hills on which the Roman city of Londinium was built. A cathedral dedicated to the saint has stood on the site since 604, when St Ethelbert, king of Kent and the first English king to embrace Christianity, founded a place of worship here. A wooden church was built on the site in 604 by Mellitus, Bishop of the East Saxons. The Vikings ruined its replacement in 962, and yet another church was built, only to be destroyed by fire in 1087. This Saxon church was replaced with a Norman cathedral, which had a generous benefactor in William II. It was made of Caen stone and became one of the largest buildings in England at the time.

As one of the most important places of worship in England, Old St Paul's was no stranger to royalty. In 1415, Henry V prayed here before he departed for France and his triumph at the Battle of Agincourt. He returned here after his victory and took part in a service of thanksgiving. In November 1501, Prince Arthur (1486–1502), the eldest son of Henry VII, married Katherine of Aragon (1485–1536) in the cathedral. Arthur died five months later and, in 1509, Katherine married his younger brother, Henry VIII.

It was this marriage that led to the English Reformation, when Henry VIII created the Church of England in defiance of the Pope's refusal to grant him a divorce from Katherine so he could marry Anne Boleyn. Every church and cathedral in England suffered, as Henry stripped them of their valuables, and Old St Paul's was no exception. In 1549, the altar was removed and replaced by an ordinary table, and the nave became a popular short cut, known as

TOP *The dome of St Paul's Cathedral.* ABOVE *The glorious interior of the cathedral.*

Paul's Walk, between Carter Lane and Paternoster Row. The tombs and font were used as shop counters, horses and mules clip-clopped their way along Paul's Walk, and lawyers met their clients here.

Such secular events ceased when Mary I became queen in 1553, and she reintroduced Catholic services at St Paul's. However, this second flowering of the Roman Catholic church ended in 1558 when Mary died and her Protestant half-sister, Elizabeth,

succeeded to the throne. She enjoyed worshipping at Old St Paul's, although she was perfectly prepared to interrupt the dean's sermon when she felt it necessary. Elizabeth donated £6,000 towards the repair of the cathedral roof after it was damaged in a disastrous fire in 1561, but this was a drop in the ocean compared to the amount of money that was needed.

A New Beginning

The cathedral's situation worsened during the English Civil War, when Parliamentarian troops used the nave as a barracks and the building became the haunt of shop-owners and traders once again. By the time Charles II was restored to the throne in 1660, the cathedral was a virtual ruin. Sir Christopher Wren (1632–1723) was consulted and in 1666 he recommended that St Paul's should be demolished and rebuilt. This was not a popular suggestion and he was told to repair the existing cathedral instead. However, matters were taken out of everyone's hands just a few days later when the Great Fire swept through the City, destroying the cathedral in the process. Wren therefore had his wish and was able to rebuild the cathedral. It took several years before his designs were accepted. He received the royal warrant giving him permission to start work on his third design in 1675, yet the finished cathedral bears little resemblance to this design, being much more modest. The first service was held in the cathedral, which at this time did not have its famous dome, in December 1697. The slow progress of the work infuriated the authorities, who decided to speed up progress by halving Wren's annual salary until the

cathedral was finished. Astonishingly, considering the beauty and complexity of Wren's design, the new St Paul's was completed in 1710 and was officially declared finished in 1711. As for Wren's missing salary, he was not reimbursed until he petitioned Queen Anne, who was then on the throne, for the arrears.

A statue to Queen Anne stands outside the west front of the cathedral, although it is a copy by Richard Belt, dating from 1886. The original was fashioned by the sculptor Francis Bird and erected in 1712 to commemorate the completion of the cathedral. It deteriorated so badly over the years, doubtless harmed by the noxious London air, that it had to be removed.

A Hero Rests

Unlike Westminster Abbey, which is crammed with memorials, tombs and monuments, St Paul's is relatively free of such things. However, the tomb of Admiral Lord Nelson (1758–1805) lies in the crypt. It is a black sarcophagus that was originally intended for Cardinal Wolsey (c.1472–1530), who was Henry VIII's

chief minister. Henry took a liking to the casket himself, and later considered that it might be suitable for him and his third wife, Jane Seymour (c.1507–37). However, in the end it gathered dust in Windsor Castle for nearly three centuries before it was used for Lord Nelson's burial in January 1806.

State Ceremonies

Tradition dictates that the great royal ceremonies, such as coronations and funerals, take place in Westminster Abbey, but several state occasions have been held in St Paul's Cathedral. For instance, there was a thanksgiving service, over which Queen Anne presided, for the British victory at the Battle of Blenheim in 1704 and another thanksgiving service at the end of the Napoleonic Wars in 1814, which was attended by the Prince Regent. In 1872, there was a service of thanksgiving for the safe recovery of Edward, Prince of Wales (later Edward VII), who had nearly died from typhoid the previous year. This service was remarkable because Queen Victoria emerged from her deep mourning,

following the death of Prince Albert in 1861 (also from typhoid), in order to attend it, and in doing so managed to quash the republican sentiment that was sweeping the country at the time. She retained her throne, and celebrated her Diamond Jubilee in 1897 with another service of thanksgiving at the cathedral. The sermon was given on the steps of St Paul's, while the queen listened from her open carriage. In 1901, a memorial service for Victoria was held at the cathedral at the same time as her burial service in Windsor.

In July 1981, Prince Charles was the focus of world attention when he married Lady Diana Spencer at St Paul's. The wedding captured the imagination not only of Britain, but of the world – 750 million people watched the service on television. The cathedral was also the venue for services to celebrate the 80th and 100th birthdays of Queen Elizabeth the Queen Mother in 1980 and 2000 respectively. On 4 June 2002, Queen Elizabeth II and the Duke of Edinburgh attended a Golden Jubilee service at St Paul's, having travelled here in the Gold State Coach.

Temple Bar

Paternoster Square, EC4M 8AD; www.thetemplebar.info;
open daily (upper chamber not open to public); ADMISSION: free;
TUBE: St Paul's; RAIL: City Thameslink

Until the end of the 18th century, the boundary of the City of London was marked by eight gates: Aldgate, Aldersgate, Bishopsgate, Cripplegate, Ludgate, Moorgate, Newgate and Temple Bar. They are remembered in nearby street names but only Temple Bar has physically survived, even though it no longer stands on this original spot.

Temple Bar marked the westernmost boundary of the City of London, and from the 14th century it comprised a wooden gate topped with a prison. It was the scene of some very important occasions in the history of London, including the triumphant entry into the City of Edward, the Black Prince, on 19 September 1356 when he rode through Temple Bar accompanied by his prisoner, King John of France. In February 1503, the funeral procession of Elizabeth of York, the wife of Henry VII, stopped here on its way from the Tower of London, where she had died, to Westminster Abbey, where she was buried. In June 1533, the coronation procession of Anne Boleyn passed through the gate, which had been repaired and painted specially for the occasion. However, one of the most significant royal events took place on 24 November 1588 when Anne's daughter, Elizabeth I, rode in a chariot through Temple Bar on her way to St Paul's Cathedral (see pages 61–3) for a service of thanksgiving for the defeat of the Spanish Armada. This is thought to be the first time that the Lord Mayor of London waited at Temple Bar so he could present the keys of the City to his sovereign. Elizabeth responded by handing him a pearl-encrusted sword. This was the start of the tradition in which the sovereign has to halt at Temple Bar and ask the Lord Mayor's permission to enter the City. He hands his Sword of State to his sovereign as a sign of his loyalty, and it is then handed back to him and carried at the head of the royal procession to show that the sovereign is in the City under the protection of the Lord Mayor.

Temple Bar survived the Great Fire of 1666, but it could not withstand Charles II's desire to rebuild it. It had become so shabby that Charles overruled the Lord Mayor's insistence that he had other things to spend the City's money on, and promised that he would make up the difference between the actual cost of the replacement and the £1,005 that the Commissioners had offered. Sir Christopher Wren was commissioned to design the replacement Temple Bar, and the rebuilding work was carried out from 1669 to 1672. The new Temple Bar was made from Portland stone taken from the royal quarries in Dorset, and was adorned with four statues of Stuart sovereigns crafted by John Bushnell: Charles I, Charles II, James I and Anne of Denmark. Between 1684 and 1745, the Bar received extra decorations in the form of the severed heads and bodies of traitors, which were first boiled in salt to make them unpalatable to birds and then impaled on spikes on the Bar. Canny shopkeepers rented telescopes so passers-by could get a better look.

Temple Bar continued to mark one of the City boundaries until January 1878, when it was dismantled as part of the improvement schemes that were being carried out in London. The Bar was causing too much traffic congestion, it looked old-fashioned and its

maintenance was expensive, so down it came. In 1880, the brewer Sir Henry Meux bought the stones, which were lying in a builder's yard, and had them reassembled as the gateway to his estate at Theobalds Park, Cheshunt, Hertfordshire. The original site of Temple Bar is marked by a monument to Queen Victoria.

The Return of Temple Bar

However, the story has a happy ending, because Wren's Temple Bar returned to the City of London in November 2004. Its new home is the southern gateway in Paternoster Square. It has its four Stuart statues, plus new statues of royal beasts by Tim Crawley. Stone C45 contains a time capsule of such objects as a mobile phone, an Egyptian sixpence and photographs of Temple Bar being reassembled in Paternoster Square.

Ireland Yard

EC4V 5EH; TUBE: Blackfriars, St Paul's;
RAIL: Blackfriars, City Thameslink

Queenhithe

EC4V 3RL; TUBE: Blackfriars, Cannon Street,
Mansion House; RAIL: Blackfriars, Cannon Street

A fragment of wall in Ireland Yard is the only remaining trace of Blackfriars Monastery, which stood on the site between 1221 and 1538. The monastery was run by Dominican monks who, as the name suggests, wore black habits. Their first monastery was in Shoe Lane but they moved to the area around Ireland Yard in 1278. The monks grew rich under the patronage of Edward I, and became so influential that Parliament met here in 1311.

In 1529, a court at Blackfriars heard the divorce proceedings between Henry VIII and Katherine of Aragon. Henry wanted to divorce his wife because she had failed to provide him with a male heir. He claimed that the marriage was void on the grounds of consanguinity, as she had briefly been married to his late brother, Prince Arthur. Henry's marital problems led to the end of Blackfriars Monastery, as he broke with the Church of Rome when the Pope refused to sanction his divorce. In the late 1530s, Henry dissolved England's monasteries, robbing them of their considerable influence and financial assets. The church plate from Blackfriars was among the treasures he seized. The buildings were given to Sir Thomas Cawarden, Keeper of the Royal Tents and Master of the Revels, although they were demolished soon after. When Mary I came to the throne, she allowed Cawarden to construct a new church, St Ann Blackfriars, which was destroyed during the Great Fire in 1666.

The monastery is remembered in place names nearby, including Friar Street, and also by the abutments, which resemble pulpits, that run along nearby Blackfriars Bridge.

This is one of the ancient quays that punctuate the banks of the River Thames: they have long since lost that original function. Before the 12th century, London residents called this quay Ethelredshythe, after the Alderman of Mercia, who was the son-in-law of King Alfred (c.846–99). However, its name was changed in honour of Queen Matilda (1080–1118), the wife of Henry I, who built the first public lavatory here in the early 12th century. There was an announcement that the lavatory was for 'the common use of the citizens', which was a revolutionary idea at the time.

After Matilda's great-grandson, King John (r.1199–1216), succeeded to the throne, he gave the quay to his mother, Eleanor of Aquitaine (c.1122–1204). She collected customs tolls here in such an exacting fashion that she made herself extremely unpopular. Ownership of Queenhithe passed to each ruling queen in turn, and by the 15th century it had become the most important of the London docks. However, it had reached its zenith, because by this time the boats had become too large to dock in this small medieval quay, and their owners preferred to berth in nearby Billingsgate. This had the added advantage of being downstream from London Bridge, so boats were spared the tricky business of navigating their way through its arches and the dangerous currents that these created.

Williamson's Tavern

1 Groveland Court, Bow Lane, EC4M 9EH;
☎ 020 7248 5750; www.nicholsonspubs.
co.uk; licensed opening hours; TUBE: Bank,
Mansion House

This old inn has a fascinating history. It was built on the site of a house owned by Sir John Falstaff and some authorities claim that the new building was the original official residence of the Lord Mayor of London before the Mansion House was built in the first half of the 18th century. On one occasion, the Lord Mayor gave a dinner here for William III and Mary II, who presented him with a pair of wrought-iron gates. The story goes that the mayor accepted the gates, but then ordered that they should be taken outside, which incensed Mary so much that she insisted they were brought inside again. They now have a permanent resting place outside, and can still be seen at the end of the alley.

The building was bought by Robert Williamson in 1739, which is the year when the foundation stone for the present Mansion House at Bank was laid. Williamson turned the house into a tavern, naming it after himself.

Many modern pubs have various machines that can entertain the clientele, but Williamson's Tavern has the distinction of containing a stone that is said to mark the centre of the City of London.

St Lawrence Jewry

Guildhall Yard, EC2V 5AA; ☎ 020 7600 9478;
www.stlawrencejewry.org.uk; open Mon–Fri;
ADMISSION: free; TUBE: Bank, St Paul's

Edward I was not a tolerant man. He reigned from 1272–1307, during which time he quelled a number of uprisings in Scotland and Wales, thereby displaying his tremendous gifts as a military tactician. In 1291 Edward was responsible for the violent expulsion of the Jewish community living in this area of London. They occupied a site that centred around Old Jewry, which allowed them to retain an independent community, but it also left them vulnerable to attack by anyone who took against them. The Crown made them pay extortionate taxes and they were also scapegoats for many anti-Semitic fears. Finally, the Jewish people of the area were expelled by Edward, who showed no mercy in his treatment of them. He subsequently acquired their property, which he sold for a healthy profit.

The church of St Lawrence Jewry, first built in 1136, stood on the fringe of this Jewish ghetto, hence its name. It was dedicated to St Lawrence, who was roasted alive on a gridiron in the 3rd century AD. Sir Thomas More (1478–1535), who fell foul of Henry VIII and was eventually executed on his orders, once preached at this church.

St Lawrence Jewry was destroyed during the Great Fire of London in 1666, but it was rebuilt in Portland stone by Sir Christopher Wren in 1671–87. Wren's great patron, Charles II, was present at the rededication ceremony. Only the walls and tower were left standing after the church was bombed during the Blitz in 1940, but it was rebuilt by Cecil Brown in 1954–7 to Wren's designs. It has been the official church of the Corporation of London since 1822, when the Guildhall Chapel was demolished.

Church of St Mary-le-Bow

Cheapside, EC2V 6AU; ☎ 020 7248 5139; www.stmarylebow.co.uk; open Mon–Fri, guided tours available in summer; closed weekends and bank holidays; ADMISSION: free; TUBE: Bank, Mansion House, St Paul's

Any child born within the sound of Bow bells can claim to be a true Cockney. The Bow bells in question belong to those of the church of St Mary-le-Bow, although today it is a wonder that they can be heard at all above the rumble of the traffic in Cheapside.

The church, which dates from Norman times (c.1080), was originally called Sancta Marie de Arcubus, because of the arches (or bows) that can still be seen in the crypt. The earliest mention of the church dates from 1091 when it lost its roof during a violent storm. Some unfortunate incidents took place in the church: 20 people died when the tower collapsed in 1271, and a goldsmith was murdered here in 1284, after which the church had to be reconsecrated. In 1331, a joust was held to celebrate the birth of Edward of Woodstock (1330–76), the eldest son of Edward III. He later became known as the Black Prince because of the colour of his armour. His mother, Philippa of Hainault (c.1314–69), was watching the entertainment from a wooden balcony with her ladies-in-waiting when it collapsed under them. They survived, and the rebuilt balcony continued to be used by other monarchs who enjoyed watching City pageants from its lofty position.

The church was one of the casualties during the Great Fire in 1666, and was rebuilt in 1670–83 by Sir Christopher Wren, who based his design on the Basilica of Maxentius in Rome. He retained the balcony, in memory of the dramatic incident of 1331,

and it was from here that Queen Anne watched the Lord Mayor's procession in 1702, the same year that she succeeded to the throne. Luckily for her, the balcony remained securely in place.

Although Wren had allowed space for 12 bells in the famous tower, only 8 were installed in 1680. These were replaced with 10 bells in the 1750s. They were first rung together on 4 June 1762 to celebrate George III's 25th birthday. In 1881 the number of bells was increased to 12.

ABOVE *The dragon weathervane on top of the church.*
RIGHT *The celebrated bell tower.*

Guildhall

Gresham Street, EC2V 7HH; ☎ 020 7606 3030;
www.guildhall.cityoflondon.gov.uk; open all year Mon–Sat, May–Sept
Sun (subject to events taking place in Guildhall); ADMISSION: free;
TUBE: Bank, Mansion House, Moorgate, St Paul's; RAIL: Blackfriars,
Cannon Street, Liverpool Street

Guildhall is the administrative headquarters of the Corporation of the City of London and has therefore been of great importance ever since the present building was erected in 1411. Its size is an indication of its significance, as the Great Hall is the third largest hall in England after Westminster Hall and the Great Hall of the Archbishop's Palace in Canterbury. Lord Mayors and Sheriffs were elected in Guildhall, and the Court of Common Council (the governing body of the City of London, led by the Lord Mayor) met here.

In medieval London, important trials were also held at Guildhall. One of the most notable occurred in 1553, when Lady Jane Grey and her husband, Lord Guilford Dudley, were tried for treason. Lady Jane was the granddaughter of Henry VIII's sister Mary, Duchess of Suffolk, and therefore the king's great-niece. When Henry died in 1547, his will stated that the line of succession should pass in the following order – to his son, Edward; his daughter, Mary; his second daughter, Elizabeth; their heirs; and then to the heirs of his sister, Mary. Edward VI duly inherited the throne, but he was only nine and so John Dudley, Duke of Northumberland, was appointed Lord Protector. When Edward, always a sickly child, lay dying in 1553, Northumberland saw this as a chance to continue his power and to ensure the success of the newly established Protestant religion. He persuaded the young king to change his father's will. Mary was barred from the succession on the grounds of her Catholicism and Elizabeth was barred because she had not stated her religious convictions, so the crown conveniently passed to Lady Jane Grey – who just

TOP *Carvings of the giants Gog and Magog adorn Guildhall.* ABOVE *The sumptuous interior of Guildhall.*

happened to be Northumberland's daughter-in-law. Northumberland had ensured this connection by marrying his son, Guilford, to Jane in May 1553, a few weeks before the death of Edward VI. Lady Jane reigned for nine days before being deposed by Mary I on 19 July 1553. Lady Jane and her husband were found guilty of treason, and both were executed on Tower Hill in February 1554. Archbishop Cranmer (1489–1556), who was one of the many people who countersigned Edward VI's will, was also hauled off to Guildhall where he was tried and found guilty of treason, and burnt at the stake in Oxford.

Clockmakers' Company Museum

Guildhall Library, Aldermanbury, EC2V 7HH;
☎ 020 7332 1868; www.clockmakers.org; open
Mon–Sat; ADMISSION: free; TUBE: Bank, Moorgate,
St Paul's; RAIL: Cannon Street

London is full of interesting little corners and places that deserve a second look, and this is definitely one of them. As its name suggests, this is the museum of the Worshipful Company of Clockmakers, which was founded in 1631. It can be found in the public library next to Guildhall (see page 69), which is appropriate because the members of the guild have always worked close to Guildhall.

The museum contains a skull watch that was believed to have been given to a maid-of-honour by Mary, Queen of Scots (r.1542–67) but was actually made in the 18th century. It also displays the H5 chronometer, which was one of the marine timepieces that John Harrison (1693–1776) developed in order to find a sure means of measuring longitude at sea. The H5 was tested by George III, who was fascinated by science and scientific apparatus.

Aldermanbury also has an interesting history, because it is believed to have been the site of a royal castle that stood here long before Edward the Confessor built his palace at Westminster in 1060. One of its residents may have been Ethelbert, the king of Kent (r.580–616). He was the first English king to convert to Christianity. Aldermanbury means 'alderman's manor' and dates from the 14th century, when the alderman in question may have been Ethelred, the son-in-law of Alfred the Great.

Statue of Queen Alexandra

The Royal London Hospital, Whitechapel Road,
E1 1BB; ☎ 020 7377 7000; www.bartsandthe
london.nhs.uk; TUBE: Aldgate East, Whitechapel;
RAIL: Bethnal Green

The Royal London hospital was founded in 1740, at which point it was known as the London Infirmary and was situated in Prescot Street. It became the London Hospital in 1748, and then moved to its present position, surrounded by what were then green fields, in 1753. The hospital grew in size and was granted a royal charter by George II in 1758. In 1876 Queen Victoria opened the Grocers' Wing, which made it the largest hospital in Britain. In 1903 King Edward VII and Queen Alexandra opened the new outpatients' department, and the following year the queen became the hospital's president. The Alexandra Wing was named after her, and specialized in accommodation for Jewish patients, including a kosher kitchen. In July 1990, the hospital was granted a royal title and became the Royal London Hospital. Queen Elizabeth II visited it to commemorate its 250th anniversary.

The bronze statue of Queen Alexandra in the courtyard to the rear of the hospital is by George Edward Wade and was cast in 1908. It shows the queen in her coronation robes and the inscription explains that she 'introduced to England the Finsen Light cure for lupus and presented the first lamp to this hospital'. This is just one example of her charitable work because Alexandra was a very conscientious Queen Consort. She had particular sympathy with people who were ill as she suffered from a series of health problems herself, including deafness and lameness. Her mother-in-law, Queen Victoria, once wrote of her that she was 'one of those sweet creatures who seem to come from the skies to help and bless mortals'.

Bank of England

Threadneedle Street, EC2R 8AH; ☎ 020 7601 5545; www.bankofengland.co.uk/education/museum/index.htm; museum open Mon–Fri; closed weekends, public holidays and bank holidays; ADMISSION: free; TUBE: Bank, Mansion House, Monument; RAIL: Cannon Street, Liverpool Street

It took a Dutchman to create the Bank of England. When William III, the Prince of Orange, sailed from the Netherlands to Britain to take the throne in 1688, he did so thanks to a loan from a Sephardic Jew, Francisco Lopez Suasso. A few years later, in 1694, William was attempting to raise sufficient money to fund a war with France. Two City merchants, William Patterson and Michael Godfrey, suggested that a national bank should be founded, which could then loan the necessary money to the government. William agreed, taking the structure of the Bank of Amsterdam as his inspiration.

The Bank of England was incorporated by Royal Charter on 27 July 1694 and was an instant success. The bank began trading at Mercers' Hall, Cheapside, but moved to the Grocer's Hall in Princes Street a few months later, where it stayed until 1734 when it moved to its present site.

One of the functions of the bank is to issue banknotes and coins. The coins have always been stamped with a portrait of the head of the reigning monarch, although banknotes did not carry a portrait of the sovereign until 17 March 1960, when it appeared on a one-pound note.

The bank itself is the hub of the UK's financial sector and therefore is not open to the public, but the bank's museum is well worth a visit.

BELOW *The Bank of England is popularly called The Old Lady of Threadneedle Street.*

Royal Exchange

Royal Exchange Avenue, EC3V 3LR; open daily;
TUBE: Bank, Monument; RAIL: Cannon Street

The Royal Exchange stood on this spot between 1566 and 1939. It began life when Thomas Gresham, a successful London trader who owned a shop in nearby Lombard Street, recognized the need for a meeting place in which merchants and adventurers could conduct business with each other. Gresham laid the first brick in June 1566 and the building was ready by the winter of 1567. Statues of English monarchs were set in niches overlooking the courtyard, but Nicholas Stone's statue of Elizabeth I was deemed unsuitable and was moved to the Guildhall Chapel; it now stands on the staircase leading to the old library in Guildhall (see page 69).

When Elizabeth I visited what was then called the Exchange in January 1570, an accompanying herald proclaimed that it was henceforth to be known as the Royal Exchange. It was one of the many buildings destroyed during the Great Fire of London in 1666 but it was quickly rebuilt. A further collection of statues of monarchs graced the courtyard, and more were added until the reign of George IV. In January 1838, fire once again destroyed the Royal Exchange and many of the royal statues were sold at auction that April. The third building was completed in 1844 and was opened by Queen Victoria, who followed the tradition set by her ancestor, Elizabeth I, and proclaimed that the building should henceforth be called the Royal Exchange. More royal statues appeared, including those of Victoria, Prince Albert and Elizabeth I.

Such was the importance of the Royal Exchange that it was one of the places in London where a new sovereign was proclaimed. Today, however, it has been developed into a complex of shops and restaurants and is therefore fulfilling a different function for Londoners.

BELOW *The frieze on top of the Royal Exchange.*

43

Tower of London

Tower Hill, EC3N 4AB; ☎ 0844 482 7777 (from the UK), +44 (0)20 3166 6000 (from outside the UK); www.hrp.org.uk/toweroflondon; open daily; closed 24–26 Dec and 1 Jan; ADMISSION: adults £££, concessions £££, children ££; TUBE: Tower Hill, Tower Gateway DLR; RAIL: Fenchurch Street, London Bridge

One of the most celebrated and distinctive buildings in the world, the Tower of London occupies a majestic position on the banks of the Thames just outside the City of London. For centuries, the sight of its rising towers and thick walls struck terror in the hearts of many Londoners because the Tower was a fortified prison as well as a royal palace. Many royal personages were held against their will here, and two kings are believed to have been murdered within its walls. The Tower was also a place of official execution for those of noble birth, and it was where three queens of England were beheaded. Other prisoners were executed in public on Tower Hill, outside the fortress's walls.

A Norman Conquest

From its earliest days, when Norman builders started to construct the keep, (which we now know as the White Tower), soon after William the Conqueror had successfully invaded England in 1066, the main purposes of the Tower of London were subjugation and control. The new regime knew it had to keep strict control of its conquered people, despite William's assurances that he would be 'a gracious liege Lord' to the English. Blood had already been spilt at William's coronation on

TOP *The battlements of the Tower of London.*
ABOVE *The winter ice rink in the Tower's moat.*

Christmas Day 1066, when Norman soldiers misinterpreted the watching crowd's hurrahs as cries of defiance and promptly killed them. This was not the most auspicious beginning to William's reign, yet he wanted to ensure that the English people understood that he and his men would not hesitate to quell any insurrection.

William died in 1087 and his son and successor, the highly unpopular William II (called William Rufus because of his red hair), continued the building project that had been started by his father. The keep was completed during his reign. In 1240, it was whitewashed, after which it became known as the White Tower. Successive kings added to the complex of buildings within the fortress as the need arose. During the 13th and 14th centuries, the outer wall, the inner curtain wall and the moat were created. Such powerful defensive structures were needed to combat the constant threat of uprisings from malcontents and pretenders to the throne. As the centuries progressed, the buildings within the Tower were adapted, enlarged or demolished and replaced, according to the needs and styles of the period and the whims of the reigning monarch.

Royal Residents

One of the main requirements of the Tower of London was to serve as a royal palace; its secure fortifications were a necessary precaution in medieval England where the threat of plagues, revolt and other trouble was never far away. The Tower's first royal resident was King Stephen (1135–54), who stayed here at Whitsun 1140. In January 1236, the newly married Henry III accompanied his bride, Eleanor of Provence, from the Tower to her coronation in Westminster Abbey. This was the first time that the coronation procession started from the Tower, where the royal couple had stayed the night before, and it set a precedent that continued until 1604, when James I was the last monarch to spend his pre-coronation night at the Tower. By this time, the buildings were in such a bad state that they were not considered a safe or comfortable place in which a monarch should sleep. However, Charles II paid lip-service to this old tradition at his coronation in April 1661 when the royal procession rode to the gates of the Tower at dawn, so it could at least be seen to start from here.

A Bloody History

Although the Tower has served many purposes in its existence, including providing a home for the Royal Menagerie, the Royal Mint and the Crown Jewels, two of its most colourful and notorious functions were as a prison for royalty and a place of execution. In 1241–4, the Tower was the prison of Llywelyn ap Gruffydd, who was the Welsh Prince of Wales (the English did not appoint their own Prince of Wales until 1301, when the infant Prince Edward, son of Edward I, was given this title). He fell to his death while trying to escape from the Tower. Richard II was the first English king to be imprisoned in the Tower in 1399, and he was forced to abdicate during his stay. Prince James of Scotland was locked in the Tower in 1406, having been abducted on his way to France. On 21 May 1471, Henry VI was murdered in the Tower while he was at prayer. It is alleged that his murderer was the Duke of Gloucester – the future Richard III – who is also believed to have dispatched Edward V and his brother, Richard, Duke of York, in the Tower in 1483. Princess Elizabeth was imprisoned in the Tower by her half-sister, Mary I, in 1554, but was released and lived to become Elizabeth I.

In addition to all these royal prisoners, three official executions of queens were carried out on Tower Green within the walls of the Tower. Anne Boleyn, the second wife of Henry VIII, was executed on 19 May 1536; Henry's fifth wife, Catherine Howard, suffered the same fate on 13 February 1542; and Lady Jane Grey, who was queen for nine days in July 1553 but never crowned, was executed on 12 February 1554. They, and the four other people who are known to have been beheaded on Tower Green, were buried in the Chapel of St Peter ad Vincula, which stands nearby.

The Crown Jewels

The Tower is known worldwide as the home of the English Crown Jewels, which have been on public display since the 17th century. Most of the collection is known as the Coronation Regalia, as it is used in coronations, and includes the Orb and Sceptre that were made for Charles II's coronation in 1661, after the restoration of the monarchy the previous year. Most of the Coronation Regalia dates from this time, as it replaced the regalia that was melted down after the execution of Charles I, when Britain

was briefly a republic under the rule of Oliver Cromwell. Later additions to the Coronation Regalia include St Edward's Crown, which was made in 1661 for Charles II, and the Imperial State Crown, which was worn by George VI at his coronation in 1937 and, after remodelling, by his daughter, Elizabeth II, in 1953. It is so heavy that Elizabeth had to practise wearing it for several hours at a time.

It is tempting to imagine that the Tower is a series of buildings that now function as little more than a busy tourist attraction. In fact the Tower is still a fortress that is protected by Yeomen Warders round the clock, ending each day with the highly atmospheric Ceremony of the Keys in which the outer gates are locked for the night.

Monument

Monument Street, EC3R 8AH; ☎ 020 7626 2717;
www.themonument.info; open daily; closed 24–26 Dec and 1 Jan;
ADMISSION: adults £, concessions £, children £; TUBE: London Bridge,
Monument, Tower Gateway DLR; RAIL: Cannon Street, Fenchurch
Street, London Bridge

Shortly after midnight on 2 September 1666, during what was proving to be a very hot and dry summer, a small fire started in a bakery in Pudding Lane. The business was owned by a royal baker named Thomas Farriner (or Farynor), who led his family across the rooftops, away from the blaze and to safety. At first, despite a strong easterly wind that was fanning the flames, the fire was not taken seriously. When the Lord Mayor, Sir Thomas Bloodworth, was summoned and it was suggested that he should order the demolition of buildings to provide a much-needed firebreak, he airily dismissed the idea: 'Pish! A woman might piss it out!'

Royalty Rallies Round

However, the fire rapidly took hold and by the time the diarist Samuel Pepys (1633–1703) visited Charles II and his brother, James, Duke of York (later James II), at Whitehall later that morning, over 300 houses and half of London Bridge had been reduced to ash. Charles II told Pepys to instruct the Lord Mayor to pull down houses in order to create a firebreak, but Bloodworth was still prevaricating and on Sunday night Charles II took control. But by then it was too late because London was in the grip of a firestorm. The Duke of York was put in charge of fighting the fire, and Charles II helped soldiers attack the blaze, but the flames still raged out of control. The fire finally ended on 5 September, by which time it had burned 162 hectares (400 acres) within the City walls and 25.5 hectares (63 acres) beyond them, destroying nearly 14,000 homes and 87 churches. It had also fumigated a city that was still recovering from the ghastly effects of the Great Plague the summer before, and destroyed most of the rats that had caused it. Homeless Londoners camped out in fields and were visited by Charles II on horseback, who promised that they would be fed and reassured them that the fire was not the result of a foreign or Catholic plot. Nevertheless, a Frenchman called Robert Hubert confessed to the fire (even though he only arrived in London two days after the fire had started), thereby offering himself as a convenient foreign scapegoat. He was duly hanged.

Rebuilding the City

When an Act of Parliament was passed about the rebuilding of London, it also ruled that a monument to the fire should be erected. It was designed by Sir Christopher Wren, in conjunction with his friend, Robert Hooke. It stands 61 metres (202 feet) high, which is the distance between the Monument and the baker's shop in Pudding Lane, and is the tallest isolated stone column in the world. A series of panels around its base records the events of September 1666 and also notes the part played by Charles II in London's reconstruction. He saw this as an opportunity to build a properly planned city, rather than to reproduce the rabbit warren of narrow streets that had existed before the fire. Another panel, created by Caius Gabriel Cibber (1630–1700), shows Charles and his brother conducting the firefighting operations.

ABOVE *The panels around the base of the Monument.*
RIGHT *The flaming urn of fire, made from copper, on top of the Monument.*

London Bridge

SE1; TUBE: London Bridge, Monument;
RAIL: Cannon Street, London Bridge

This is one of the most famous bridges in the world, even though the present structure, opened in 1973, hardly merits such an accolade. Actually, it is the history of London Bridge that is so thrilling. We remember it in the nursery rhyme, 'London Bridge is falling down', even if we do not know exactly what it refers to.

In fact, the nursery rhyme commemorates one of the earliest incidents in the long history of the bridge. In 994, London was attacked by Olaf Tryggvason of Norway and Sweyn Forkbeard of Denmark, who managed to extract large amounts of money, or 'danegeld', from the city during the following 20 years. Ethelred II (r.978–1016), who was King of England at the time, was unable to stand up to this aggressive treatment and was usurped by Sweyn Forkbeard in 1013. Sweyn was never crowned and died in 1014, allowing Ethelred to take back the English throne. That same year, Ethelred joined forces with King Olaf of Norway to repel the Danes, and succeeded by burning down the wooden London Bridge while the Danes were on it. This was celebrated by a Norse poet named Ottar Svarte, and his poem was adapted in the 17th century to the version we know now.

The Medieval Bridge

The first stone bridge across the Thames at this point was erected in the 1170s and the first houses were built on it a few years later. In the centre of the bridge was a chapel dedicated to St Thomas à Becket, who had been murdered in Canterbury Cathedral by supporters of Henry II (r.1154–89).

During the Barons' War, Henry III was taken prisoner in 1264 by Simon de Montfort (c.1208–65). When de Montfort tried to cross London Bridge with his royal prisoner, the Lord Mayor pulled up the drawbridge and locked the gates. However, Londoners then knocked down the gates to let de Montfort into the city.

One of the more colourful traditions of medieval London involved beheading prisoners, boiling their heads in tar to preserve them, and then sticking these on poles above the bridge's gatehouse. Edward II's great Scots enemy, William Wallace, who was the first man to be hung, drawn and quartered in Smithfield, was also the first man whose head was treated in this way, but he was by no means the last. Sir Thomas More, who was Henry VIII's trusted adviser before he offended the king by refusing to agree to his divorce from Katherine of Aragon, was also beheaded and his head was impaled above the gatehouse in 1535. Five years later, Thomas Cromwell (c.1485–1540), who had supported More's execution, received exactly the same treatment.

London Bridge was also the setting for happier events. When Henry V returned victorious from the Battle of Agincourt in France in 1415, he rode over the bridge with the Lord Mayor. Upon his restoration to the throne in 1660, Charles II rode into London over the bridge accompanied by a massive retinue.

Footpads and Frost Fairs

London Bridge was the only structure to span the Thames until 1738, when work began on Westminster Bridge, which was completed in 1750. This was followed by Blackfriars Bridge, which opened in 1769. London Bridge was long considered a dangerous haunt of footpads (robbers) and other insalubrious characters, and Elizabeth I, among others, refused to cross it, always using a ferry instead. However, London Bridge did have something to recommend it, because its many piers slowed the flow of the river to such an extent that the Thames often froze hard from bank to bank in winter. This is the reason for the many frost fairs that took place on the Thames during bitter winters. In 1683,

ABOVE *This is the third London Bridge to span the Thames.*

Charles II visited that winter's frost fair and, along with many other Londoners, bought a certificate with his name printed on it to testify to his attendance. The last frost fair was held in the winter of 1813.

London Bridge, Arizona

The 19th century saw the end of the medieval London Bridge, with a replacement bridge built upstream by Sir John Rennie (1794–1874) in 1823–31. The bridge was opened on 1 August 1831 by William IV and Queen Adelaide and one of its approach roads, King William Street, was named after the monarch. The bridge was replaced by the current structure in 1973. The old bridge was sold for $2.4 million and re-erected in Lake Havasu City, Arizona. Popular gossip at the time speculated that the purchasers had confused their London bridges and thought they were buying the much more interesting Tower Bridge.

PICCADILLY TO HACKNEY

This section of London incorporates parts of the West End as well as corners of the City of London. The Strand runs through it like a long spine, connecting secular sites, such as Somerset House, with sacred places like the church of St Bride's.

46
Queen Street

Mayfair, W1; TUBE: Green Park, Hyde Park Corner, Piccadilly Circus; RAIL: Victoria

47
St Anne's Church

55 Dean Street, W1D 6AF; ☎ 020 7437 8039; www.stannes-soho.org.uk; open daily; ADMISSION: free; TUBE: Leicester Square, Piccadilly Circus, Tottenham Court Road; RAIL: Charing Cross

Queen Street lies between Charles Street and Curzon Street, in a very exclusive part of Mayfair. William IV lived at 22 Charles Street for a short time in 1826, when he was the Duke of Clarence, and many other illustrious people lived around here in the 19th century.

However, scandal surrounded the occupants of 6 Queen Street, because it was the home of a grandson of George III, George, Duke of Cambridge (1819–1904), and his actress wife, Sarah Fairbrother, who became known as Mrs FitzGeorge. They were married privately in January 1847, in contravention of the Royal Marriages Act of 1772 – in other words, without the consent of the reigning monarch, Queen Victoria. They had three children, although the first two were born before their marriage, which must have been even more shocking at the time. Queen Victoria would definitely not have been amused. Mrs FitzGeorge died at 6 Queen Street in January 1890.

The duke's grandfather, George III, is alleged to have contracted his own unsuitable marriage in April 1759 to Hannah Lightfoot, the daughter of a cobbler from Wapping, by whom he is rumoured to have had three children. If this is true, his official marriage to Charlotte Mecklenburg-Strelitz in 1761 is bigamous, and all his descendants have no claim to the British throne. Ironically, it was George III who introduced the Royal Marriages Act of 1772, expressly to stop members of the Royal Family from making unfortunate marriages.

This church was built between 1677 and 1686, but it is not certain whether it was designed by Sir Christopher Wren or his assistant William Talman, or whether they both worked on it. It soon had a royal parishioner in the Prince of Wales (later George II), who had 'an Inclination to come to this Church'. It was dedicated to St Anne in honour of Princess Anne, who later became Queen Anne.

St Anne's has another royal connection. Theodore, the dethroned King of Corsica (1694–1756), was buried here and his epitaph was written by Horace Walpole.

In common with many other buildings in London, St Anne's was severely damaged during the air raids of 1940. Only the tower was left standing and at one point the church was going to be sold. However, the tower was restored and the church was finally rebuilt. The new foundation stone was laid by Princess Anne in 1990 and, appropriately, the new building was rededicated on St Anne's Day (26 July) in 1991.

Passers-by may wonder why the gardens of the church are so high. This is because they were consistently raised in order to accommodate the 10,000 bodies of parishioners who lie underneath them.

LEFT *Beautiful façade of Somerset House (see pages 92–4).*

St James's Church

197 Piccadilly, W1J 9LL; ☎ 020 7734 4511; www.st-james-piccadilly.org; open daily; church hosts lunchtime recitals and evening concerts, see website for listings; ADMISSION: free; TUBE: Green Park, Piccadilly Circus

This is one of the few churches that Sir Christopher Wren built outside the City of London, and the only one not to stand on the site of a previous church. Instead, it was built between 1676 and 1684 on land acquired by Henry Jermyn, Earl of St Albans (1605–84), on what had once been part of St James's Fields, next to St James's Palace. Wren was delighted with the church, and particularly with the acoustics.

St James's quickly became a fashionable place of worship, no doubt helped by its proximity to St James's Palace. The organ was built by Renatus Harris (one of the two greatest organ-makers of the day) and was made for the Chapel Royal in Whitehall in 1686, when James II was on the throne.

In 1691, James's daughter, Mary II, was asked by the rector, Dr Thomas Tenison, to give the organ to St James's. After it was installed in the church it was tested by both John Blow (c.1649–1708) and Henry Purcell (c.1659–95). Grinling Gibbons (1648–1721) carved the gilded organ case.

St James's Church was badly damaged during the Second World War and rededicated in 1954. The churchyard was turned into a garden of remembrance, in honour of the courage of Londoners during the Blitz, and was opened by Queen Mary in 1946. It is now the venue for a daily craft market.

BELOW *St James's Church still thrives in the bustle of Piccadilly.*

Soho Square

W1; TUBE: Leicester Square, Oxford Circus,
Tottenham Court Road; RAIL: Charing Cross

ABOVE *The mock-Tudor shed and the restored statue of Charles II in the middle of Soho Square.*

In the days of Henry VIII, long before London was covered by concrete and high-rise buildings, the area around what we now know as Soho was used for hunting. Various calls were used during hunts, one of which was 'So Ho!' It became the rallying cry of Charles II's illegitimate son, the Duke of Monmouth (1649–85), at the Battle of Sedgemoor in 1685.

Monmouth knew this area of London well. In the 1660s, his father had given him the land around what is now Soho Square. He built a suitably impressive mansion on the site called Monmouth House.

The square was laid out in the 1670s and 1680s, and was initially called King Square in honour of Charles II; a stone statue of the monarch, which was fashioned by Caius Gabriel Cibber, stood in the garden at the centre. Thanks to the hard work of Richard Frith, the bricklayer who gave his name to nearby Frith Street, the square contained a total of 41 houses by 1691, including Monmouth's own residence. The square quickly became a very fashionable address and attracted some very important people.

In the 1870s the dilapidated statue of Charles II was removed and replaced by the mock-Tudor gardener's shed that still stands here. The statue was given a new home at Grimsdyke House in Harrow, where it stayed in private ownership (its last owner was the librettist, W. S. Gilbert) until it was returned to the square in 1938.

National Portrait Gallery

St Martin's Place, WC2H 0HE; ☎ 020 7306 0055; www.npg.org.uk;
open daily; ADMISSION: free; TUBE: Charing Cross, Embankment,
Leicester Square; RAIL: Charing Cross

If you want to view portraits of virtually every monarch from Richard III to Elizabeth II and her immediate family, this is the place to come. The portraits are arranged chronologically and are a fascinating insight into the kings and queens of Britain because they tell us so much about them. A wily Henry VII looks sideways at us, a Lancastrian red rose in his hand as a reminder of his rather shaky claim to be the rightful heir to the throne through the House of Lancaster. History tells us that he was mean with money, and a quick glance at his pinched face seems to confirm this. Charles I, painted by Daniel Mytens in 1631, stares straight ahead, looking slightly hesitant but the essence of romantic innocence; 18 years later he was executed after losing a power struggle with Parliament. The heavily lined face of his son, Charles II, in a portrait painted by John Michael Wright or his studio in the 1660s, is the epitome of world-weary dissipation. He was only in his early 30s, but it is evident that he had packed a tremendous amount into those years.

There are many photographs, too, which date from the Victorian age onwards. Queen Victoria is pictured with John Brown and later Abdul Karim (known as her Munshi), the two notorious servants who won her affections and caused scandal in the process.

The National Portrait Gallery even had a royal backer in Prince Albert, who in 1856 approved the suggestion of Philip, 5th Earl of Stanhope, that there should be 'a gallery of the portraits of the most eminent persons in British history'. When it opened in 1859, the gallery had 57 portraits; today, it has over 9,000 in its collection.

BELOW *The gallery contains many royal portraits.*

St Giles-in-the-Fields

60 St Giles High Street, WC2H 8LG; ☎ 020 7240 2532;
www.stgilesonline.org; open daily; ADMISSION: free; TUBE: Covent Garden,
Leicester Square, Tottenham Court Road

St Giles is the patron saint of outcasts, which gives a clue about the name of this church and the original nature of this area. The land once comprised fields that stood outside the city wall. In 1101, it became the site of a leper hospital founded by Matilda, wife of Henry I. It was a miserable place, not only because of the lepers, but because prisoners from Newgate passed by the hospital chapel on their way to their execution at Tyburn.

The chapel soon became a place of worship for parishioners as well as patients, and it continued as a church even after Henry VIII closed the hospital in 1539. Another church was built on the site in the 1620s, but it had to be rebuilt the following century, as the foundations had been undermined by the extraordinary number of burials in the churchyard. The new church was built by Henry Flitcroft (1697–1769), who was the architect son of William III's gardener, and was completed in 1734.

St Giles was an insalubrious district for centuries – it was the setting for William Hogarth's illustration, *Gin Lane*, and Byron described the area as one of 'squalid wretchedness' – which is why the church had no royal visitors or patrons after Matilda. There are some royal connections – Catherine Sedley, an unpopular mistress of James II, was baptized here in 1657. There is also a tombstone bearing the name of Richard Pendrell, one of the men who risked their lives after the Battle of Worcester in September 1651 by hiding the fugitive Charles II in the tree that became known as the Boscobel Oak.

RIGHT *A view across Phoenix Garden to St Giles-in-the-Fields.*

Trafalgar Square

WC2; TUBE: Charing Cross, Embankment, Leicester Square, Piccadilly Circus; RAIL: Charing Cross

Today, despite the best efforts of the London Mayor to discourage them, Trafalgar Square is overrun with pigeons. They are part of the square's character and are a direct avian link with its original purpose. During the reign of Edward I in the 12th century, what we now know as Trafalgar Square was the King's Mews and home of the royal falcons. The poet Geoffrey Chaucer (c.1343–1400) was, at one point, Clerk of the Mews.

The royal mews had vanished by the time Henry VII came to the throne in the 15th century and was replaced by the royal stables. These burned down in 1534, while Henry VIII was on the throne, but they were rebuilt by his daughter, Elizabeth I. During the English Civil War in the 1640s, the stables were initially turned into barracks for the Parliamentary army. They were subsequently converted into a prison for 4,500 Royalists who had been captured at the Battle of Naseby in 1645.

Following the Restoration in 1660, there were grand plans for Sir Christopher Wren to rebuild the stables; however, these did not materialize. Instead William Kent rebuilt the main stable block, in 1732, on the site now occupied by the National Gallery.

The site was redeveloped during the reign of George IV, and the National Gallery was founded in 1824, with the acquisition of a set of paintings intended to be the nucleus of a national collection. The Corinthian columns supporting the portico of the main entrance were taken from George IV's private London residence, Carlton House, when it was demolished to help finance the building work at Buckingham Palace.

The square was officially named in 1830, in honour of Britain's victory at the Battle of Trafalgar in 1805.

BELOW *Trafalgar Square, with the National Gallery to the left of the fountain and St Martin-in-the-Fields to the right.*

Statue of Charles I

Trafalgar Square, WC2; TUBE: Charing Cross, Embankment, Leicester Square, Piccadilly Circus; RAIL: Charing Cross

Marooned on a traffic island to the south of Trafalgar Square, a bronze equestrian statue of Charles I stares down Whitehall towards the scene of his execution, which took place on 30 January 1649, outside the Banqueting House (see pages 46–7). You might take your life in your hands by trying to dodge the buses and taxis in order to inspect the statue at close range, but it's worth it because there are three fascinating stories connected with it.

The statue was cast in bronze by Hubert Le Sueur in 1633, and was commissioned by Lord Weston, High Treasurer, who intended to erect it in his garden at Roehampton. However, trouble was already brewing for Charles I and it was considered politic to hide the statue. Royalists stashed it away in the crypt of St Paul's Church, Covent Garden, where it was discovered by the Parliamentarians in 1655. The Civil War was still raging, and a brass-worker from Holborn, named John Rivett, was instructed to melt down the statue. Instead, he hid it while making a tidy sum from selling pieces of what was alleged to be the statue of the 'late king and martyr'. After the Restoration in 1660, Rivett refused to give the statue to Weston's son. Nevertheless, Charles II eventually acquired it and it was finally erected at its present site in 1676. The choice of site was no accident: it marks the place where eight of the regicides and signatories to Charles I's death warrant were disembowelled in 1660.

The site is important for another reason, as the original Charing Cross stood here until 1647. This was the last of the series of stone crosses erected by Edward I to mark the resting places of the

TOP *The statue of Charles I.* ABOVE *The statue stands on a site of great historical importance.*

funeral cortège of his first wife, Eleanor (c.1244–90), when her body was brought back to Westminster from Nottinghamshire in 1291. A Victorian replica of the stone cross now stands outside Charing Cross station, from which it got its name.

As if all that were not enough, the statue of Charles I has a third significance: it stands at the point from which all distances to London are calculated.

St Martin-in-the-Fields

Trafalgar Square, WC2N 4JJ; ☎ 020 7766 1100; www2.stmartin-in-the-fields.org; open daily; ADMISSION: free; TUBE: Charing Cross, Embankment, Leicester Square, Piccadilly Circus; RAIL: Charing Cross

This is the parish church of Buckingham Palace and in the 1700s it even had a king – George I – as its churchwarden. He was the only reigning monarch ever to have been given such a post, and it seems that he was not very assiduous at the task because he rarely put in an appearance. By way of compensation, he donated an organ to the church.

George's Royal Arms adorn the pediment above the Corinthian columns of the entrance and his portrait hangs in the south-west porch.

There are many royal connections with St Martin-in-the-Fields. The original Norman church was pulled down and rebuilt by Henry VIII around 1542. A new chancel was built between 1606–09 and paid for by Prince Henry (1594–1612), the eldest son of James I. St Martin-in-the-Fields was the church in which the infant Prince Charles, later Charles II, was christened in 1630. One of Charles's most famous and popular mistresses, Nell Gwyn, was buried in the churchyard in 1687.

The church was once again pulled down and rebuilt in 1722–6. It was designed by James Gibbs, who initially wanted to make the building circular. However, he had to alter his plans to fit in with the strict budget imposed by the Commissioners for the Building of Fifty New Churches. His eventual design – a large rectangular church with a portico and a tall steeple – was much imitated in New England.

Inside the church, the Royal Box is on the left of the high altar and the Admiralty Box (the Admiralty in Whitehall is contained within the parish) is on the right. The Royal Arms from 1725 are situated on the arch above the altar.

LEFT *Many monarchs have worshipped in St Martin-in-the-Fields, including George I.*

Statue of George III

Pall Mall East, WC2; TUBE: Charing Cross, Embankment, Piccadilly Circus; RAIL: Charing Cross

Coutts & Co

440 Strand, WC2R 0QS; ☎ 020 7753 1000; www.coutts.com; open Mon–Fri; closed bank holidays; TUBE: Charing Cross, Covent Garden, Embankment, Waterloo; RAIL: Charing Cross, Waterloo

Although George III was the third Hanoverian king to occupy the British throne, he was the first one to be born in England. He was also the first Hanoverian king whose first language was English rather than German.

For many years his life was blighted by what is now believed to have been porphyria, but which at the time was considered to be insanity. He had several episodes of extreme illness, during which he appeared to be mentally ill. He always recovered from these illnesses, but in November 1810 the death of Amelia, his youngest and most beloved daughter, was the final straw. He became so ill that he was no longer fit to rule, and his eldest son, George, was created the Prince Regent on 5 February 1811. George III died on 29 January 1820 at Windsor Castle (see pages 152–3) after a decade of chronic illness, and the Prince Regent became George IV.

A public subscription was set up that same year to raise funds for a statue of the late king, which was installed near the junction of Pall Mall East and Cockspur Street in 1836. The finished article was a bronze equestrian statue by Matthew Cotes Wyatt (1777–1862), with the horse's tail raised horizontally. This led to a popular verse of the time:

Here stands a statue at which critics rail
To point a moral and to point a Tail.

Characterized by its oversized chequebooks, Coutts is one of the oldest banks to survive in London. Founded in 1692 by Scottish goldsmith John Campbell, it was situated at 'the sign of The Three Crowns in the Strand'. This was an apt address, considering the bank's later list of royal clients.

The first of these arrived in 1716, when the Prince of Wales (later George II) bought some silver dressing plate. The bank flourished, attracting political and aristocratic clients over the following years, including George III who opened an account with them. Since then, every succeeding sovereign has had a bank account with Coutts. There is even a Coutts ATM (automatic teller machine) in the basement of Buckingham Palace for the staff to use. The bank is no longer privately owned, as it is now part of the Royal Bank of Scotland, but it is still considered to be very prestigious. Until 1993, Coutts sent a horse-drawn carriage to deliver royal correspondence, but unfortunately that tradition has now ended.

There is a fascinating royal story connected with Coutts. In 1917, during the First World War, the parents of Elizabeth Bowes-Lyon, later Queen Elizabeth the Queen Mother, discovered that their son, Michael, was still alive through a Coutts cheque. He had been declared missing in action on the Western Front and his family feared that he had suffered the same fate as his brother, Fergus, who had been killed. In fact, Michael was a prisoner of war in Germany, and he succeeded in drawing some money from his captors by writing them a cheque. When the cheque was presented at Coutts, the manager rang the Bowes-Lyon family to give them the good news.

Savoy Chapel

Savoy Hill, WC2R 0DA; www.duchyoflancaster.com/about-the-duchy/historic-properties/london/; open Tue–Sun; ADMISSION: free; TUBE: Aldwych, Charing Cross, Covent Garden, Embankment, Waterloo; RAIL: Charing Cross, Waterloo

Centuries before this corner of London was covered by the luxurious Savoy Hotel, it was the site of the Savoy Palace, which was owned by one of Edward III's sons, John of Gaunt, Duke of Lancaster (1340–99). The palace had an accompanying chapel, dedicated to St John the Baptist, but both chapel and palace were destroyed during the Peasants' Revolt of 1381. The buildings lay in ruins until 1505 when Henry VII announced that a hospital for the poor should be built here, once again dedicated to St John the Baptist. It had three chapels, including the Savoy Chapel, which is now all that remains of the medieval palace. The chapel is a royal peculiar, which means that it is privately owned by the reigning sovereign in his or her role as the Duke of Lancaster.

The 16th century was a tumultuous time, thanks to the many disputes about the national religion, and all religious institutions suffered the consequences of these arguments. The hospital was no exception. It was closed down by Edward VI (r.1547–53) in 1553, only to be opened again by his half-sister, Mary I (r.1553–8), three years later. However, the hospital soon fell into disrepute, with claims that it was the 'chief nurserie of evil men', as criminals took refuge from the law there. In the 17th century it became first a barracks for Foot Guards and then a Jesuit school. After a disastrous fire in 1776, the site was cleared in 1816–20 and redeveloped as the approach road to Waterloo Bridge. Only the Savoy Chapel was left standing.

The chapel has had as colourful a history as the palace. Illegal marriages were performed here in the 1750s, which brought the building a certain notoriety. It was badly damaged by fire in 1843 and 1864, after which only the outer walls were left intact. However, the chapel was rebuilt by Robert Smirke (1780–1867), an architect who had carried out a great deal of restoration work on it in the 1820s.

In 1937, the building became the chapel of the Royal Victorian Order. This was founded by Queen Victoria in 1896, and enabled her to confer personal honours on people who had served her. The order was, and still is, entirely within the sovereign's personal gift and has nothing to do with ministerial advice or recommendation. Its anniversary is 20 June, the day on which Victoria became queen. When the number of members of the Order became too great for the Savoy Chapel, the service was relocated to St George's Chapel at Windsor Castle (see pages 152–3). Nevertheless, the Savoy is still the Order's official chapel.

Among the recipients of the Order was Lionel Logue (1880–1953), whose work as a speech therapist enabled George VI, who had a severe stammer, to master public speaking.

ABOVE *The beautiful chancel of the Savoy Chapel. The church's ornate ceiling was restored for the Queen's Golden Jubilee.*

Theatre Royal, Drury Lane

Catherine Street, WC2B 5LA; ☎ 0844 412 4648;
www.reallyuseful.com/theatres/theatre-royal-drury-lane; open daily
during performances; ADMISSION: contact box office; TUBE: Aldwych,
Covent Garden, Temple; RAIL: Waterloo

Two of the many women in Charles II's life are associated with this famous theatre. The street is named for his queen, Catherine of Braganza, while the theatre itself was where one of his mistresses, Nell Gwyn, was an actress. Nell knew the area around Drury Lane well as she had lodgings here; Samuel Pepys records seeing her in her doorway in 1667.

Charles II was keen to enjoy himself whenever the opportunity arose, and once he was safely back on the throne following the Restoration, he had no truck with the prevailing Puritan aversion to theatrical displays. Many theatres had been closed in London during the Civil War to stop them being used for public meetings that might provoke unrest. However, Charles was determined to reverse this trend and in 1662 he conferred a theatrical patent on two actor-managers, which licensed them to set up their own theatres. Thomas Killigrew (1612–83), who ran the King's Company, built a theatre on the site of the present playhouse. His fellow actor-manager, Sir William D'Avenant (1606–68), who ran the Duke's Company, built a theatre in Lincoln's Inn.

Players and Kings

Charles disliked the British theatrical convention of employing men to play women's roles on stage and announced that actresses should be used in future. He was not called 'the Merry Monarch' for nothing, and there was doubtless a great deal of self-interest in his new ruling. Sure enough, in 1668 he first met Nell Gwyn at the Duke's Theatre; she had made her debut at the Theatre Royal in 1665, in Dryden's *Indian Queen*. Nell and Charles II soon became lovers and she moved to a much more respectable address in Pall Mall (see page 38), which was conveniently located close to St James's Palace, although she continued her successful theatrical career.

Charles was not the only monarch to fall in love with an actress. In 1791, the Duke of Clarence (who was later William IV) first saw the comic actress, Mrs Jordan (1761–1816), on stage at the Theatre Royal. They conducted a long and happy love affair, during which Mrs Jordan bore him 10 children.

Theatrical Dramas

Theatregoers to Drury Lane sometimes had very eventful experiences that bore no relation to the plays they were seeing. In 1716, a man called Freeman tried to shoot the Prince of Wales (the future George II) in the theatre. History repeated itself in 1800, when George III also survived an attempt on his life here. George III enjoyed visiting the Theatre Royal, as did his son, the Prince of Wales (later George IV). However, after they had a row in the foyer, the theatre's management decided to build two royal boxes so the king and his son need not sit together in future.

The present theatre is the fourth building to stand on this spot. The original theatre was closed down in 1664–5 during the Great Plague, which was at its most virulent in the area around Drury Lane. It subsequently burnt down in 1672. The theatre was rebuilt by Sir Christopher Wren in 1674 but it was finally demolished in 1791. The third theatre was designed by Henry Holland (1745–1806) and opened in 1794. This burnt down in 1809 and the present theatre, designed by Benjamin Dean Wyatt, was opened in 1812.

Somerset House

Strand, WC2R 1LA; ☎ 020 7845 4600; www.somersethouse.org.uk; open daily; ADMISSION: Courtauld Gallery adults £, concessions £, children free; TUBE: Charing Cross, Covent Garden, Embankment, Temple; RAIL: Blackfriars, Charing Cross, Waterloo

In 16th-century London, the Strand was a very fashionable address because it was conveniently close to the Palaces of Westminster and Whitehall. It was thronged with houses belonging to bishops and various members of the aristocracy, so it was the obvious choice for Edward Seymour (c.1506–52), the ambitious uncle of the young Edward VI, when he wanted to build a palace for himself in 1547. Henry VIII was dead, and Seymour was created Lord Protector and Duke of Somerset. He was looking forward to the power he would be able to exercise on behalf of his nine-year-old nephew, and decided to build a suitably grand house for himself on land he already owned between the Thames and the Strand. Various old churches and chapels already stood on the land, but Somerset soon got around such nuisances by having everything demolished. This was long before the days of preservation orders and listed buildings, of course, but nevertheless Somerset's actions provoked a furore and he enjoyed a brief spell of incarceration in the Tower of London in 1549.

Two years later, Somerset was back in the Tower, this time on a charge of treason, and was executed in January 1552. His glorious new palace was almost finished, having cost £10,000, and was given to the Crown. Princess Elizabeth lived in it until she became queen in 1558, when she moved to Whitehall and St James's Palaces. Somerset House was then used for meetings, and provided accommodation for visiting foreign diplomats.

The building became a palace again when James I came to the English throne in 1603. His queen, Anne of Denmark, happily settled into Somerset House, which she renamed Denmark House and where she entertained lavishly. The house was remodelled for the queen, to designs by Inigo Jones, who was pressed into service once again in the 1620s by Henrietta Maria, the French wife of Charles I. One of Jones's commissions was to build her a Roman Catholic chapel. This made both Henrietta Maria and her husband deeply unpopular and mistrusted in a country that was almost rabidly Protestant.

Denmark House was taken over by Parliament during the Civil War, and returned to its original name of Somerset House, becoming the quarters for General Thomas Fairfax (1612–71), who was commander of the Parliamentarian army. It was also the repository for the royal treasures that were collected by the Parliamentarians during the war, and from where they were sold. When Oliver Cromwell died in September 1658, his coffin lay in state at Somerset House until November. He was following a royal tradition, as the bodies of Anne of Denmark and James I had also lain in state here. However, it is thought that his coffin may have contained someone else's corpse because his body may have already been buried in a secret location in Westminster Abbey. Therefore, the corpse that was exhumed in January 1661 and hanged at Tyburn before being beheaded may not have been Cromwell's at all.

RIGHT *The jets of water in the Edmond J. Safra Fountain Court rise and fall in an orchestrated sequence.*

Somerset House was built as a royal palace.

After the Restoration in 1660, Henrietta Maria moved back to Somerset House, although she was forced out by the Great Plague in 1665 and never returned. The following year, the Great Fire burnt itself out just before it reached the building. When Charles II died in 1685, his Catholic widow, Catherine of Braganza, moved to Somerset House. While living here she quarrelled with the Protestant monarchs, William III and Mary II, when they took over the throne in 1689. This personality clash was only resolved in 1693, when Catherine was invited to become Regent of Portugal and left the country.

Changing Roles

Somerset House lost its popularity with widowed queen consorts after this and was used as grace-and-favour apartments. By 1775, the building was in such a state of disrepair that George III agreed for it to be demolished and for its replacement to contain purpose-built public offices, such as the Navy Board. He reserved the right for space to be created for the three societies he patronized – the Royal Academy of Arts, the Royal Society and the Society of Antiquaries. The new Strand frontage was based on the 17th-century remodelling of the riverfront façade and was designed by Sir William Chambers. In 1788, John Bacon the Elder cast the full-length bronze statue of George III, wearing a toga, which stands in the courtyard. Queen Charlotte obviously did not think much of it because she asked Bacon why it was so ugly. He replied, 'Art cannot always effect what is ever within reach of Nature, the union of beauty and majesty.'

Among the public offices to occupy Somerset House in succeeding years was the General Register of Births, Deaths and Marriages, the Principal Probate Registry and the Inland Revenue. However, some of these offices have since moved and the building is now home to the Courtauld Gallery, and hosts summer film seasons and an ice rink in winter. Somerset House may no longer be a royal palace but it is still suitably regal, and full of history.

Temple Church

Temple, EC4Y 7BB; ☎ 020 7353 3470; www.templechurch.com;
open Mon–Fri, Sat and Sun for services only; ADMISSION: adults £,
senior citizens and under-21s free; TUBE: Blackfriars, Temple;
RAIL: Blackfriars

Only four round churches are still standing in Britain, one of which is Temple Church. Legend has it that it was modelled on the Church of the Holy Sepulchre in Jerusalem, although some authorities say it is more likely that it was modelled on the Dome of the Rock. It was built between 1160 and 1185, when it was consecrated by Heraclius, the Patriarch of Jerusalem, in the presence of Henry II.

Temple Church owes these very auspicious beginnings to the fact that it is the church of the Order of the Knights Templar. This order of knights was formed c.1118 in order to protect Christian pilgrims who were journeying to the Holy Land. They wore white tunics adorned with red crosses, which proclaimed that they were answerable only to the Pope. Human nature being what it is, such absolute power was bound to be a temptation, even to an order of knights who prided themselves on their piety and sanctity. They did not baulk at inflicting punishment if they thought it necessary, as they did when they imprisoned Walter-le-Bacheler, the Grand Preceptor of Ireland. He was held in the penitential cell in Temple Church where he starved to death for disobeying the Master of the Order.

Eventually, such behaviour caught up with the knights. Their property was confiscated during the reign of Edward II and passed to the Knights Hospitaller (also known as the Order of St John of Jerusalem). These new owners leased Temple Church to local lawyers, an arrangement that continued until 1540 when Henry VIII abolished the Hospitallers and helped himself to their property. However, James I reversed this measure in 1608,

ABOVE *Temple Church has a fascinating history.*

when he gave the freehold of Temple Church to the neighbouring lawyers, provided that they maintained the church in perpetuity. He divided it between the Inner Temple, who received the southern half of the church, and the Middle Temple, who received the northern half. Accordingly, the south window bears the crest of the Inner Temple (Pegasus, the winged horse of Greek mythology), and the north window displays the crest of the Middle Temple (the Holy Lamb and Flag). A further reminder of royal involvement is that the appointment of a new Master or chaplain is carried out by the reigning sovereign, rather than by the Bishop of London.

In common with so many City churches, Temple Church received the attentions of Sir Christopher Wren in 1682 when he was asked to improve it. Repairs were carried out in 1825 and again in 1841–2. The church was badly damaged by bombing in May 1941 during the Second World War, but it has since been completely restored.

St Mary le Strand

Strand, WC2R 1ES; ☎ 020 7836 3126; www.stmarylestrand.org;
open Tue–Sun; ADMISSION: free; TUBE: Charing Cross, Covent
Garden, Embankment, Holborn, Temple; RAIL: Blackfriars,
Charing Cross, Waterloo

When the Lord Protector, the Duke of Somerset, decided to knock down all the buildings that stood on the site of what is now Somerset House (see pages 92–4) in 1549, one of the churches that he demolished was the Nativity of Our Lady and the Innocents. It is claimed that one of its early rectors was Thomas à Becket. Somerset's promise to rebuild the church went unfulfilled and the parishioners had to wait until the 1710s before they were given a replacement.

St Mary le Strand was designed by James Gibbs and was one of the Fifty New Churches planned for London. A 76-metre (250-foot) tall column, topped by a brass statue of Queen Anne, was going to stand next to the church, but the idea was scrapped when the queen died in August 1714 and the church was given a modest spire instead because it was too late to strengthen the foundations for anything more lavish.

It is claimed that Bonnie Prince Charlie (1720–88), the grandson of the deposed James II, who spent his life trying to reclaim the British throne for his father, 'The Old Pretender', made a secret visit to St Mary le Strand in 1750. He allegedly renounced his Catholic faith here and was received into the Church of England. This is quite a claim, as it meant he essentially renounced the Jacobite cause for which he had fought all his life. We may never know the truth of this rumour, but it certainly adds to the atmosphere and interest of this unusual church.

RIGHT *St Mary le Strand stands amid the noise of the Strand.*

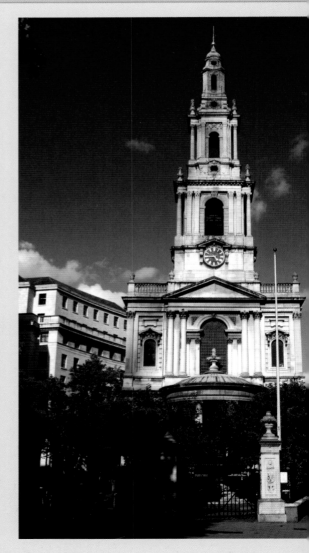

St Dunstan-in-the-West

186a Fleet Street, EC4A 2HR; ☎ 020 7405 1929;
www.stdunstaninthewest.org; open Mon–Fri; ADMISSION: free;
TUBE: Chancery Lane, Temple; RAIL: Blackfriars, City Thameslink

In 1666, the Great Fire of London burned itself out a short distance from this Fleet Street church. Parishioners were so grateful for their escape that they clubbed together to buy a clock for the church. It was erected in 1671, and was the first public clock in London to be given a minute hand.

In 1760, almost all the city gates that had once defended the entrances to the City of London were pulled down, including the Lud Gate, which stood on what is now Ludgate Hill. This gate had been decorated with statues of Elizabeth I, King Lud (who was believed to have reigned in about 66 BC) and his two sons, and these were all preserved and moved to St Dunstan's church, where they can still be seen. The statue of Elizabeth I is the oldest stone statue of her in existence. It was carved by William Kerwin and dates from 1586.

Fleet Street was widened in 1832 and the old church had to be demolished. It was rebuilt in Gothic revival style by John Shaw the Elder (1776–1832) and completed by his son, John Shaw the Younger (1803–70). The statues of Elizabeth I and King Lud and his sons were erected in the new church. The famous clock, however, was bought by the Marquess of Hertford for his house in Regent's Park (see pages 104–5). Happily, in 1935, Lord Rothermere, who presided over his newspaper empire in Fleet Street, bought the clock and returned it to St Dunstan's.

BELOW *The figure of Elizabeth I is thought to be the oldest stone statue of her in existence.*

St Bride's Church

Fleet Street, EC4Y 8AU; ☎ 020 7427 0133; www.stbrides.com;
open daily; ADMISSION: free; TUBE: Blackfriars, St Paul's; RAIL: Blackfriars,
City Thameslink

We owe our tradition of tiered, elaborately iced wedding cakes to the spire of St Bride's Church. In the late 18th and early 19th centuries, the aptly named William Rich was a pastry cook in Fleet Street, and he based the design of his wedding cakes on the spire of his nearby church. Perhaps the appropriate name of the church acted as the spur to his inspiration.

A building has stood on this site since Roman times: the remains of a Roman house are preserved in the crypt, having been discovered there by an archaeologist after the church was demolished during an air raid in 1940. W. F. Grimes, the archaeologist who worked on the project, also uncovered clear evidence of six different churches that have stood on this site since Saxon times.

It was obviously a place of importance, as King John held a parliament in the Norman church in 1210. In 1666, the 15th-century church burnt down in the Great Fire of London, and Sir Christopher Wren was commissioned to design its replacement in 1671. Wren added the famous spire in 1701–03, making it the tallest of all his steeples.

Natural Disaster

Disaster struck in 1764 when the spire was hit by lightning, which knocked off the top 2.5 metres (8 feet). It was widely agreed that the answer was to fit a lightning conductor, but there was enormous controversy over its design. George III was a keen amateur scientist so he took great interest in the lightning conductor, and decided that it would be best to install one with blunt ends. However, perhaps not trusting his own conclusions, he consulted several scientists, including the American polymath, Benjamin Franklin, who was the inventor of lightning conductors. Franklin favoured a conductor with pointed ends. This was a gift to Fleet Street's newspapers, which wrote of 'sharp witted colonists' as opposed to 'good, honest, blunt King George'.

Despite being reduced to rubble on the night of 29 December 1940 (a fate suffered by many other buildings in London), St Bride's was lovingly restored over 17 years, and was finally rededicated in a ceremony attended by Elizabeth II and the Duke of Edinburgh in 1957.

BELOW *St Bride's steeple, with its hotly debated lightning conductor.*

York Watergate

Watergate Walk, WC2; TUBE: Charing Cross, Embankment;
RAIL: Charing Cross, Waterloo

This area of the Embankment has changed dramatically since Charles I's day, but one thing that remains is the York Watergate, which was built in 1626. It was once the direct link between the Thames's north bank and the garden of York House in the Strand, but it's now stranded quite a long way from the river as a result of the Victorian development of the Thames Embankment.

York House was originally the home of the Bishops of Norwich, but after the Dissolution of the Monasteries in the 1530s Henry VIII gave the property to his brother-in-law, Charles Brandon, Duke of Suffolk. He, in turn, gave it to Mary I, who presented it to the Archbishop of York in 1556.

A Favourite of James I

In 1621, the house was acquired by George Villiers, 1st Duke of Buckingham (1592–1628), who is usually described as one of the 'favourites' of James I. This appears to be a euphemism for 'lover', as the two men had a very close friendship, which only ended when James died in 1625. When James conferred the earldom on Buckingham in 1623, he told the assembled Lords of the Council: 'I, James, am neither God nor angel, but a man like any other … I love the Earl of Buckingham more than anyone else and more than you who are here assembled. I wish to speak in my own behalf and not to have it thought a defect, for Jesus Christ did the same, and therefore I cannot be blamed. Christ had his John, and I have my George.' Buckingham, who was deeply disliked by a great many people, was assassinated in 1628 and his son, also named George (1628–87), became 2nd Duke of

Buckingham. He was brought up by Charles I while his mother continued to live at York House, which was popularly called Buckingham House.

Buckingham Lives On

York House was considered sufficiently royal to be confiscated during the Civil War and later taken over by General Fairfax, who was also making use of nearby Somerset House (see pages 92–4). Rather cleverly, the young 2nd Duke of Buckingham married Fairfax's daughter, Mary, in 1657, thus ensuring that his property would be returned to him after the Restoration.

The house was demolished in the 1670s and the land built on by Nicholas Barbon (c.1640–c.98), who was the main property developer of the age. Buckingham's house might have vanished but he insisted that his name should live on in the local street names, such as Villiers Street and Buckingham Street. His coat of arms can still be seen over the central archway of York Watergate, and the two lions on top, holding shields with anchors, commemorate his position of Lord High Admiral.

ABOVE *York Watergate still stands in Victoria Embankment Gardens.*

Holborn Circus

EC1; TUBE: Chancery Lane, Farringdon;
RAIL: City Thameslink, Farringdon

Gray's Inn

High Holborn, WC1V 6BS; www.graysinn.info/;
TUBE: Chancery Lane, Holborn

One of the boundaries of the City of London slices straight through Holborn Circus, therefore dividing it between the City and Camden. The circus takes its name from the Holebourne, a tributary of the Fleet River. It is the point at which Holborn, New Fetter Lane, St Andrew Street, Holborn Viaduct, Charterhouse Street and Hatton Garden all meet.

Holborn Circus is also the site of a bronze equestrian statue of Prince Albert, who is wearing his field-marshal's uniform and doffing his cap to the City. The statue was cast by Charles Bacon and presented to the City of London in 1874, 13 years after the prince's death, courtesy of Charles Oppenheim. Plaques at the base of the statue show the prince laying the foundation stone of the Royal Exchange in 1842, and also depict Britannia distributing awards at the 1851 Great Exhibition, over which the prince presided so successfully.

There are four Inns of Court: Gray's Inn, the Inner Temple, Lincoln's Inn and the Middle Temple. They are all places where lawyers have worked and studied for centuries, and each of them is formally referred to as an 'Honourable Society'. They are all completely independent, and are governed by the Benchers (judges from the High Court and senior barristers) who are the only people allowed to call students to the Bar.

Gray's Inn was founded in about 1370 on the site of a manor house that was the London residence of Sir Reginald le Grey, who was the Chief Justice of Chester, Constable and Sheriff of Nottingham. The Inn prospered, and in the 16th century it counted Thomas Cromwell as one of its members until he was beheaded on the orders of Henry VIII. During her reign, Elizabeth I was the Inn's Patron Lady and many of her advisers were members. It is said that the screen at the west end of the hall was made from the timbers of a Spanish galleon that was captured during the Armada, and was given to the Inn by Elizabeth herself.

Ely Place

EC1N 6RY; TUBE: Chancery Lane, Farringdon;
RAIL: City Thameslink, Farringdon

This was the site of Ely House, the London palace of the Bishops of Ely for five centuries, between the late 13th century and 1772. It was an important building; Philippa of Hainault spent Christmas 1327 here, shortly before her marriage to Edward III. She was not the only royal visitor; her son, John of Gaunt, had to move here in 1381 after the Savoy Palace was destroyed during the Peasants' Revolt. It remained his residence until his death in 1399.

In 1576, Elizabeth I instructed the Bishop of Ely to lease part of the property to Sir Christopher Hatton (1540–91), who was her Lord Chancellor at the time. In the 1580s, Hatton took advantage of a vacancy at the see and built a house in the garden of the bishop's palace. This was taken over temporarily by the Parliamentarians during the Civil War, who used it is a jail for Royalist prisoners. After the Hatton line died out in 1772, the property reverted to the Crown. Ely House, which had been the home of the Bishops of Ely for so long, was by now in such a dreadful state that it was pulled down and replaced by brick-built, terraced houses. The Bishops of Ely moved to a new Ely House at 37 Dover Street.

A Saintly Relic

St Etheldreda's Church, which was built in Ely Place in about 1293 as a private chapel for the Bishop of Ely, is the only part of the original Ely House still standing. It was named for the abbess who founded the monastery at Ely in 673, and part of her hand is kept as a relic in the church. In common with parts of Westminster Abbey (see pages 48–51), the church is one of the very few surviving buildings in London to contain Gothic architecture from the reign of Edward I in the 11th century. After the Protestant Reformation in 1538, St Etheldreda's became the first church in England to revert to the Roman Catholic faith. Despite being sold to Welsh Episcopalians in 1836, St Etheldreda's is once again a Roman Catholic church.

Geographical Curiosities

Ely Place is still owned by the Crown, and is a private road whose iron gates are locked at 10 o'clock each evening. The Lord Mayor of London has no jurisdiction over the street, and even the police are not allowed to enter unless invited to do so by one of the commissioners who manage Ely Place. This is interesting enough, but even more curious is the fact that Ely Place is technically in Cambridgeshire because it was originally part of the diocese of Ely.

There is another geographical curiosity just around the corner. The Olde Mitre Tavern stands in Ely Court, which is a narrow passage leading from Ely Place to Hatton Garden (named after Sir Christopher Hatton and now the centre of London's diamond trade). The pub was built on part of the site of Ely House, and is therefore another little piece of London that belongs to Cambridgeshire. The preserved trunk of an old cherry tree, which once marked the boundary of the diocese of Ely, stands in the front bar. Legend has it that Elizabeth I and Sir Christopher Hatton once danced the maypole around the tree. Whether or not this is true, they had a close relationship and he was one of her most trusted advisers. When he lay dying in Ely Place at the end of 1591, Elizabeth visited him and fed him broth.

MARBLE ARCH TO HIGHGATE

Marble Arch, once the impressive entrance to Buckingham Palace until it was relocated to its present position, marks the southern boundary of this section, while Lauderdale House marks the northern extent.

Marble Arch

Oxford Street, W1R 1DD; TUBE: Marble Arch

Most of us imagine that London landmarks have always stood in the same spot. We arrange to meet friends by them, safe in the knowledge that we will all arrive in the same place. But if a friend from the early Victorian era could somehow arrange to meet us at Marble Arch, we would find ourselves standing in different locations.

In 1827, Marble Arch was erected outside Buckingham Palace (see pages 24–6) and it stood in the position that is now occupied by the east front of the building – which is the side that looks out on to the Queen Victoria Memorial. It was designed in white Carrara marble by John Nash, who was busy remodelling Buckingham Palace at vast expense for George IV at the time, and was based on the Arch of Constantine in Rome. The arch formed the main entrance to the palace, and it cost £10,000. In 1829,

George IV commissioned Sir Francis Chantrey (1781–1841) to cast a bronze equestrian statue of himself, which he intended to place on top of Marble Arch. George died before the statue was completed and it was finally erected in Trafalgar Square.

By the time Queen Victoria and Prince Albert started their family, it was obvious that Buckingham Palace was far too small for them and would have to be extended. The most sensible solution was to move Marble Arch and turn what had been a U-shaped palace into a quadrangle by building a fourth side. In 1851, Marble Arch was relocated to its present position at the north-east corner of Hyde Park, very close to where the Tyburn gallows once stood.

Marble Arch was given its own traffic island in 1908, and now the traffic rushes around it day and night. It has three archways but only senior members of the Royal Family – in other words, the most important ones – and the King's Troop Royal Horse Artillery are allowed to pass through them.

LEFT *Statues on the frieze in Cumberland Terrace (see pages 104–5).* BELOW *Marble Arch was completely restored in 2004.*

Regent's Park

NW1 4NR; ☎ 020 7486 7905; www.royalparks.gov.uk;
TUBE: Baker Street, Camden Town, Great Portland Street,
Regent's Park, St. John's Wood

Centuries ago this was part of the ancient Forest of Middlesex. However, by 1066 it was incorporated into the Manor of Tyburn and owned by the Abbess of Barking. This ownership continued for centuries but it cut no ice with Henry VIII when he set about dissolving the monasteries: he simply appropriated the land for himself in 1539 and turned it into a hunting ground.

At the time, the land was known as Marylebone Park Fields, and it remained a royal chase until 1646, when Charles I pledged the land to Sir George Strode and John Wandesford as security for the ammunition and arms he needed to fight the Civil War. In common with virtually every other piece of Crown property, the park was sold after Charles's execution in 1649, although it was bought back after the Restoration in 1660.

A Princely Pleasure Ground

By the 1790s, it was obvious that development of Marylebone Park would not only increase the Crown's revenue, but also improve this area of London. John Nash won the resulting competition to create the most attractive and profitable scheme with his design that involved a continuous series of terraces with 2 circuses and 56 villas. It is appropriate that the architect of what became Regent's Park was Nash, as he had such strong connections with the Prince Regent; it was Nash who helped the prince to convert the Royal Pavilion in Brighton from a small farmhouse into a fantasy palace.

One of the prospective projects for Regent's Park was a pleasure ground for the prince, which would be linked by Regent Street to Carlton House. George supported Nash while the project was being planned. Inevitably, it attracted plenty of criticism. Not all of Nash's plans were carried out in the end, and some of the land that had been intended for terraces of houses became the site of London Zoo (see page 106). Only eight of the villas were ever built and only two of these remain – St John's Lodge and The Holme.

Regent's Park remained private until 1845, when it was opened to the public for the first time, although initially they were allowed in for just two days each week. In the 1930s, Queen Mary's Rose Garden was developed in honour of George V's consort.

Edward and Mrs Simpson

Cumberland Terrace is the most impressive of Nash's terraces and was built from 1826 to 1828. It was named for Ernest, Duke of Cumberland, who was a younger brother of George IV. The original plan was for this terrace to stand opposite the Petit Trianon, which was the small palace that Nash planned to create for the king, but which was never built. However, another king was a frequent visitor to Cumberland Terrace. In 1936, Edward VIII visited his American mistress, Mrs Simpson (1896–1986), at a flat at No. 16. The story of their love affair was a hot news item in America and Europe, but it had been kept from the general public in Britain until late that year, when news of the 'abdication crisis', as it was called, broke in *The Times* newspaper. Shocked and angry crowds gathered outside Mrs Simpson's flat and threw bricks through her

windows; she was smuggled out of the country and travelled to France, where she waited for her divorce to be made absolute. On 11 December 1936, Edward VIII abdicated, having made an announcement to the nation on the radio that evening, explaining that he was abdicating so he could marry 'the woman I love'. His position as king, and therefore head of the Church of England,

OPPOSITE *The Holme was the first villa to be built in Regent's Park.* ABOVE *Avenue Gardens, Regent's Park.*

prevented him marrying a divorcée. Now styled the Duke of Windsor, he left England for Austria, where he also waited for Mrs Simpson's divorce to be finalized. They were married in France in June 1937 and spent the rest of their lives in exile from Britain.

London Zoo

Regent's Park, NW1 4RY; ☎ 020 7722 3333; www.zsl.org/zsl-london-zoo; open daily except Christmas Day; ADMISSION: adults £££–££££, concessions ££–£££, children ££–£££, under-3s free (prices vary according to season); TUBE: Camden Town, Regent's Park

St Katharine's

4 St Katharine's Precinct, Regent's Park, NW1 4HH; ☎ 020 7935 7584; www.danskekirke.org; open daily; ADMISSION: free; TUBE: Camden Town

The story of London Zoo began at the Tower of London (see pages 73–5) in 1235, when Frederick II, the Holy Roman Emperor, presented three leopards to Henry III. This was the birth of the Royal Menagerie, which was housed at the Tower until August 1835.

The Zoological Society of London was founded in 1826, and two years later it opened London Zoo in part of Regent's Park. Initially, the zoo was not open to the public, as it had been created so that scientists could study the exotic creatures before them.

London Zoo finally opened to the public in 1847 and was an instant success. In 1962–4, the pioneering Snowdon Aviary, which was constructed from aluminium, was erected. It was designed by Princess Margaret's husband Antony Armstrong-Jones (who had been created the 1st Earl of Snowdon) in conjunction with Cedric Price and Frank Newby.

St Katharine's Church was moved to Regent's Park from its original site at St Katharine's Dock in the 1820s. The original chapel was founded in 1148 by Matilda (c.1103–52), the wife of King Stephen, to look after 'thirteen poor persons'. Since then, it has been under the patronage of the queens of England. Although most churches were stripped of their valuables and their property sold off during the Dissolution of the Monasteries in the late 1530s, St Katharine's evaded such a fate and retained Henry VIII's divorced wife, Katherine of Aragon, as its patron.

Today, the chapel is the principal Danish place of worship in London. Edward VII's widow, Queen Alexandra, granted it to her fellow Danes during the First World War. Outside the church is a copy of the rune stone that was erected in about 980 at Jelling, Denmark, by Harald Bluetooth (c.958–c.85).

St George's Church

7 Little Russell Street, WC1A 2HR (the church's entrance is in Bloomsbury Way); ☎ 020 7242 1979; www.stgeorgesbloomsbury.org.uk; open daily; ADMISSION: free; TUBE: Tottenham Court Road

Queen Square

WC1; TUBE: Holborn

'**A** masterpiece of absurdity' is how Horace Walpole described the statue of George I that adorns the top of the pyramid-shaped steeple of St George's Church. Walpole was not the only critic of this church, which was one of the eight to be built by Nicholas Hawksmoor (*c*.1661–1736) between 1716 and 1731, as it excited a great deal of adverse comment at the time. The government were not very happy about the building either, as it went wildly over budget and eventually cost £31,000 instead of the estimated £9,000.

The unusually shaped steeple was inspired by Pliny's description of the Mausoleum at Halicarnassus, and its base was originally decorated with images of lions and unicorns. Unfortunately, toxic fumes ate away at the carvings and their mouldering remains were removed in 1871. The statue of George I, who had succeeded to the British throne in 1714 without being able to speak a word of English, was donated by Mr Hicks, who was brewer to the Royal Household and presumably doing his best to curry favour with the new king. George I was depicted in Roman dress, posing as St George, the patron saint of England. The message to his subjects was clear – this man might be German but he had every right to assume the British throne and was the country's new saviour.

LEFT: *Giraffe House, London Zoo.*

The queen in question is Queen Anne, who was on the throne when work began on this square in 1708. However, she had died by the time the square was completed in 1720. Another queen is commemorated in the middle of the square, where a lead statue of Queen Charlotte, wife of George III, was erected in about 1775. A few years later, Charlotte became very familiar with the square because it was here in 1788 that George III stayed with his physician, Dr Francis Willis, when he became ill with what was probably porphyria, a disease of the blood that causes bizarre mental and physical symptoms. It is said that his devoted wife used to prepare his favourite food for him, while he stayed in Queen Square, in the cellars of what is now the Queen's Larder pub.

British Library

96 Euston Road, NW1 2DB; ☎ 0843 208 1144; www.bl.uk; Reading
Rooms open Mon–Sat; closed on public holidays; ADMISSION: free;
TUBE: Euston, Euston Square, King's Cross St Pancras; RAIL: Euston,
King's Cross St Pancras

The abiding folk memory of George III is of a mad king who lost the American colonies. Although George did have periods of insanity and Britain did lose the War of Independence during his reign, there is still a great deal to be said in his favour. He was highly intelligent and cultured, fascinated by science and art, and his collections of books and scientific instruments now belong to the nation. His scientific instruments are part of the collection at the Science Museum in London and his books can be found in the King's Library, at the British Library.

The British Library only came into existence in 1973, when the British Museum Library, the National Central Library and the National Lending Library for Science and Technology were brought together. The British National Bibliography and the Office for Scientific and Technical Information both joined the library in 1974, followed by the India Office Library and Records in 1982 and the British Institute of Recorded Sound in 1983. The British Library is the national library of the United Kingdom, and contains some of the most important books in the world.

The King's Library is housed in a six-storey glass tower, called the King's Library Tower. It contains books printed mostly in Britain, Europe and North America between the 13th and 19th centuries. George III started the collection because the previous royal library (known as the Old Royal Library and now also part of the British Library) had been given to the new British Museum by George II in 1757. There were books in the different royal residences but no properly organized library existed, so George III set about creating one. His agents travelled around Europe, buying everything from individual books to complete libraries. By the time of his death in 1820, George III's library contained about 65,000 printed books as well as pamphlets and manuscripts.

The King's Library had a fairly peripatetic existence in its early days, as it was first housed in the Old Palace at Kew, before being moved to the Queen's House (later rebuilt as Buckingham Palace, see pages 24–6). When George IV succeeded to the throne in 1820 and decided to extend the Queen's House, the books were moved once again and eventually the library was offered to the nation in 1823. After spending several years at Kensington Palace (see pages 124–6), the library was given a permanent home in the King's Library Gallery within the British Museum. A small part of the collection was damaged during a German bombing raid in September 1940, and the books were sent for safe-keeping to the Bodleian Library, Oxford, for the rest of the war. In 1998, the King's Library was moved to its present home.

Among the treasures of the collection is the prayer book of Lady Jane Grey, which she carried to the scaffold when she was executed for treason in 1554. She was a pawn in her father-in-law's plan to control the English throne and was briefly proclaimed queen of England before being imprisoned and beheaded in the Tower of London (see page 75).

Despite the rarity of many of the books in the King's Library, it continues to be a working library. Many of the books are displayed behind special glass panels so they can be easily viewed.

RIGHT *A section of the King's Library.*

Lauderdale House

Waterlow Park, Highgate Hill, N6 5HG; ☎ 020 8348 8716;
www.lauderdalehouse.org.uk; open Tue–Sun; ADMISSION: free;
TUBE: Archway

ABOVE *The house was closely connected with Oliver Cromwell.*

In Elizabethan times, this was the home of Sir Richard Martin, who was Lord Mayor of London twice and also the Master of the Royal Mint. The house subsequently had a succession of owners, and at the start of the English Civil War was the home of the Royalist John Maitland, who was the 2nd Earl of Lauderdale. However, in 1649, Lauderdale was imprisoned for his Royalist sympathies and the house passed into the hands of John Ireton, who had family connections with Oliver Cromwell (Ireton's brother, Henry, was Cromwell's son-in-law). The situation was reversed rather neatly with the Restoration in 1660, because Lauderdale was freed and Ireton became a captive. The house once again became the property of the Lauderdale family. The Earl of Lauderdale rose to a prominent position during the reign of Charles II, becoming one of the five ministers who formed Charles's Cabal (an acronym composed of the men's names). At one point, Charles's mistress, Nell Gwyn, stayed here with their small son, Charles (who later was given the title of Duke of St Albans).

Nell Gwyn was one of Charles II's favourite mistresses and, in common with several of her rivals, bore him children. This is somewhat ironic considering that all his children by his wife, Catherine of Braganza, were stillborn. Nell Gwyn was naturally very keen to ensure that her children by Charles should have secure futures, and she found ingenious means by which to do it. It is said that while staying at Lauderdale House she threatened to drop the young Charles out of a window unless his father immediately made provision for his future. Thinking quickly, Charles II shouted out 'Save the Earl of Burford!'

Today, the house mounts exhibitions of paintings and also stages regular performances of music and poetry.

WEST LONDON

Three centuries ago, West London was quiet, pretty countryside. This was what attracted William and Mary, who were looking for a home away from Central London. They chose to live in what is now Kensington Palace, and immediately put this part of West London on the world stage.

Hyde Park

W2 2UH; ☎ 020 7298 2100; www.royalparks.gov.uk;
TUBE: Hyde Park Corner, Knightsbridge, Lancaster Gate,
Marble Arch

It is often remarked that London's parks are its lungs, in which case Hyde Park contributes more than all the other green spaces to the purification of the city's air because it is the largest of all the royal parks. It appears to be even larger than it really is because its western boundary merges into Kensington Gardens, making it difficult to establish where one park ends and the other begins. In fact, the demarcation line runs from Victoria Gate on the Bayswater Road, down West Carriage Drive, across the Serpentine Bridge and south to Alexandra Gate, which sits at the point where Kensington Gore meets Kensington Road. This ceremonial gate is a remnant of Prince Albert's Great Exhibition of 1851. The park's three remaining boundaries are obvious: it is bordered to the north by the Bayswater Road, to the east by Park Lane and to the south by the Brompton Road, Knightsbridge and Kensington Road.

As with so many great London landmarks, we have Henry VIII to thank for Hyde Park. He first spotted the potential of this stretch of land in 1536, during the Dissolution of the Monasteries, when he took it from the monks of Westminster Abbey and turned it into another of his many hunting grounds. His daughter, Elizabeth I, also enjoyed hunting here. The public was given limited access to the park for the first time in the 17th century, during the reign of James I, but it was his son, Charles I, who opened it fully to the public.

Parliament sold off the park in 1652, during the Interregnum, but it became a royal possession once again after 1660 when Charles II returned from exile in Europe to claim the throne. He had a brick wall constructed to surround the park, and, presumably, to keep out the riff-raff. However, during the Great Plague of 1665, which killed off so many of his subjects, Charles allowed military encampments to set up within the park.

A Royal Water Feature

In the 18th century, gardening became one of the great royal pleasures. Queen Caroline, wife of George II, was particularly interested in landscape gardening. In the late 1720s, she decided that Hyde Park needed a lake. One of London's many rivers, the Westbourne, was dammed to create this water feature, which took three years to complete and was named the Serpentine. Whenever the lake's water level drops too low, it is topped up by a pump, which is located on Duck Island in nearby St James's Park (see pages 30–31).

Fireworks, Riots and a Crystal Palace

Hyde Park has been the scene of some memorable occasions. In 1821, the celebrations for George IV's coronation included firework displays and hot-air balloons. That same summer, there were riots when the funeral cortège of George's estranged wife, Queen Caroline, tried to pass through Cumberland Gate (named for George's brother, the Duke of Cumberland). The fighting was so intense that soldiers had to intervene. In 1851, the Great Exhibition was held in the park. Various sites were proposed for the event, including Regent's Park. Hyde Park was eventually chosen, despite scare stories in *The Times*

announcing that 'Kensington and Belgravia would be uninhabitable and the Season would be ruined'. The Great Exhibition was organized by Prince Albert, and aimed at demonstrating Britain's supremacy as a world power. The event was a wild success. It was housed within the massive Crystal Palace that was designed by Joseph Paxton (1801–65), ran between May and October 1851, and was visited by over 6 million people. Queen Victoria attended the event frequently, visiting roughly every other day during its first three months. In 1852, the Crystal Palace was dismantled and moved to a new site at Sydenham in south London, although the ceremonial entrance gate remained in Hyde Park. More recent royal events here have included the Queen's Silver Jubilee Exhibition, which took place in 1977, and the royal fireworks party, which was held in July 1981 to celebrate the marriage of Prince Charles and Lady Diana Spencer.

One of the more curious facts about Hyde Park concerns the Broad Walk, which runs to the west of Park Lane. In 1954, the elm trees that grew either side of it were cleared to create a wide path that could double as an emergency airstrip if the Royal Family needed to leave London in a hurry. So far, they have not made use of it.

Hyde Park Corner

SW1; TUBE: Green Park, Hyde Park Corner, Knightsbridge;
RAIL: Victoria

This was originally the site of a toll gate for people entering London. However, in the 18th century, it was decided that the area should be tidied up and made to look more imposing. Constitution Arch, also known as the Wellington Arch, which stands in the centre of Hyde Park Corner, was commissioned by George IV who wanted it to be part of an imposing route to Buckingham Palace. He gave the commission to Decimus Burton, who completed it in 1825. The arch was erected in 1828, close to Apsley House, the home of the Duke of Wellington (1769–1852), but it was moved to its present position in 1882 in order to line up with the top of Constitution Hill. It was originally adorned with a massive statue of the 'Iron Duke', as Wellington was popularly called, on horseback, but this was so large that it provoked an equally big controversy. When the arch was relocated in 1882, the statue was tactfully removed. Its replacement, a bronze group called *Quadriga* by Adrian Jones, was presented by Lord Michelham in 1912 in memory of his friend, Edward VII. It is the largest bronze sculpture in Europe. The Wellington Arch is now under the care of English Heritage and is open to the public (*www.english-heritage.org.uk*).

To the north of Hyde Park Corner is the Hyde Park Screen, which was also designed by Decimus Burton in the 1820s. It was intended to be an impressive link between Hyde Park and Buckingham Palace, and it incorporates a frieze based on the Elgin Marbles.

Just around the corner, at the start of Park Lane, is the Queen Elizabeth Gate that was designed by Giuseppe Lund with sculptures by David Wynne. The gate was unveiled in 1993 by Queen Elizabeth II in the presence of her mother, Queen Elizabeth the Queen Mother, whose life it celebrates.

ABOVE *The Queen Elizabeth Gates*.
BELOW *Wellington Arch*.

Mandarin Oriental Hyde Park Hotel

66 Knightsbridge, SW1X 7LA; ☎ 020 7235 2000;
www.mandarinoriental.com/london;
TUBE: Knightsbridge

Rotten Row

SW1; TUBE: Hyde Park Corner, Knightsbridge

This building began life in 1882 as a select apartment block, but it reopened as the Hyde Park Hotel in 1908. The original main entrance, which faced Hyde Park, was in Albert Gate and intended for the exclusive use of royalty; the Knightsbridge entrance was the one used by everyone else. This royal entrance is still closed to the general public, although it is occasionally opened in honour of very special visitors.

Throughout the 20th century, the Hyde Park Hotel was popular with members of the Royal Family. During the First World War, Queen Mary would visit the soldiers who stayed here when on leave. Her son, Edward VIII, used to enjoy chatting to members of staff while he was out of the public gaze. When they were young girls, the Princesses Elizabeth and Margaret had dancing lessons here from Madame Vacani. In recent years, the hotel has undergone a change of name and is now known as Mandarin Oriental Hyde Park.

On 28 April 2011, the night before Prince William's marriage to Catherine Middleton, the British Royal Family and their overseas cousins attended a dinner at the hotel. The guests arrived and departed through the Albert Gate entrance.

One of Hyde Park's main features is Rotten Row, a sand-covered bridleway that runs in a straight line near its southern boundary. There is much speculation about the origins of its name, with one theory being that it was once called 'route du roi', because it was the path that William III used to take when he walked between his home in Kensington Palace and St James's Palace. By all accounts, William seems to have been someone who enjoyed ill health and who was always waiting for the next disaster to befall him. Walking the route du roi in the dark made him intensely nervous. He was justified in fearing for his personal safety because Hyde Park was a notorious haunt of highwaymen during the late 17th century. As a result, William took the precautionary measure of having 300 oil lamps suspended from the trees along the route to light his way in the dark. Rotten Row therefore became the first English road to be illuminated at night.

If you walk through Hyde Park you will often see people riding on horseback along Rotten Row. It is particularly convenient for the Household Cavalry, whose horses are stabled nearby.

Eaton Square

SW1; TUBE: Sloane Square, Victoria;
RAIL: Victoria

King's Road

SW1; TUBE: Fulham Broadway, Sloane Square;
RAIL: Victoria

This very expensive London square was built between 1826 and 1855 by Thomas Cubitt (1788–1855). He cannily recognized the potential of the area around Buckingham Palace after serious work began on converting it into a lavish palace for George IV. The square was named after Eaton Hall in Cheshire, which is the country seat of the Grosvenor family who owned much of the land in this part of London. In common with so many other select London squares of the time, Eaton Square was built over a sewer, in an age when typhoid fever was extremely prevalent. The disease affected everyone from the poorest members of society to the Royal Family; Queen Victoria suffered from it in 1836, the year before she came to the throne and, in 1861, typhoid killed her husband, Prince Albert.

Nevertheless, its proximity to a noxious sewer did not deter members of society from moving into Eaton Square and its neighbouring streets. One of the square's earliest residents, at No. 13, was George FitzClarence, Earl of Munster (1794–1842). He was the eldest illegitimate son of William IV and Mrs Jordan, and married Mary, the illegitimate daughter of George Wyndham, 3rd Earl of Egremont.

Eaton Terrace, just around the corner, was a favourite haunt of George FitzClarence's cousin, Edward, Prince of Wales (later Edward VII). He took his mistresses to the apartments at No. 55, where the concierge, Mrs Rosa Lewis, was his friend. She later became the celebrated owner of the Cavendish Hotel in Jermyn Street. Edward's visits to Eaton Terrace ceased after he came to the throne in 1901, as he was required to lead a more discreet lifestyle.

Note the name. This is the King's Road and, until 1830, that is precisely what it was: a private road for the reigning sovereign and the privileged few who were considered important enough to be allowed to use it.

King's Road was built during the Restoration, following Charles II's succession to the throne in 1660, as a swift route for the royal party between Whitehall Palace and Hampton Court (see pages 148–50). London streets in the 17th century were narrow, uneven and congested with horses, carts, people, carriages and the smelly detritus that accompanied them, so it made sense to create a private short cut for royalty. Other well-connected people were allowed to use the road, provided that they produced a special copper pass, which bore the stamp of the monarch's monogram on one side and the words 'The King's Private Roads' on the other. George III later used the road whenever he travelled to his palace at Kew.

Royal Hospital Chelsea

Royal Hospital Road, SW3 4SR; ☎ 020 7881 5298;
www.chelsea-pensioners.co.uk; open Mon–Fri; ADMISSION: free;
TUBE: Sloane Square, Victoria; RAIL: Victoria

Popularly known as the Chelsea Hospital, its residents are called Chelsea Pensioners. They are veteran soldiers, and about 450 of them live here at any one time, divided into six companies.

The Royal Hospital has stood on this Chelsea site for over 400 years. It was established as a direct result of the English Civil War. Until then, Britain did not have a standing army, so there was no need to provide a home for its old and injured soldiers. However, all that changed after the Restoration. In 1681, Sir Stephen Fox (1627–1716), the first Paymaster General, suggested to Charles II that there should be an English equivalent of the Hôtel des Invalides in Paris. Sir Christopher Wren was appointed architect and Charles laid the foundation stone in 1682. The first soldiers took up residence in February 1692.

May Celebrations

The hospital's Figure Court contains a bronze statue of Charles II, which was designed by Grinling Gibbons (1648–1721). Each year, on 29 May, Oak Apple Day, which is Charles II's birthday and the anniversary of his formal restoration to the throne in 1660, the Chelsea Pensioners don tricorn hats, carry sprigs of oak leaves and adorn the statue with more oak leaves.

May is an important month in the calendar of the Royal Hospital because this is when the Chelsea Flower Show is held in part of the grounds. It has been held here since 1913, and is staged by the Royal Horticultural Society, one of whose former presidents was Prince Albert. There is a special

ABOVE *Charles II's statue is decorated each Oak Apple Day.*

preview on the Monday evening before the show opens the next day, which is always attended by several keen horticultural members of the Royal Family. In 2002, Prince Charles helped to design one of the gardens.

Close to the hospital is Royal Avenue. When William III and Mary II moved into Nottingham House, which became Kensington Palace (see pages 124–6) in 1689, they required a road that connected their new home with the Royal Hospital. Work started from the Chelsea end but it was never extended past the King's Road (see opposite).

Harrods

87–135 Brompton Road, SW1X 1BB; ☎ 020 7730 1234;
www.harrods.com/visiting; open daily; TUBE: Knightsbridge

You might expect to find a royal memorial in a cathedral or the chapel of a royal palace, but it is another matter to stumble across two of them when shopping in one of the world's most famous department stores. Nevertheless, shoppers in Harrods can combine some satisfying retail therapy with a thought-provoking visit to two memorials to the late Diana, Princess of Wales and her companion, Dodi Al Fayed (1955–97).

A shrine to them stands next to the Central Egyptian Escalator and was erected by Dodi's father, Mohamed Al Fayed, who owned Harrods until he sold it in 2010. On display is a wine glass that Diana used on her final evening in Paris, as well as the ring that Dodi bought for Diana on the day before their deaths. Debate still rages about whether this was an engagement ring, and also about Diana's thoughts on the matter. There is also a bronze statue of the pair, entitled 'Innocent Victims', located at Door Three.

Until December 2000, Harrods was the proud owner of four royal warrants: those of the Queen, Queen Elizabeth the Queen Mother, the Duke of Edinburgh and the Prince of Wales. A royal warrant is rather like a royal stamp of approval, as it proclaims that a particular business is patronized by a senior member of the Royal Family. The business has to apply for the royal warrant every five years and it is renewed if relations between the business in question and the royal person are still harmonious. Harrods had proudly displayed its four royal warrants for many years, not only outside the shop but also on all its merchandise, packaging and stationery. However, in January 2000, the Duke of Edinburgh announced that he would be withdrawing his royal warrant from Harrods at the end of that year because he no longer shopped there. Although this was a perfectly reasonable explanation, it was widely believed that the duke's decision did not concern his shopping habits so much as the accusations that Mohamed Al Fayed had made about his alleged involvement in arranging the car crash that killed Diana and Dodi.

The other three royal warrants were still operational, but Al Fayed announced that he would not apply for their renewal when the time came and, in December 2000, he had them all removed from the front of the building. They also vanished from everything else connected with Harrods.

Victoria and Albert Museum

Cromwell Road, SW7 2RL; ☎ 020 7942 2000; www.vam.ac.uk; open daily except 24–26 Dec; ADMISSION: free (except to some exhibitions); TUBE: Knightsbridge, South Kensington

When a building has a name like this, there is no need to ask which members of the Royal Family are associated with it. This world-class museum of the decorative arts was one of the projects that Prince Albert championed following the Great Exhibition of 1851. It was originally an amalgam of the Museum of Manufactures and the School of Design, which were both housed in rather makeshift quarters on the site now occupied by the Victoria and Albert Museum, or the V&A, as it is popularly known.

By the 1880s, it was clear that the museum's collections had swelled to such an extent that there was no longer space for them all. They needed a proper, purpose-built home, and in 1890 a competition was launched to find the best design. Aston Webb, the architect who later designed the Queen Victoria Memorial (see page 29) was the winner, but it was not until 1899 that Victoria laid the foundation stone. By now she was 90: it turned out to be the last major official engagement that she ever attended. At the ceremony, she announced that the building should henceforth be called the Victoria and Albert Museum.

The V&A was finally completed in 1909, at a cost of over £600,000, and was opened by Edward VII. As if anyone should be in any doubt about the museum's royal connections, the top of the central tower is shaped like a crown, and statues of Victoria and Albert and Edward VII and Queen Alexandra flank the main entrance. The museum contains many treasures, including some with royal connections. The Raphael Cartoons, which have

ABOVE *The V&A is a commanding architectural presence.*

their own gallery, were bought for the Royal Collection in 1623 by the future Charles I and were first lent to the museum by Queen Victoria; they are now on loan from Queen Elizabeth II. You can also see tapestries stitched by Mary, Queen of Scots, the wedding suit of James II, the Dark Jewel given to Elizabeth I by Sir Francis Drake and Holbein's miniature of Anne of Cleves.

Royal Albert Hall

Kensington Gore, SW7 2AP; www.royalalberthall.com;
☎ 020 7589 8212; open for performances; ADMISSION: contact box office
for details; TUBE: High Street Kensington, Knightsbridge

This part of London is so well stocked with memorials to Prince Albert, consort of Queen Victoria, that you might be forgiven for thinking it should be renamed 'Albertovia' or something equally appropriate. The Albert Memorial is nearby, but even its gilded magnificence pales in comparison with the vast red-brick dome of the Royal Albert Hall.

After the financial success of the Great Exhibition of 1851, Prince Albert suggested that the profits should be used to create a complex of museums, schools, colleges and a hall in South Kensington. The Kensington Gore Estate was duly bought the following year. However, the project to create a big concert hall failed to get off the ground and was still in limbo when Albert died unexpectedly of typhoid fever in 1861. Money was collected from the public to pay for the Albert Memorial and a concert hall, but it was not nearly enough to pay for both ventures. In the end, the money for the Hall of Arts and Sciences, as the Royal Albert Hall was originally called, was raised by selling 999-year leases on its seats. The design was begun by Captain Francis Fowke and completed by Lieutenant Colonel Henry Darracott Scott, and Queen Victoria laid the foundation stone in 1867. At the end of the ceremony, she dropped the bombshell that the hall should be given the prefix of 'Royal Albert'. The hall was opened four years later by Victoria's son, the Prince of Wales (later Edward VII), because his mother's emotions were so overwhelming that they prevented her being present at the opening ceremony.

ABOVE *The Royal Albert Hall viewed from Kensington Gardens.*

The Royal Albert Hall became a popular venue for concerts and balls, despite its appalling acoustics, which were not improved until 1968. In 1911, over 80 royal guests attended the Shakespeare Ball here, as they were all in London for the coronation of George V, which took place a few days later. In 1937, George VI's Coronation Ball was held here, and the tradition was continued for his daughter, Elizabeth II, in 1953.

A further memorial to Prince Albert can be found by the South Steps outside the Royal Albert Hall. This memorial was originally intended to commemorate the Great Exhibition. It was created by Joseph Durham in 1863, and was first erected in the grounds of the Royal Horticultural Society, moving to its present position in 1899.

Albert Memorial

Kensington Gardens, Kensington Gore, SW7 2AZ; ☎ 020 7495 0916; www.royalparks.org.uk; ADMISSION: fee for guided tours; TUBE: High Street Kensington, Knightsbridge

Opinion remains divided on the merits of the Albert Memorial. To some, it is a typically overblown example of the sort of mawkish, sentimental monument that Queen Victoria was so fond of erecting in memory of her dead consort, Prince Albert. To others, it is a wonderful example of High Victoriana, especially since it was restored in the late 1990s to all its original gilded glory.

At first sight, the memorial is certainly startling, especially when the sunlight catches its shiny surface. During the First World War, the gilding was removed for fear that it would act as a landmark for German Zeppelins hoping to bomb Kensington Palace. It stands 53 metres (175 feet) high, with seven tiers of statuary and enormous marble groups, which represent Asia, Europe, Africa and America. A white marble frieze runs around the base of the memorial, decorated with 187 life-size figures of celebrated musicians, poets, painters, architects and sculptors. The Gothic canopy is inlaid with semi-precious stones including jasper, onyx and carnelian, and topped with an orb and cross. In the middle of all this is a statue of Prince Albert himself, seated and wearing the collar of a Knight of the Garter, with the garter on his left leg. The catalogue of the Great Exhibition of 1851, which he championed and was held in nearby Hyde Park (see pages 112–13), lies open on his knees.

The monument cost £120,000, and some of the money was raised through subscriptions to the Royal Society of Arts, of which the prince had been president. It took 12 years to build, and was designed by George Gilbert Scott, who was knighted by his grateful queen after she first saw it in 1872. The bronze statue of Prince Albert was cast by John Henry Foley (1818–74), and was erected in 1875. To his grieving widow, the prince's memorial doubtless fell far short of reality, but at least she heartily approved of Scott's intention to create a shrine to Prince Albert's sainted memory.

ABOVE *The gilded figure of Prince Albert.*
BELOW *The memorial is ornately decorated.*

Kensington Gardens

W2 2UH; ☎ 020 7298 2000; www.royalparks.gov.uk;
TUBE: Bayswater, High Street Kensington, Lancaster Gate

In marked contrast to what often feels like the dusty sprawl of Hyde Park, Kensington Gardens seems much more intimate. Perhaps it is the knowledge that one of the great royal palaces lies within the park and that Kensington Gardens once formed its private garden.

The history of Kensington Gardens is closely linked with that of Kensington Palace (see pages 124–6), which stands near the western boundary of the gardens. The first royal occupants of the new palace were William III and Mary II, in 1689. Mary had a strong artistic and decorative eye, and she commissioned Henry Wise and George London to landscape the gardens in the formal Dutch style, with box hedging and rows of tulips. This was not a hit with the next royal incumbent, Queen Anne, who had all the plants dug up and replaced with a more relaxed, English style of planting.

However, Anne did approve of the formal wilderness, north of the palace, which William had commissioned from London and Wise. Work was interrupted by William's death, but Anne had barely succeeded to the throne before she told the gardeners to continue. The Orangery, which is still in use, was designed by Nicholas Hawksmoor and modified by Sir John Vanbrugh (1664–1726). It was built in 1704–05 near the entrance to the wilderness, and provided an outdoor room in summer and shelter for tender plants in winter. Anne was also responsible for the stone summer house, which originally stood at the south end of Dial Walk but now lies at the north end of the fountains, near Lancaster Gate.

In 1725–6, George I put his stamp on the gardens by installing some exotic animals, including wild cats, in the paddock. However, they did not stay here very long, and were relocated to the menagerie at the Tower of London (see pages 73–5) in 1727 after the death of the king. This move may have been the suggestion of Queen Caroline, wife of George II, who was a keen gardener and had her own ideas about the design of Kensington Gardens. She may have been less than enthusiastic at the idea of encountering tigers and civet cats whenever she took a stroll around the gardens of her new palace. Both the Broad Walk and the Round Pond, which was originally intended to be rectangular, were created during this time. The Queen's Temple, which still stands, was a revolving summer house designed by William Kent and built in 1734–5.

A Park for the 'Respectably Dressed'

George II followed the tradition of other royal parks by opening the gardens to the public, although he restricted the opening hours to each Saturday when the court was at Richmond. He also stipulated that only 'respectably dressed people' could be admitted, and that soldiers, sailors and liveried servants should be denied entrance. It was not until the 1830s, and the reign of William IV, that the public was allowed into the gardens at any time of the year. However, by this time the palace was no longer the home of the reigning sovereign, as Buckingham Palace (see pages 24–6) now fulfilled that function.

National Grief

In September 1997, the area of Kensington Gardens just outside the gates of Kensington Palace became the focus of an extraordinary outpouring of national mourning after the sudden death of Diana, Princess of Wales. The gardens near the Crowther Gates were covered in a blanket of tens of thousands of flowers, photos, cards and messages, all laid there in the memory of the princess, who had lived at Kensington Palace until her death.

OPPOSITE *Looking up Dial Walk.*
ABOVE *The Italian Gardens and Long Water.*

Kensington Palace

Kensington Gardens, W8 4PX; ☎ 0844 482 7777 (from UK), +44(0)20 3166 6000 (from outside UK); www.hrp.org.uk/kensingtonpalace; open daily; ADMISSION: adults ££, concessions ££, under-16s £, under-5s free; TUBE: High Street Kensington

If William III had not suffered from asthma, it is doubtful that Kensington Palace would ever have been built. When he and his wife, Mary II, came to the throne in 1689, following the hasty departure of the previous incumbent, James II, the official London palace was Whitehall. This was very near the Thames, making it convenient for visiting Parliament when it was sitting, but highly inconvenient for William whose chronic bronchial problems were exacerbated by the damp, riverside air. There was also the ticklish question of smell, as at the time the Thames was basically an open sewer into which all London's waste was eventually discharged (having polluted the city's other rivers, which flowed into the Thames, first). The royal noses would have been mightily offended by the rank stench that floated towards Whitehall on a warm day, and so William and Mary made it their first priority to find somewhere else to live.

They settled on Nottingham House, which was a Jacobean mansion in what was then the village of Kensington. It was too small, of course, so they commissioned Sir Christopher Wren to rebuild it. William and Mary must have been exacting clients for Wren, because they wanted everything done in a great hurry and Mary frequently visited the house 'to hasten the workmen'. In November 1689, her chivvying ended in disaster when some of the new buildings fell down and killed several workmen. Despite this, work continued and the Royal Family was in residence by Christmas, despite the fact that the house was far from finished.

Mary's instincts in telling the workmen to hurry were prophetic: she died of smallpox in the palace in 1694. This was a highly dangerous and disfiguring disease, and Mary insisted that everyone who had not had it should leave the palace before they caught it. William remained at the palace until his death in 1702, from complications that set in after he broke his collarbone in a fall from his horse.

Queen Anne, who suffered from ill health all her life and had to be carried to her coronation because of her degenerative arthritis, enjoyed living at the palace. Her husband, the Prince George of Denmark, was asthmatic and the 3rd Earl of Sheffield remarked that it was only the prince's heavy breathing that told his courtiers he was still alive. Anne died here in 1714, and the crown passed to her third cousin, George I.

Hanover Comes to Kensington

George, who left his divorced wife Sophia behind in Germany when he travelled to Britain to take the throne, liked Kensington Palace because it reminded him of his family home, Schloss Herrenhausen, in Hanover. His new palace needed renovating and three new state rooms were added: the Privy Chamber, the Cupola Room and the Withdrawing Room. William Kent, who at the time was barely known, made his name by painting all the ceilings and creating the *trompe l'oeil* on the King's Grand Staircase.

When George II and Queen Caroline moved into the palace on their accession in 1727, they were the last reigning monarchs to live here. Their turbulent family life was dramatically played out in the palace;

ABOVE *The gates of the palace.* RIGHT *The South Front, topped by William III's windvane.*

they had an almost pathological hatred of their eldest son, Frederick, Prince of Wales, which they made no secret of. Their enmity towards him was so pronounced that Caroline once said, 'Our first-born is the greatest ass, the greatest liar, the greatest *canaille* and the greatest beast in the world and we heartily wish he was out of it.'

When not shouting at the Prince of Wales, the king and queen kept busy by decorating the palace. They spent a lot of money on furniture and fabrics, but carried out little building work. Caroline died in 1737, after which many rooms in the palace were shut up and no longer used. When George died in his lavatory in the palace in 1760, an era ended. George III had no desire to live in the palace and it was neglected. It quickly became dilapidated, so it cost a small fortune to renovate it when some of the apartments were earmarked for various members of the Royal Family at the end of the 18th century. The Duke of Wellington was so incensed at the amount of money it cost to house the Royal Family that he described them as 'the damndest millstone about the necks of any government that can be imagined'.

One of these 'millstones' was Edward, Duke of Kent, fourth son of George III. Like his elder brother, who later became George IV, the duke had a talent for spending money that he did not own, and even had to leave the country at one point to escape his creditors. He returned in 1818 after the sudden death of Princess Charlotte, the heir to the throne, a year before. A new heir was needed, and quickly, so the duke married Victoria, Dowager Princess of Leiningen and on 24 May 1819 their daughter, Princess Victoria, was born in Kensington Palace. Her christening took place that June in the Cupola Room. The duke died the following January and his widow raised Victoria in the palace, having altered the State Apartments, against the wishes of William IV, so they could live in them.

The Victorian Age Begins

On the momentous morning of 20 June 1837, Princess Victoria was woken with the news that her uncle, William IV, had died and she was now queen. She and her mother moved into Buckingham Palace the following month, but Kensington Palace was still lived in by other members of the Royal Family, including the Duke and Duchess of Teck and their daughter, Princess Mary, who was born here. As a young woman, she became engaged first to Prince Eddy, Duke of Clarence, but he died in 1892, giving Mary a lucky escape from marriage to a man who was never far away from scandal. The following year, she married his brother, George, Duke of York (later George V). In the early 1930s, Queen Mary, as she was by then, was instrumental in renovating Queen Victoria's Apartments. By this time, the State Apartments were open to the public, having first been opened on Queen Victoria's 80th birthday on 24 May 1899.

Kensington Palace Today

Today, Kensington Palace is still home to some members of the Royal Family. 'KP', as it is popularly known by its inhabitants, has to combine three main functions: it is a private residence; a major tourist attraction; and a working palace. It is also a fascinating building, full of architectural and historical interest.

Diana, Princess of Wales Memorial Playground

Kensington Gardens, W8 4PX; ☎ 0300 061 2001; www.royalparks.org.uk; open daily; ADMISSION: free; TUBE: High Street Kensington

St Mary Abbots Church

Kensington High Street, W8 4LA; ☎ 020 7937 5136; www.stmaryabbotschurch.org; open daily; ADMISSION: £££ for concerts; TUBE: High Street Kensington

This is one of several London memorials to Diana, Princess of Wales. The playground is close to Kensington Palace, where she used to live, and is a place where children (up to the age of 12) can run around and enjoy themselves while their parents relax nearby. The playground includes a pirate ship, teepees and other structures that were all inspired by J. M. Barrie's *Peter Pan*. There is also a café.

Several churches have stood on this site, after the first one was built in the 12th century. Its replacement was built in 1370, but this was pulled down and replaced in the 1690s to create a suitably impressive church for William III and Mary II, who had moved into nearby Nottingham House (which later became Kensington Palace, see pages 124–6), which lacked a private chapel. William contributed towards the building costs and donated the pulpit and reading desk. However, this church was demolished in 1772 and rebuilt, before George Gilbert Scott was commissioned to build the present church in 1869–72.

In 1821, Kensington Church Street lay on the route of Queen Caroline's funeral cortège. Her funeral should have been a solemn occasion but the public treated it as a chance to vent their fury at what they saw as George IV's appalling treatment of her. He had prevented her taking any part at all in his coronation only a few weeks before, and had also instigated a trial at the House of Lords to investigate her supposedly adulterous behaviour – which many thought was a classic case of the pot calling the kettle black. When the funeral cortège entered Kensington Church Street it was greeted by a mob that threw obstacles in the way of the horses. The funeral procession had no option but to double back and go past Hyde Park (see pages 112–13), where further disruptions took place.

SOUTH LONDON

South-east London (see pages 129–38) is dominated by Greenwich, where the original palace was built in the 15th century. South-west London (see pages 139–50) has its own distinctive character and offers leafy royal parks and breathtaking vistas of the Thames.

Prince Consort Lodge

Kennington Park, SE11 4AS; not open to public; TUBE: Kennington, Oval

Lambeth Palace

Lambeth Palace Road, SE1 7JU; ☎ 020 7898 1200; www.archbishopofcanterbury.org; not open to public; TUBE: Lambeth North, Waterloo, Westminster; RAIL: Waterloo

If you are a prince consort you can pull strings that are not available to other people. This is why Prince Albert was able to persuade the organizers of the Great Exhibition of 1851 to allocate the adjoining site in Kensington Gardens (see pages 122–3) to the Society for Improving the Conditions of the Labouring Classes.

At the time, the conditions of the working classes in Victorian Britain were a national scandal – they were damp, insanitary, crowded and often inhumane. By contrast, the Model Lodge that was displayed at the Great Exhibition was designed by Henry Roberts to provide decent habitation, including what was then the luxury of an indoor lavatory. The design was subsequently used for housing in various parts of London.

After the exhibition closed, the lodge was moved to its present position in Kennington Park, where it became the home of two park attendants in addition to being a museum. An inscription below the balcony states 'Model houses for families erected by HRH Prince Albert'.

This has been the official residence of the Archbishops of Canterbury since 1207, when it was called Lambeth House and was the home of Stephen Langton (c.1157–1228). The oldest surviving part of the palace is the crypt, which dates from the 13th century; the chapel was built soon afterwards. The palace has been extended and modernized on various occasions over the centuries, including in 1553 when Queen Mary ordered that it should be refurbished for Cardinal Pole (1500–58); strangely enough, they died within hours of each other in 1558.

Drama was played out in the Guard Room in 1534 when Thomas More was interrogated by Thomas Cromwell after he refused to sanction Henry VIII's decision to appoint himself head of the Church. When the English Civil War broke out in 1642, Lambeth House, as it was still called, was taken over for public service and became a prison during the Commonwealth, with the chapel being used for dances. Naturally, the building was greatly damaged, and after the Restoration in 1660 the Great Hall had to be rebuilt under Archbishop Juxon (1582–1663).

Today, the Great Hall is a library that contains the leather gloves that Charles I is alleged to have handed to Archbishop Juxon on the scaffold, shortly before his execution in January 1649. The library also houses the medical reports of George III, whose life was blighted so severely by what is believed to have been porphyria.

OPPOSITE *The intricate façade of Hampton Court Palace (see pages 148–50).*

Old Royal Naval College

Greenwich, SE10 9LW; ☎ 020 8269 4747; www.oldroyalnaval
college.org; Painted Hall and chapel open daily
except 24–26 Dec; ADMISSION: free; TUBE: Cutty Sark DLR;
RAIL: Greenwich

This complex of four buildings is all that remains of the medieval Greenwich Palace, which was a favourite residence of the Tudor sovereigns. The original palace was built by Humphrey, Duke of Gloucester (1390–1447), who was the youngest brother of Henry V. He called it Bella Court and, as its name suggests, it was considered to be one of the most beautiful houses in medieval England. Humphrey was a cultured man and was the first private individual in England to create an important library, which he bequeathed to Oxford University, where it became the centre of what is now the Bodleian Library.

Humphrey was also a generous man. In 1445, he lent Bella Court to his nephew and niece, Henry VI (r.1422–61, 1470–71) and Margaret of Anjou (1429–82), for their honeymoon. Such kindness counted for nothing two years later when Humphrey fell out with Margaret, and she had him imprisoned and – it is said – murdered. Henry and Margaret moved into Bella Court with unseemly haste a few days after Humphrey's death. Henry VII had the palace rebuilt in 1490, renaming it Placentia, 'the pleasant place'. It was here that his son, the future Henry VIII, was born in June 1491 and married his first wife, Katherine of Aragon, in June 1509 and his fourth wife, Anne of Cleves, in January 1540.

Henry VIII loved Greenwich Palace. It was here that his daughters, Mary and Elizabeth, were born in February 1516 and September 1533 respectively. Henry's sole legitimate son, Edward VI, died at the palace in July 1553. He would have been appalled at the fate of the palace during the Civil War, when it was first put up for sale and then, when there were no takers, turned into a biscuit factory. After the Restoration in 1660, Charles II decided to rebuild the palace and call it the King's House, but only one block was completed when the project had to be suspended in 1669 for lack of money.

The Birth of the Naval Hospital

When William and Mary succeeded to the throne in 1689, they had little interest in the King's House because they feared that its proximity to the dank and smelly Thames would exacerbate William's asthma. Mary wanted the house to be demolished, which it was in 1694, and rebuilt as a naval hospital. However, the original design would have blocked the view of the river from the Queen's House (see pages 134–5), and vice versa, so the buildings were split into their current arrangement. Mary died before the work began, and the foundation stone for the new hospital was laid by Sir Christopher Wren, as architect, and John Evelyn (1620–1706), as treasurer, in June 1696. Work continued for the next 50 years, under a variety of different architects, including Sir John Vanbrugh, Nicholas Hawksmoor and James 'Athenian' Stuart. There are four blocks: King Charles's building, Queen Anne's building, King William's building and Queen Mary's building. Together, the buildings are considered to be the finest example of Baroque architecture in England. The only trace of Greenwich Palace still standing is the undercroft of Queen Anne's building.

The naval hospital was not a complete success and it was closed in 1869 amid accusations of ill-treatment and corruption. In 1873, the Royal Naval College moved here from Portsmouth, where it stayed until 1998. The buildings have since been taken over by the University of Greenwich and Trinity College of Music. Nevertheless, the grounds of the Old Royal Naval College, plus the Painted Hall and the chapel, are open to the public.

The Elephant and the Maypole

Nearby is Five Foot Walk, which is where George I landed on 18 September 1714, having succeeded to the British throne after the death of Queen Anne the previous month. He left his divorced wife in Hanover and brought with him two women, who must have been a comical sight as one was extremely fat and the other immensely thin. Sophia von Kielmansegg (assumed to be his mistress but

OPPOSITE *The ceiling of the Painted Hall.* ABOVE *King William Court is on the left and Queen Mary Court on the right.*

allegedly his half-sister), who was later created Countess of Darlington, was known as 'The Elephant' at court because of her size. Horace Walpole gave a vivid description of her: 'the fierce black eyes, large and rolling between two lofty arched eyebrows, two acres of cheeks spread with crimson, an ocean of neck that overflowed & was not distinguished from the lower part of her body, and no part restrained by stays.' The other woman was Ehrengard Melusina, Baroness von der Schulenburg, later created Duchess of Kendal, who was popularly called 'The Maypole' because she was so tall and thin. George had at least two daughters by her. Walpole had a strong opinion of her, too, describing her as 'a very tall, ill-favoured old Lady'.

Greenwich Park

SE10 8QY; ☎ 020 8858 2608; www.royalparks.gov.uk;
TUBE: Cutty Sark DLR; RAIL: Blackheath, Greenwich, Maze Hill

The oldest of the enclosed royal parks, Greenwich Park has stunning views across the Thames. It was created in 1433 when Humphrey, Duke of Gloucester, the brother of Henry V, enclosed the land around his home, which later became Greenwich Palace.

The park and the palace became favourites of that keen hunter of deer and women, Henry VIII; he managed to satisfy both appetites at Greenwich. May Day was a time of celebration, when Henry held regular sporting events in the park. On May Day 1515, Henry and his first wife, Katherine of Aragon, held a sumptuous picnic in the park for the Venetian ambassador. Every comfort had been provided, even to the extent of placing caged songbirds in the trees above the guests' heads. By contrast, the May Day revels of 1536 were an occasion for tension and fear for Henry's second wife, Anne Boleyn: it was the last time she ever saw her husband, as she was arrested for treason and sent to the Tower of London (see page 75) the following day. Soon after the accession of Anne's daughter, Elizabeth I, in 1558, the City of London held a magnificent party for her in Greenwich Park.

When Charles II returned from exile to take the throne in 1660, he commissioned the French landscape gardener André Le Nôtre to redesign the park. Many elms and Spanish chestnuts were planted during the same decade. In 1675, the Royal Observatory (see page 133) was built on the site of the Duke of Gloucester's home.

Greenwich Park was first opened to the public in the 18th century, but people really began to flock here a century later, as the railway line between Greenwich and London Bridge opened in 1838, and a steamboat service between Greenwich and Central London began in 1854. By this time, the park was still owned by the Crown, although the palace had long since been deserted by its royal residents.

The Sailor King

In 1935, the statue of William IV, which had originally been erected in King William Street in the City of London, was moved to King William Walk in Greenwich. This statue was created by Samuel Nixon (1803–54) in Foggit Tor granite. It is an appropriate site for the man who had joined the Navy as a midshipman at the age of 13 and became known as the 'Sailor King', as the National Maritime Museum is situated nearby.

BELOW *The statue of William IV in King William Walk.*

Royal Observatory

Blackheath Avenue, Greenwich, SE10 8XJ; ☎ 020 8858 4422; www.nmm.ac.uk/places/royal-observatory; open daily, except 24–26 Dec; ADMISSION: Astronomy Centre free; Flamsteed House and Meridian Line Courtyard adults ££, concessions £, under-15s free; Planetarium adults £, concessions £, children £; TUBE: Cutty Sark DLR; RAIL: Greenwich, Maze Hill

ABOVE *The time-ball on top of Flamsteed House.*

In March 1675, Charles II appointed John Flamsteed (1646–1719) the first Astronomer Royal. The next step was to build a suitable observatory in which Flamsteed could work. Various sites were proposed, but Sir Christopher Wren swayed the argument in favour of Greenwich Hill. On 22 June that year Charles duly founded the observatory. Flamsteed's first brief was 'to apply himself with the most exact care and diligence to the rectifying of the tables of the motions of the heavens, and the places of the fixed stars, so as to find out the so-much desired longitude of places for the perfecting of the art of navigation'.

Charles promised to buy some of the astronomical instruments that would be required, but, as happened so often with him, he failed to provide the money, so Flamsteed had to purchase the equipment himself. The astronomer carried out most of his work in the Sextant House.

In 1833, a time-ball – the first of its kind in the world – was erected on the top of Flamsteed House. This signalled the time to ships travelling along the Thames so they could adjust their chronometers if necessary. This time-ball still drops at precisely 1 o'clock each afternoon. Another important event took place in 1884, when it was formally announced that the Prime Meridian should run through Greenwich, giving it the longitude of 00° 00' 00". A brass strip on the ground marks this point.

London's appalling light pollution led to the transfer of the Royal Observatory from Greenwich to Herstmonceux, Sussex, in the late 1950s, and from here it later moved to Cambridge. The observatory buildings at Greenwich were taken over by the National Maritime Museum, which displays many important historical astronomical instruments.

Queen's House

Greenwich, SE10 9NF; ☎ 020 8858 4422;
www.nmm.ac.uk/places/queens-house; open daily; ADMISSION: free;
TUBE: Cutty Sark DLR; RAIL: Greenwich, Maze Hill

In 1605, James I gave Greenwich Park (see page 132) and Greenwich Palace to his wife, Anne of Denmark. This was probably intended as some consolation for their rather unsatisfactory marriage: modern historians consider that James was probably homosexual. In 1616, Inigo Jones was commissioned to build a new house for Anne in the grounds of Greenwich Park. However, work on the Queen's House did not progress far before she died in 1619.

'The House of Delights'

In 1629, Anne's son, Charles I, gave the unfinished building to his queen, Henrietta Maria, commissioning Jones to complete the project. The building was completed in 1640, much to the joy of Henrietta Maria who called it 'the house of delights'. Unfortunately, the Civil War intervened and in 1642 Henrietta Maria left England for Holland, where she hoped to raise the money to buy arms and equip Royalist soldiers. In November that same year, Parliamentary forces searched the Queen's House for weapons; they found no trace, but they confiscated the building. Many of the treasures within the house were sold, but the house was retained and used for the lying-in-state of Commonwealth generals.

Greenwich Palace was badly damaged during the Commonwealth and in 1662 Charles II decided that it would have to be pulled down and rebuilt. At the same time, he commissioned John Webb to enlarge the Queen's House, as this was to serve as a royal residence while Greenwich Palace was being reconstructed. After the Restoration, Charles's mother, Henrietta Maria, briefly returned to her old house in 1662, before moving to Somerset House (see pages 92–4). She died in Paris in 1669. In 1663, the Queen's House was given to Charles's wife, Catherine of Braganza, and in 1685 it became the property of James II's second wife, Mary of Modena (1658–1718), but she had little use for it. It was the same story when William and Mary came to the throne in 1689, so in 1690 it was given to the Earl of Dorset, who was the first Ranger of Greenwich Park.

In the meantime, work on rebuilding Greenwich Palace had come to a halt in 1669 through lack of money after only one wing was built, and it did not start again until 1694 by which time it had been decided to convert the palace into the Royal Naval Hospital (see pages 130–31). The design for the new hospital placed the Queen's House at its central point, so there would still be an uninterrupted space between the house and the Thames. The house became part of the hospital but its upkeep was very expensive.

When George I landed at Greenwich on 18 September 1714, he held his first official reception in the Queen's House the following day. In 1805, George III appointed Princess Caroline of Brunswick, the estranged wife of the Prince of Wales, as Ranger of Greenwich Park. The house became her official residence, but in 1806 she leased it to the Royal Naval Asylum, a school for sailor's orphans, in an attempt to clear her debts. The school moved out in 1933 and in 1937 the Queen's House was opened as part of the National Maritime Museum. It has since been restored to its 17th-century appearance.

RIGHT *The house was a royal residence from 1640–1806.*

Eltham Palace

Court Yard, Eltham, SE9 5QE; ☎ 020 8294 2548;
www.english-heritage.org.uk; open Sun–Wed; ADMISSION: adults ££,
concessions ££, children £, free to members of English Heritage;
RAIL: Eltham, Mottingham

There has been a royal connection with Eltham since at least 1086, when the Domesday Book recorded that the manor of Eltham was owned by Odo, Bishop of Bayeux and half-brother of William the Conqueror. In 1305, the manor house was rebuilt by Anthony Bek, Bishop of Durham, and given to Edward, Prince of Wales, who later reigned as Edward II. He presented it to his wife, Isabella of France (c.1294–1358), after their marriage in 1308 and she was a frequent visitor; the couple's second son, John, was born here in 1316.

Succeeding kings played their part in the history of Eltham Palace. Richard II instigated some improvements to the palace, which were carried out under the supervision of Geoffrey Chaucer, who was the Clerk of Works. The Great Hall, which is the most impressive part of the palace to have survived, was built in the 1470s, during the reign of Edward IV (r.1461–70, 1471–83). It still has the third largest hammerbeam roof in the country.

Medieval Modernism

The role of Eltham Palace as a favoured royal residence effectively came to an end during the reign of Henry VIII. He spent a great deal of time here as a boy, but in later life he much preferred nearby Greenwich Palace. His daughter, Elizabeth I, also favoured Greenwich over Eltham. The palace was sold off during the Interregnum, which followed the execution of Charles I, and was partially pulled down by its new owner. The Great Hall was used as a barn for the next two centuries and the rest of the palace was left in ruins.

This once-great palace would probably have rotted away had it not been for Stephen and Virginia Courtauld, who bought it in 1931 and began a lengthy restoration programme. Although it seems an extraordinary act in today's architectural climate of preservation orders and listed buildings, the Courtaulds built a highly contemporary, Art Deco house right next to the Great Hall so they could move seamlessly between the 15th and 20th centuries. They also landscaped the gardens, which included converting what was once the moat into a sunken garden. This extraordinary combination of medieval and modern was requisitioned by the army during the Second World War, but Eltham Palace is now owned by English Heritage and is open to the public.

TOP *Medieval and modern at Eltham Palace.*
BELOW *The palace was transformed in the 1930s.*

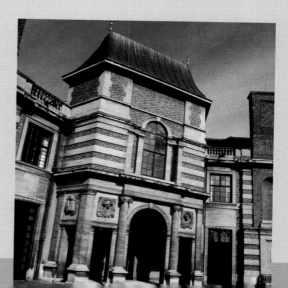

Rotherhithe

SE16; TUBE: Rotherhithe

This old area of London dockland was originally called Redriffe. Samuel Pepys knew it by this name, but it had already been thriving for centuries. In fact, it is believed that early in the 11th century, King Canute (r.1016–35) laid siege to London from here when he dug a trench that stretched from Rotherhithe to Vauxhall.

When the Domesday survey was carried out in 1086, Rotherhithe was part of the royal manor of Bermondsey. In the 14th century, a royal fleet was fitted out at Rotherhithe on the orders of the Black Prince and John of Gaunt, who were both sons of Edward III. Early in the 1400s, Henry IV (r.1399–1413) retreated to Rotherhithe, suffering from what was thought to be leprosy and which apparently killed him. An examination of his corpse in 1832 refuted this.

ABOVE *The South Dock Marina, Rotherhithe.*

The Cuckolding King

Downriver of Rotherhithe is Limehouse Reach, which begins at Cuckold's Point. This site was once marked by a pair of horns (the symbol of a cuckold) mounted on top of a pole. This was the starting point of the annual Horn Fair that proceeded to Charlton. According to legend, Cuckold's Point gets its name because King John seduced the wife of a local miller and, in order to pacify him, gave him this stretch of land.

The remains of a moated manor house, which was built for Edward III in 1361 and excavated in the 1980s, can be found at Bermondsey Wall East and Cathay Street.

Blackheath

SE3; RAIL: Maze Hill

Blackheath was once notorious for the highwaymen that made this stretch of the journey between Dover and London so dangerous. The road did not become safe until the surrounding area was developed into a residential suburb in the 18th century, and when the railway arrived in 1849 another wave of building commenced. Blackheath's position on the London–Dover road means that it has been the scene of important events in British history. In 1415, Henry V rode through Blackheath on his return to England after his victory at the Battle of Agincourt. During the Cornish Rebellion of 1497, Henry VII defeated Michael Joseph and his fellow Cornish rebels in a battle on the heath. In January 1540, Henry VIII travelled to Blackheath to meet his new queen, Anne of Cleves. The Elizabethan historian, William Lambard, wrote: 'Blackheath hath borne some gorgeous and pleasant spectacles but none so magnificent as that of King Henry VIII, when he brought in the Lady Anne of Cleves.' It was a splendid scene, in which Henry glittered with jewels and cloth of gold, and his bride-to-be was also in her finest clothes. Tents made from cloth of gold were pitched, and it was here that Henry and Anne met for the first time. The meeting was a diplomatic success, but it was a romantic and dynastic failure. The couple divorced within six months.

There was more spectacle and rejoicing on Blackheath when Charles II rode here on horseback to meet General Monck and his army on his restoration to the throne in May 1660. Cloth of gold might not have adorned the scene, but the route was thronged with happy people who were

ABOVE *The view across Blackheath, which has witnessed many royal events.*

longing to see their new ruler, delighted that the monarchy, and their old way of life, had returned.

The Ranger's House

Nearby is the Ranger's House, which was built in 1699–1700. It was the home of the Duchess of Brunswick, mother of Caroline, Princess of Wales, from 1807 to 1814. The duchess wanted to be near her daughter, whose marriage to the Prince of Wales (later George IV) was by then over in all but name and who attracted scandal. In 1815, the house became the official residence of the ranger of Greenwich Park (see page 132). The first resident ranger was Princess Sophia Matilda, the great-granddaughter of George II, who lived here until her death in November 1844. In 1902, the Ranger's House became a café after it was sold to the London County Council. It has now been restored and converted into an art gallery (run by English Heritage) that houses the Wernher Collection of silver and paintings.

Royal Botanic Gardens

Kew, TW9 3AB; ☎ 020 8332 5655; www.kew.org; open daily except 24–25 Dec; ADMISSION: adults ££, concessions ££, children free; TUBE: **Kew Gardens**; RAIL: **Kew Bridge**

In the 18th century, this area formed the private gardens of Frederick, Prince of Wales, which are today known as the Royal Botanic Gardens. At the time, Kew was a place of political intrigue, having grown in importance during the previous two centuries because of its close proximity to nearby Richmond Palace. Whenever the court sailed downstream to Richmond for the summer, away from the threat of plague and the stench of the Thames at Whitehall, all the courtiers followed and many of them settled in Kew.

Frederick was a very keen gardener, having already created a landscaped garden at Carlton House in London, and he set about doing the same thing at Kew. Frederick was greatly aided in this task by John Stuart, the 3rd Earl of Bute (1713–92), who was briefly prime minister in 1762–3. He helped the prince to design the gardens and to collect many of the plants and trees that became the basis of the world-renowned collection of the Royal Botanic Gardens. On 31 March 1751, Frederick died from complications that set in after he caught a chill while gardening in the rain. His widow, Augusta, continued to live at the White House, which was one of the residences within the gardens. She also continued to work on the gardens with Bute, prompting some ribald gossip about the nature of their relationship. Their work at Kew was helped by William Chambers (1723–96), who was the architectural tutor to Augusta's son, George, Prince of Wales, and a noted expert on Chinese culture. He undoubtedly had a very strong influence on the plethora of Chinese-inspired buildings that sprang up in the grounds of

Kew – the Chinese Pagoda is one of the few extant buildings from that time. Other buildings at Kew were inspired by other cultures as well. In 1761, Chambers also designed for Augusta the building that is now known as the Orangery; at the time, such structures were becoming the places in which to play cards, drink tea and entertain one's friends.

By the end of her life, Augusta was only an occasional visitor to Kew, but she had helped to landscape over 40.5 hectares (100 acres), which contained more than 2,700 species of plants. It was a colossal achievement and is commemorated in the Princess of Wales Conservatory at the Royal Botanic Gardens, which was opened by Diana, another Princess of Wales, in 1987.

ABOVE *The Palm House.* BELOW *The Chinese Pagoda dates from the time of George, Prince of Wales.*

Kew Palace

Royal Botanic Gardens, Kew, TW9 3AB; ☎ 020 8332 5655;
www.hrp.org.uk/kewpalace and www.kew.org; open Apr–Sept;
ADMISSION: adults £, concessions £, under-16s free (note, you must
buy a ticket to the Royal Botanic Gardens too); TUBE: Kew Gardens;
RAIL: Kew Bridge

Kew Palace is set like a miniature jewel within the vast expanse of the Royal Botanic Gardens (see page 139). The palace began life as the Dutch House and was built in red brick in around 1613 by a Dutch merchant called Samuel Fortrey. It was one of the first examples in Britain of a style of brickwork known as 'Flemish bond', in which the bricks are laid with their sides and ends alternating. The rounded gables gave the house its distinctive Dutch appearance. Fortrey lived here with his wife, Catherine, and their initials can still be seen above the entrance.

The Dutch House was leased in 1728 by Queen Caroline, who intended to use it as a royal annexe whenever she and her husband, George II, were staying at nearby Richmond Lodge. The Dutch House became a nursery for the royal children, and George III spent a lot of time here as a boy. Caroline also leased several other buildings and plots of land, including the White House which stood nearby. In 1731, the White House became the home of Frederick, Prince of Wales. He was the despised eldest son of George II and Queen Caroline, so even the thought of his nearby presence must have been vexatious to them. However, he and his wife, Augusta of Saxe-Gotha-Altenburg, were rare visitors to Kew until the death of Caroline in 1737. After that, they lived at Kew, devoting much of their time to creating what are now the Royal Botanic Gardens.

In 1772, the White House was taken over by Frederick and Augusta's son, George III, and his young family. George, Prince of Wales (who became the Prince Regent in 1811 and George IV in 1820) and his younger brother, Frederick, lodged nearby at Kew Palace. The freehold of the property was given to their mother, Queen Charlotte, in 1781.

Although the life of what we now know as the Royal Botanic Gardens continued to develop, and still flourishes today, Kew Palace enjoyed only a brief flowering. By 1818, it was the end of an era. On 13 July 1818, William, Duke of Clarence, and his younger brother, Edward, Duke of Kent, were both married in a joint ceremony at Kew Palace. A crisis had been triggered the previous year by the death of Princess Charlotte, the daughter of the Prince Regent, in childbirth. The Royal Family needed more heirs, and in effect the two brothers embarked on a race to see who could produce a child first. It was a sad irony that the Duke of Clarence had fathered numerous healthy, illegitimate children, most notably by his long-time mistress, Mrs Jordan, but none of his legitimate children survived early infancy. The Duke of Kent and his wife, Victoria, were more fortunate and produced a daughter who grew up to become Queen Victoria.

On 17 November 1818, Queen Charlotte died at Kew Palace, and it was closed. The Royal Botanic Gardens acquired the palace, with Queen Victoria's permission, in 1896, and it was opened to the public two years later. The present garden behind the palace, known as the Queen's Garden, was opened by Elizabeth II in 1969 and contains the classical busts of figures that originally stood in the innovative gardens of Carlton House, created in the 18th century by the Queen's ancestor, Prince Frederick.

RIGHT *Kew Palace was once a nursery for George II's children.*

Richmond Park

Richmond-upon-Thames, TW10 5HS; ☎ 020 8948 3209;
www.royalparks.gov.uk/Richmond-Park.aspx; TUBE: Richmond
(then bus); RAIL: Richmond (then bus)

Richmond Park has been a favourite royal hunting ground since the 13th century, when it was still known as Shene Chase. If you can manage to screen out the noise and sight of passing cars and aircraft, it is comparatively easy to picture the park as it might have been when Edward I knew it, thanks to its mixture of ancient broadleaf trees, wild deer and stretches of bracken.

In 1637, Charles I acted against the wishes of local residents and his own advisers by enclosing the park with a high wall that still stands today. At least he allowed pedestrians the right to walk through the park, which was a privilege that Princess Amelia (1711–86), one of George II's daughters, rescinded after she became the ranger of the park in 1747. Only her closest friends were allowed access to the park, a stricture that aroused so much local antagonism that she was forced to resign her position. Ladderstile Gate, near Kingston Hill, commemorates this victory of the people against the Crown.

TOP *Deer in Richmond Park.* ABOVE *Beverley Brook in Richmond Park.*

Richmond's Lodges

Princess Amelia lived at White Lodge, to the east of the park, while she was ranger. This Palladian villa was also a favourite residence of her mother, Queen Caroline, and had been commissioned by George II. In the 1870s–1900, White Lodge was the home of the Duke and Duchess of Teck, whose daughter, Mary, married the future George V in 1893. It was here, in June 1894, that Mary gave birth to her eldest son, who later became Edward VIII. In the 1920s, White Lodge was the home of the Duke and Duchess of York who, much to their horror, became

King George VI and Queen Elizabeth after the abdication of Edward VIII in 1936. In the mid-1950s White Lodge was taken over by the Lower School of the Royal Ballet School, and they are still here.

Pembroke Lodge, to the west of the park, also has an interesting history. It was originally the home of the park's molecatcher, but in 1780 George II gave the house to his friend, the Countess of Pembroke, after whom it became known. It later became the home of Elizabeth, Countess of Errol, who was the illegitimate daughter of the Duke of Clarence (later William IV) and his long-standing mistress, Mrs Jordan.

Richmond Palace

Old Palace Yard, Richmond-upon-Thames, TW9 1HP;
TUBE: Richmond; RAIL: Richmond

Once one of the great medieval royal palaces, all that remains now of Richmond Palace is the old gatehouse on the south side of Richmond Green, and a trio of houses in Old Palace Yard, which date from the reign of the Tudors. Old engravings of the palace show a sprawling building of several storeys, with many turrets and chimneys, standing on the banks of the Thames. There is a model of the palace at the nearby Richmond Museum.

Richmond Palace started life as a manor house in the 12th century. At the time, this area was known as Shene and was a popular hunting ground. Henry I acquired the manor house in 1125, although Edward III was the first king to spend a lot of time here and he also lavished money on the place. Edward died here in June 1377, dependent on his ambitious mistress, Alice Perrers, who had persuaded the servants to wrench the rings from his fingers. Edward's grandson, Richard II, inherited the throne and, with it, Shene Palace. It was his favourite summer residence, where he and his first wife, Anne of Bohemia (1366–94), entertained. However, medieval summers always brought the plague, and the disease killed Anne in June 1394. Richard experienced such intense grief that he ordered the destruction of Shene Palace. Nevertheless, some parts of it were left standing and were used by Henry V as the basis for a major programme of restoration.

Tudors and Stuarts

Shene was a particular favourite with Henry VII, and he had the palace rebuilt in grand style after it burnt down in 1499. It was at this point that its name was changed to Richmond, after Henry's earldom in Richmond, Yorkshire. Two of Henry VIII's children by Katherine of Aragon were born and died here, and in 1554 his daughter, Mary I, spent part of her honeymoon here after her marriage to Philip of Spain. In March 1603, the dynasty of the Tudors ended when Elizabeth I died in Richmond Palace.

Richmond Palace passed to the Stuart kings and was therefore an inevitable casualty of the Civil War of the 1640s. Most of the palace was destroyed after the execution of Charles I in 1649, and although Charles II later had it restored for his mother, she found it too bleak. The palace gradually fell down, until more memories than stones remained.

BELOW *The gatehouse is all that's left of Richmond Palace.*

Syon House

Brentford, TW7 6AZ; ☎ 020 8560 0882; www.syonpark.co.uk;
open Mar–Oct Wed, Thur, Sun and bank holiday Mon; ADMISSION: adults
££, concessions ££, children £; TUBE: Boston Manor (then bus);
RAIL: Kew Bridge (then bus)

Syon House has been the London residence of the Percys, the Dukes of Northumberland, for over 400 years. Contained within more than 80 hectares (200 acres) of parkland, the present house was built by Robert Adam in the 1760s and stands on the site of an abbey dedicated to St Bridget and named after Mount Zion, which was founded by Henry V in 1415. However, in common with so many similar English properties, Henry VIII acquired the abbey in 1539 during his Dissolution of the Monasteries. The Father Confessor of the nuns had already been executed in 1535 on Henry's orders for refusing to accept the king as the head of the new Church, and his body was exhibited on the gateway to the abbey to set an example to everyone else. In November 1541, Henry's fifth wife, Katherine Howard (c.1525–42), was accused of high treason and sent to Syon Abbey, to await the outcome of the investigations that were conducted into the behaviour of her alleged lovers; she was beheaded at the Tower of London in 1542. There is a rather macabre ending to Henry's association with the area. When he died in 1547, grossly overweight and suffering from complications caused by a leg ulcer, his body was carried from Whitehall Palace to Windsor Castle (see pages 152–3). En route it rested overnight in the ruined chapel at Syon Abbey. During the night, his lead coffin burst open and the following morning dogs were found lapping up his blood on the floor of the church.

Between 1547 and 1552, Edward Seymour, 1st Duke of Somerset, who was the Lord Protector of Henry's heir, Edward VI, built a house on the site. This passed to John Dudley, Duke of Northumberland (c.1502–53) – no relation of the current family – after Somerset's execution in 1552. He had aspirations to become the power behind the throne by making his daughter-in-law, Lady Jane Grey, queen. She was offered the crown in the Long Gallery at Syon and accepted it reluctantly: she was right to be wary, as she only reigned for nine days before being overthrown by Mary I and sent to the Tower, where she was executed. In 1594, Syon House passed into the hands of Henry Percy, 9th Earl of Northumberland (1564–1632), and it has remained in the family ever since.

There seems to be a path that leads from Syon House to the Tower, and the 9th Earl trod it in 1605 through no fault of his own. His cousin, Thomas Percy (1560–1605), dined with the earl at Syon and then travelled up to London where he joined forces with his fellow Roman Catholic conspirators, among whom was Guy Fawkes, and attempted to blow up Parliament the following day. Thomas Percy was shot while trying to escape and his hapless cousin, the 9th Earl, was considered to be guilty by association, and was detained in the Tower for 15 years on the orders of James I.

The 10th Earl, Algernon (1602–68), had happier royal connections, being the governor to Charles I's younger son, James, Duke of York from 1646–9. The duke and his siblings lived at Syon House in 1646 and Charles was able to visit them from time to time. The 3rd Duchess of Northumberland continued this educational tradition when she was official governess to the young Princess Victoria in 1831–7, at which point her 18-year-old charge became Queen Victoria.

Marble Hill House

Richmond Road, Twickenham, TW1 2NL;
☎ 020 8892 5115; www.english-heritage.org.uk;
open Sat and Sun for guided tours only;
ADMISSION: adults £, concessions £, children £,
free to members of English Heritage;
TUBE: Richmond; RAIL: St Margaret's

Marble Hill House was built in 1729 for Henrietta Howard (c.1689–1767), later the Countess of Suffolk, with money given to her by George II. She was the king's mistress for over 20 years and, as if that were not galling enough for his wife, Caroline, she was also one of her ladies-in-waiting. In the 1790s, the house was taken by another royal mistress, Mrs Fitzherbert. In 1785, she had entered into an illegal marriage with the then Prince of Wales, later George IV.

After being allowed to fall into a state of disrepair for a number of years, Marble Hill House has now been restored by English Heritage and one of its highlights is Lady Suffolk's Bedchamber.

Orleans House Gallery

Riverside, Twickenham, TW1 3DJ; ☎ 020 8831 6000; www.richmond.gov.uk/orleans_house_gallery; open Tue–Sun and bank holidays; ADMISSION: free; RAIL: St Margaret's

A 16th-century villa originally stood on this site, leased in 1702 by James Johnston, who was the Joint Secretary of State for Scotland under William III. A few years later Johnston commissioned James Gibbs to build a Baroque garden pavilion known as the Octagon. It was intended to amuse Caroline, Princess of Wales, who was married to the future George II, during a visit to the house.

In 1815–17, Orleans House was the home of the exiled Duc d'Orléans (1773–1850), who later returned to his native France and reigned as Louis Philippe I, King of the French, from 1830–48. Most of the house was demolished in the 1920s, although Gibbs's Octagon survived and is now part of the Orleans House Gallery, which stands on this site.

Bushy Park

Hampton Court Road, Hampton, TW12 1EJ; ☎ 020 8979 1586; www.royalparks.gov.uk/Bushy-Park.aspx; RAIL: Hampton Court, Hampton Wick, Teddington

This is the second largest of the royal parks and it spreads north of its nearest green neighbour, Hampton Court Park. These two parks have always been connected historically because originally they both belonged to the Knights Hospitallers of St John. In 1514, the land was acquired by Cardinal Thomas Wolsey. Irreconcilable differences between Wolsey and Henry VIII led to the cardinal's downfall, and in 1528 he gave all the land, along with his palace, to the king. Henry had the parks enclosed so he could use them for his favourite sport of hunting.

Bushy Park was now a royal possession and so it passed from sovereign to sovereign. Over the centuries, three of those monarchs made an important contribution to the park. The first king to make his mark was Charles I, who decided to create the artificial stretch of water in Bushy Park that we now know as Longford River.

The other main feature of the park was created on the orders of William III and Mary II, who were both keen gardeners. They ordered Sir Christopher Wren to design an avenue, which would provide a formal approach to Hampton Court Palace, running from Teddington Gate on the northern boundary of Bushy Park. This long avenue is lined on each side with a single row of horse chestnut trees and four rows of lime trees, and circles a small lake.

During the First World War, parts of Bushy Park were dug up and used to grow crops as part of the war effort. George V gave permission for Upper Lodge, one of the buildings in the park, to become a home for convalescent Canadian soldiers. Areas of the park were again put under the plough during the Second World War, and in 1942 it became the site of a US base called Camp Griffiss. The park was the headquarters of various Allied departments, and was where Operation Overlord, which was the codename for the D-Day landings of 1944, was planned.

ABOVE *Deer roam in the park.* BELOW *Heron Pond.*

Ham House

Ham, Richmond-upon-Thames, SW10 7RS;
☎ 020 8940 1950; www.nationaltrust.org.uk;
open Apr–Oct Sat–Thur; ADMISSION: adults ££,
children £, free to members of National Trust;
TUBE: Richmond; RAIL: Richmond

Coronation Stone

High Street, Kingston upon Thames, KT1 1EU;
RAIL: Kingston

Today, when we talk of someone being a 'whipping boy', we mean that they are taking the punishment or blame for something. But when Charles I was a boy, he had a real whipping boy who received punishments on his behalf. This was William Murray, who became a friend of the young prince.

Murray acquired Ham House in 1626 and had a good deal of the house remodelled in the following decade. During the Civil War, Murray became a Royalist and was made 1st Earl of Dysart. After his death in 1655, Ham House passed to his daughter, Elizabeth, who became the Countess of Dysart. She is believed to have been a member of the Sealed Knot, which was a secret organization that supported the exiled Charles II. It is also thought that she might have murdered her first husband in order to marry her second, who was the 1st Duke of Lauderdale, Secretary of State for Scotland. His high position gave the couple plenty of contact with Charles II and his consort, Catherine of Braganza. What is now the first-floor drawing room at Ham House was once the Queen's Bedchamber, furnished for Catherine.

Is this the coronation stone upon which seven Saxon kings were crowned? Yes, according to the names carved on the plinth at its base. This lump of sandstone, fenced in by faux Saxon railings, graces Kingston's High Street outside the Guildhall. Kingston is the oldest of only three Royal Boroughs in England, having gained its charter from King John in 1200, so it definitely has important royal connections. The name of the town suggests that the provenance of the stone may be correct, for surely 'Kingston' could be a corruption of 'King's Stone'? In fact, 'Kingston' comes from the town's Saxon name of Cyningestum, which meant the 'King's Estate'.

According to *The Anglo-Saxon Chronicle*, which was a contemporary account of events, there is no doubt that King Athelstan (r. *c.*925–39) and Ethelred the Unready (r.978–1016) were crowned in Kingston. There is less certainty about the other kings named on the plinth: Edward the Elder (r.899–924), Edmund (r.939–46), Eadred (r.946–55), Eadwig (r.955–9) and Edward the Martyr (r.975–8).

Kingston upon Thames has other royal connections. Elizabeth I founded Kingston Grammar School in 1561, and in 1628 Charles I granted a charter that allowed the town to hold the only market within an 11-kilometre (7-mile) radius. The present bridge was built in 1825, replacing the old stone bridge, and was opened by the Duchess of Clarence, who was later to become Queen Adelaide.

Hampton Court Palace

East Molesey, KT8 9AU; ☎ 0844 482 7777 (from UK),
+44 (0)20 3166 6000 (from outside UK); www.hrp.org.uk/
hamptoncourtpalace; open daily; ADMISSION: adults £££,
concessions ££, under-16s ££, under-5s free;
RAIL: Hampton Court

When Thomas Wolsey took out a lease on Hampton Court in 1514, he acquired a relatively modest building. However, his plans were far from modest, because not only was he highly ambitious in his career, but he also wanted to create one of the most splendid houses in Britain. He certainly succeeded in his aims, as he became a Cardinal and the Lord Chancellor in 1515, and his house gained the grandeur and opulence that matched his elevated position. Sadly for Wolsey, his status and eminence did not last. In 1528, he gave Hampton Court to Henry VIII in a vain attempt to appease the king who was incensed that Wolsey could not negotiate his divorce from Katherine of Aragon. Henry seized the house greedily, and had Wolsey imprisoned in the Tower of London (see pages 73–5).

Henry at Hampton Court

Henry set about turning Hampton Court into a royal palace. He loved the place, although it had unhappy memories for him because it was here in October 1537 that his third wife, Jane Seymour, died from complications after giving birth to the son he had craved for so long. In the autumn of 1541, Henry's fifth wife, Katherine Howard, was accused of adultery, a crime of high treason that was punishable by death. Ironically, Henry was given the news of her infidelity that November at Hampton Court, minutes after the couple had attended a thanksgiving service for their marriage. Katherine was confined to her rooms at the palace, but one day she managed to break free and ran along what is now called the Haunted Gallery to the door of the Chapel Royal, where Henry was

attending a service. Before Katherine was able to reach the door she was captured by the guards and dragged back to her quarters. Legend has it that her ghost can still be seen and heard, rushing up and down the gallery. There is a curious coda to this story. In December 2003, it was announced that security cameras at the palace had picked up some ghostly activity, and clearly showed a figure in a cloak opening and shutting the doors in one of the exhibition areas. Although some of the guides at the palace wear period costume, none of them wear anything like the clothes that were pictured on camera.

Hampton After Henry

After Henry VIII's death in 1547, Hampton Court continued to be a favourite royal palace, partly because Henry had created such a lavish set of buildings that they were the acme of comfort in what was often a very uncomfortable age. Although many of Henry's rooms were either demolished or altered during the modernizations carried out by Sir Christopher Wren at the behest of William III and Mary II in the 1690s, enough of them still stand to give a good idea of life at the Tudor court. For instance, Elizabeth I enjoyed attending elaborately produced plays in the Great Hall.

When James VI of Scotland succeeded to the throne of England in 1603 and became James I of England, he delighted in developing the surrounding land so he could enjoy his favourite sport of hunting.

ABOVE *A carving of one of the King's Beasts.* RIGHT *Henry VIII's coat of arms above the doors of the central gateway.*

His son, Charles I, spent his honeymoon in the palace in 1625 and later commissioned ornamental lakes and ponds for the grounds. However, Hampton Court switched from being a palace to a prison during the English Civil War, when Charles was detained here on the orders of Oliver Cromwell in 1647. In the year of Charles I's execution, 1649, Parliament put Hampton Court on the open market, saying that the profits would be used to clear the royal debts and 'for the benefit of the Commonwealth'. The palace was sold in 1652 but bought back the following year, after Oliver Cromwell became Lord Protector. He moved into the palace with his family, and lived here until his death in 1658.

After the Restoration in 1660, Hampton Court once again became a royal palace, and Charles II tried to trace all the royal treasures that had been sold during the Civil War. Like his father, Charles spent his honeymoon at Hampton Court. However, he was hardly the most faithful husband and later installed various mistresses in lodgings on the estate, including Barbara Villiers, Lady Castlemaine (1641–1709).

When William III and Mary II came to the throne in 1689, they quickly commissioned Wren to modernize Hampton Court. The original plan was to raze all the buildings, with the exception of the Tudor Great Hall, but a combination of Mary's early death and an ever-diminishing budget prevented such radical changes taking place. William was intimately involved in Wren's improvements, but he did not live long enough to enjoy them as he fell from his horse while out riding in Hampton Court Park in 1702, and died a short while afterwards.

The Last of Hampton Court's Kings

The first two Hanoverian kings were the last monarchs to live at Hampton Court. George I's court was considered dull, but his son made up for that when he became king in 1727. George II brought his family here every summer, and commissioned William Kent to design the rooms now known as the Cumberland Suite for his second son, the Duke of Cumberland. George had no desire to build anything similar for his eldest son, Prince Frederick, whom he despised.

Hampton Court's life as a royal palace that housed the full court came to an abrupt end in 1737 when Queen Caroline, wife of George II, died. George continued to visit the palace, but never again with a full retinue. George III had no desire to live here and 40 members of staff were left to look after the palace. Gradually, the furniture and treasures were removed to other palaces, although these were later returned to Hampton Court during a long phase of restoration in the 19th century.

The palace survived the two world wars almost unscathed, despite the number of bombs that rained down on London in the 1940s. It was not so lucky in March 1986 when a fire broke out, causing damage to the King's Apartments. Restoration took six years but enabled the rooms to be returned to their 18th-century appearance. The restored King's Apartments were reopened by the Queen in July 1992. Ironically, a serious fire broke out in Windsor Castle in November that same year, causing extensive damage. Many of the craftsmen who had worked with such care at Hampton Court were once again pressed into service at Windsor.

DAY TRIPS FROM LONDON

The places described in this chapter can be reached by train from London in less than an hour. They include the iconic Windsor Castle and the glorious Jacobean splendour of Hatfield House.

Windsor Castle

Windsor, Berkshire, SL4 1NJ; ☎ 020 7766 7304; www.royalcollection.org.uk; open daily; ADMISSION: prices vary according to areas of castle visited – adults ££–££££, concessions ££–££££, under-17s £–££, under-5s free; RAIL: Windsor

Windsor Castle has been standing for over 900 years, making it the oldest occupied palace in Europe. It is also the largest palace in the world, and fulfils the twin roles of being a private weekend home for the Queen and a royal palace in which state duties are carried out. The castle's most iconic image is the Round Tower, which was built in the 1170s to replace the original wooden structure erected during the reign of William the Conqueror.

Windsor Castle has much to offer, including the medieval gem of St George's Chapel. This is the resting place of 10 monarchs (Edward IV, Henry VI, Henry VIII, Charles I, George III, George IV, William IV, Edward VII, George V and George VI). The chapel is dedicated to St George, who is the patron saint of the Order of the Garter. This is the oldest order of chivalry in Britain and was founded by Edward III in 1348. The order consists of the reigning monarch and 24 knights, plus royal knights.

Windsor Castle is a working palace, so some areas of it, such as the State Apartments, may be closed to the public at certain times of the year because they are in use. The Semi-State Apartments, which were George IV's private apartments, are open during the winter.

Queen Victoria loved the castle. On 14 December 1861 her adored husband, Prince Albert, died here. For the rest of her life she kept his bedroom, the Blue Room, exactly as he had left it. She developed a lifelong dislike of the colour blue because of its association with Albert's death.

One of the most famous showpieces at the castle is Queen Mary's Dolls' House, whose miniature world (the scale is 1:12) is so perfect that it even has flushing lavatories. The architect, Sir Edwin Lutyens (1869–1944), built it for Queen Mary in 1921–4. It was created as a showcase for the very best British artists and craftsmen, and over 1,500 of them worked on its contents.

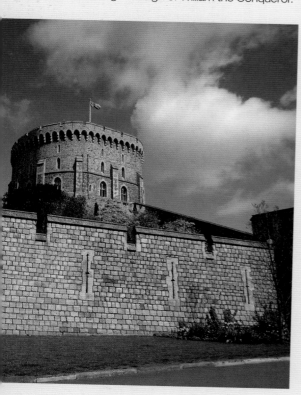

PREVIOUS PAGE *Hever Castle (see page 155).* ABOVE AND LEFT *Windsor Castle is an imposing building.* RIGHT *The Long Walk.*

Runnymede

Old Windsor, SL4 2JL; ☎ 01784 432891; www.nationaltrust.org.uk;
open daily except 25–26 Dec and 1 Jan; ADMISSION: free; RAIL: Egham

This beautiful stretch of countryside was once the site of the Witan Council, which was the council of Anglo-Saxon kings, during the reign of Alfred the Great in the ninth century. His castle was in Old Windsor. However, Runnymede is most famous for its associations with another king and what is, to date, the closest Britain has ever got to a written constitution.

In the early 13th century, King John's leadership and foreign policy left a lot to be desired. As a result of his actions, he found himself in a headlong clash with the barons, who held estates given to them by the monarchy, and in May 1215 the rebellious barons declared war against the king. After endless negotiations, both sides met at Runnymede on 15 June 1215 to sign an agreement called Magna Carta. It contained 63 clauses that aimed to control the powers of the ruling monarch as well as his sheriffs. The final section declared that a council of 25 barons would be entitled to declare war on the king if he infringed Magna Carta.

And infringe it he did, because John soon obtained the Pope's condemnation of the agreement. The barons took up arms, leading to civil war, and offered the crown to Prince Louis of France. Louis was poised to arrive on English shores when John died suddenly in 1216. His son took the throne, becoming Henry III, and the barons united to repel the impending invasion of Louis and his men.

Although Magna Carta held little significance in England for centuries, it is now regarded as an important influence on the English constitution and has been used as a model by many developing nations when creating their own constitutions.

ABOVE *The Magna Carta Memorial at Runnymede.*

Hever Castle

Hever, near Edenbridge, TN8 7NG; ☎ 01732 865224;
www.hevercastle.co.uk; open daily Apr–Oct, restricted opening
Nov–March; ADMISSION: adults ££, concessions ££, under-15s ££;
RAIL: Edenbridge (then taxi), Hever (then walk)

Two of Henry VIII's wives are associated with Hever Castle. It was the family home of the Bullen family from the early 1500s, and is where Anne Boleyn (her surname had various spellings, as was common at the time) grew up. Her father, Sir Thomas, was a courtier to Henry VII and embarked on many diplomatic missions on the king's behalf. As a result of her father's connections, Anne became part of the household of Archduchess Margaret of Austria and later became a maid of honour to Henry VIII's sister, Mary, who was married to Louis XII of France (r.1498–1515). After Anne returned to the English court she became a lady-in-waiting to Queen Katherine, and it was then that Henry VIII began to notice her. His marriage to Katherine had been happy at first but now it was blighted by her apparent inability to bear him a son and heir. Henry knew that he had to secure the succession, and the only way to do that was to find another wife. Anne seemed the perfect choice, and the couple were married in secret in January 1533, several months before Henry was divorced. Anne was crowned in June 1533 and gave birth to a daughter, Elizabeth (later Elizabeth I), that September. Unfortunately for her, she failed to produce a living male heir. Henry had to get rid of her, and she was tried and found guilty of treason on 15 May 1536. Four days later, Anne was executed at the Tower of London (see page 75).

After the death of Anne's parents in 1538, Henry took over the castle. His fourth marriage, to Anne of Cleves, was annulled within six months. The castle was given to her as part of her divorce settlement.

BELOW *Hever Castle is surrounded by a moat.*

Hatfield House

Hatfield Park, Great North Road, Hatfield, AL9 5HX; ☎ 01707 287010; www.hatfield-house.co.uk; open Apr–Sept Wed–Sun and bank holiday Mon; ADMISSION: prices vary according to areas visited – adults ££–£££, concessions ££–£££, children £–££; RAIL: Hatfield

ABOVE *The east façade and gardens at Hatfield House.*

Hatfield House is closely linked with Elizabeth I. She spent much of her childhood here with her half-brother Edward (later Edward VI). Life became more difficult after her half-sister, Mary, became queen in 1553, and at one point she was sent to the Tower of London (see pages 73–5), having been accused of taking part in a rebellion against Mary. She was freed and returned to live at Hatfield Palace, as it then was, in 1555.

Elizabeth was sitting under an oak tree in the garden on the morning of 17 November 1558 when she heard the news that her sister was dead and she was queen. She is reputed to have said 'It is the Lord's doing, and it is marvellous in our eyes'. The new Queen Elizabeth held her first Privy Council in the Great Hall three days later. She appointed William Cecil (later Lord Burghley) as her Principal Secretary, a post he held for the rest of his life. When he died in 1598, his son, Robert, took over the position. One of his duties was to ensure the smooth succession of James VI of Scotland to the English throne (as James I) on Elizabeth's death.

James did not care for Hatfield. He preferred Theobalds House, which was owned by Robert Cecil and had been refurbished to make it suitable for visiting royalty. James suggested that they swapped properties. When Robert Cecil took over the property, he had three sides of the palace pulled down and a new house built in the latest style. Only the Great Hall remained from the old palace, and it can still be visited today.

Among the rooms on show at Hatfield House is King James's Drawing Room, with a life-size statue incorporated into the chimney piece. In the garden, an oak tree marks the spot where Princess Elizabeth was told that she had become queen.

Further Reading

Arnold-Baker, Charles, *The Companion to British History*, Routledge, 2001

Bird, Charles, *Curiosities of London and Westminster*, S.B. Publications, 2003

Buckingham Palace, Royal Collection Enterprises, 2002

Clarence House, Royal Collection Enterprises, 2003

David, Saul, *Prince of Pleasure*, Little, Brown, 1998

Fraser, Antonia, *King Charles II*, Weidenfeld & Nicolson, 1979

Fraser, Antonia, ed., *The Lives of the Kings & Queens of England*, Weidenfeld & Nicolson, 1975

Glinert, Ed, *The London Compendium*, Penguin, 2004

Hampton Court Palace, Historic Royal Palaces, 2002

Hampton Court Palace, The King's Apartments, Historic Royal Palaces

Hibbert, Christopher, *London*, Penguin Books, 1980

Hilliam, David, *Crown, Orb and Sceptre*, The History Press, 2009

Hilliam, David, *Kings, Queens, Bones and Bastards*, The History Press, 2004

Humphreys, Rob, *The Rough Guide to London*, Rough Guides, 2003

Kensington Palace, Historic Royal Palaces, 2001

Impey, Edward, and Parnell, Geoffrey, *The Tower of London*, Merrell Publishers, 2000

Lamont-Brown, Raymond, *Royal Poxes and Potions*, Sutton, 2001

Longford, Elizabeth, *The Oxford Book of Royal Anecdotes*, Oxford University Press, 1991

Panton, Kenneth, *London*, Tempus Publishing, 2001

Prochaska, Frank, *Royal Lives*, Oxford University Press, 2002

Robinson, John Martin, *Buckingham Palace*, Royal Collection Enterprises, 2000

Tames, Richard, *London*, The Windrush Press, 2002

The Banqueting House, Historic Royal Palaces, 2000

The Banqueting House in the Seventeenth Century, Historic Royal Palaces, 1996

The Tower of London, Historic Royal Palaces, 2002

Weinreb, Ben, and Hibbert, Christopher, ed., *The London Encyclopedia*, Macmillan Reference Books, 1995

Weir, Alison, *Britain's Royal Families*, The Bodley Head, 1989

Weir, Alison, *The Six Wives of Henry VIII*, Vintage, 2007

Wittich, John, *Discovering London Curiosities*, Shire, 1997

Acknowledgements

I grew up listening to stories about London. They were told to me by my grandfather, father and mother, who all had a particular love and fascination for the City of London in which they worked. Later, when I lived in London, I became completely captivated by its romance and history, and the knowledge that reminders of its story were everywhere, from thought-provoking street names to medieval jetties poised above modern shop-fronts. So I was thrilled when Jo Hemmings at New Holland asked me to write this book. I would like to thank her for giving me the chance to write it, and to Guy Hobbs for inviting me to revise it for this new edition. I would also like to thank the rest of the New Holland team who have worked on the book, especially my editors Camilla MacWhannell, Rose Hudson and Gareth Jones on the first edition and Clare Hubbard for this revised edition, for all their help and expertise. Many thanks, too, to Ricky Leaver for his wonderful photographs, and to Chelsey Fox and Bill Martin who, as ever, provided exactly the right support and encouragement.

All photographs by Ricky Leaver except for the following: p 1: stuartrtaylor/iStockphoto; pp 2–3: Graeme Robertson/Getty Images; p 11: Anwar Hussein Collection/WireImage; p 14: Anwar Hussein/WireImage; pp 16–17: LEON NEAL/AFP/Getty Images; p 18: Getty Images; pp 20–21: Tim Graham/Getty Images; p 87 bottom: DavidCallan/iStockphoto; p 90: Duchy of Lancaster; p 91: Alberto Arzoz; p 104: godrick/iStockphoto; p 106 Kamira/Shutterstock; p 109: © Robert Stainforth/Alamy; p 118: Qweek/iStockphoto; p 119: track5/iStockphoto; p 127: Photolibrary/Travelshots; p 130: peterspiro/iStockphoto. p 131: stocknshares/iStockphoto; p 139 top: Kamira/Shutterstock; p 151: whitemay/iStockphoto; p 154: Adrio/iStockphoto; p 155: grahamheywood/iStockphoto; p 156: stocknshares/iStockphoto.

Index

Adam, Robert 144
Adelaide, Queen 36, 39, 79, 147
Albert Memorial 120, 121
Albert, Prince Consort 26, 72, 84, 112, 116
Alexandra, Queen 37, 39
    statues of 70, 119
Alfred, Duke of Edinburgh 36
Amelia, Princess (daughter of George II) 142
Andrew, Duke of York 10, 11, 15
Anne, Queen 30, 34, 39, 51, 55, 131
    Kensington Gardens 122
    Kensington Palace 124
    and London churches 68, 81, 96
    Queen Square 107
    St Paul's Cathedral 62, 63
Anne of Bohemia 143
Anne of Cleves 51, 119, 130, 138, 155
Anne of Denmark 51, 64, 92
    and the Queen's House 134
Anne, Princess Royal 10, 11, 13, 14–15, 36
    christening 26
    and St Anne's Church 81
    wedding 51
Arthur, Duke of Connaught and Strathearn 36
Arthur, Prince (son of Henry VII) 61, 66
Athelstan, King 147
Augusta, Princess of Wales 139, 140

Bank of England 71
Banqueting House 6, 34, 44, 46–7, 54
Birdcage Walk 28
Blackheath 138
Boleyn, Anne 52, 64, 75, 132
    and Hever Castle 155
British Library 108–9
Buckingham Palace 24–6, 30, 36
Bushy Park 36, 146

Canute, King 137
Carlton House Terrace 41, 56
Caroline of Brunswick 34, 38, 40, 48–51, 138
    funeral cortege 112, 127
    and Queen's House 134
Caroline, Queen (wife of George II) 32, 51, 112
    Hampton Court 150
    and Henrietta Howard 145
    Kensington Gardens 122
    Kensington Palace 124–6

Kew Palace (the Dutch House) 140
    Orleans House 145
    Richmond Park 142
Catherine of Braganza 37, 91, 94, 110, 134, 143
Catherine, Duchess of Cambridge 16, 17, 51
Charles I, King 21, 37, 119
    statue of 87
    trial 52–3
Charles II, King 23, 28, 30, 34, 37, 40, 51
    coronation 74, 75
    statues of 83, 117
Charles, Prince of Wales 10, 11, 13–14
    and the Chelsea Flower Show 117
    christening 26
    and Clarence House 36
    wedding 63, 113
Charlie, Bonnie Prince 96
Charlotte, Princess (daughter of George IV) 39, 56, 126, 140
Charlotte, Queen (wife of George III) 24, 81, 94, 107, 140
Churchill, Arabella 40
Cibber, Caius Gabriel 76, 83
Clarence House 14, 36
Clockmakers' Company Museum 70
Constitution Hill 23, 32
Cornwall, Duchess of (Camilla Parker Bowles) 14
Coronation Stone 147
Coutts & Co 89
Crown Jewels 75
Crystal Palace 113
Cumberland Terrace 102, 104

Diana, Princess of Wales 14, 16, 17, 33
    funeral 51
    and Kensington Palace 123
    memorial in Harrods 118
    Memorial Playground 127
    Royal Botanic Gardens 139
    wedding 63, 113
Duke of York Column 41

Eadred, King 147
Eaton Square 116
Eddy, Prince, Duke of Clarence 126
Edmund, King 147
Edward I, King 51, 60, 66, 67, 74, 86, 101
    and Charing Cross 87
    Richmond Park 142
Edward II, King 51, 78, 95, 136

Edward III, King 54, 101, 137, 143, 152
Edward IV, King 136, 152
Edward V, King 48, 51, 75
Edward VI, King 69, 92, 144
    Greenwich Palace 130
    Hatfield House 156
    Savoy Chapel 90
Edward VII, King 26, 29, 63, 114, 152
    lying-in-state 52
    as Prince of Wales 39, 116, 120
    and the Royal London Hospital 70
    statue of 41
    and the Victoria and Albert Museum 119
Edward VIII, King 10, 48, 104, 115
    and the Abdication Crisis 39, 104–5
    Richmond Park 142
Edward, the Black Prince 64, 68, 137
Edward the Confessor 48, 52, 70
Edward, Duke of Kent (son of George III) 126, 140
Edward the Elder 147
Edward the Martyr 147
Edward, Prince, Earl of Wessex 10, 11, 15
Eleanor of Aquitaine 66
Eleanor of Provence 74
Eleanor, queen of Edward I 87
Elizabeth I, Queen 30, 34, 51, 58, 59, 60, 69
    statue of 72, 97
Elizabeth II, Queen 10, 11, 84, 119
    birth 155
    coronation 51, 75
    Golden Jubilee 42, 51, 63
    as Princess Elizabeth 10, 115
Elizabeth, Queen, the Queen Mother 13, 36, 89
    lying-in-state 52
    and the Queen Elizabeth Gate 114
    Richmond Park 142
    St Paul's Cathedral 63
    statue of 37
Elizabeth of York 51, 64
Eltham Palace 136
Ely Place 101
Ernest, Duke of Cumberland 104
Ethelbert, King of Kent 70
Ethelred II, King 78

FitzClarence, George, Earl of Munster 116
Fitzherbert, Mrs Maria 145

Frederick, Duke of York 41
Frederick, Prince of Wales 56, 126, 139, 140, 150

George of Denmark, Prince 51, 124
George, Duke of Cambridge 81
George I, King 88, 107
  mistresses 131
George II, King 24, 32, 70, 81, 89, 91
  Hampton Court 150
  and Henrietta Howard 145
  Kensington Gardens 122
  Kensington Palace 124-6
  Kew Palace 140
  King's Library 108
George III, King 24, 27, 38, 40, 41, 51, 56, 70
  British Library 108
  statue of 89
George IV, King (Prince Regent) 24, 30, 40, 41, 72, 89
  coronation 48, 112
George V, King 10, 29, 39, 120, 142
George VI, King 10, 13, 36, 39
  coronation 75, 120
Gibbs, James 58, 88, 96, 145
Gold State Coach 27, 63
Gray's Inn 100
Great Exhibition (1851) 100, 112–13, 119, 120
  and the Albert Memorial 121
  the Model Lodge 129
Great Fire of London (1666) 66, 67, 68, 72
  Monument to the 76–7
  and St Bride's Church 98
  and St Dunstan-in-the-West church 97
  St Paul's Cathedral 62
  and Somerset House 94
  and Temple Bar 64
Great Plague 76, 91, 94
Green Park 32
  Royal Gun Salutes 19
Grey, Lady Jane 48, 69, 75, 108, 144
Guards' Museum 28
Guildhall 56, 69, 70, 72
Gwyn, Nell 38, 88, 91, 110

Ham House 147
Hampton Court Palace 116, 148–50
Harrods 118
Harry, Prince 17, 36
Hatfield House 156
Hawksmoor, Nicholas 107, 122, 130
Helena, Princess 38
Henrietta Maria, Queen 37, 92, 94, 134, 143

Henry I, King 52, 58, 59, 66, 142
Henry II, King 78, 95
Henry III, King 48, 74, 78, 106, 154
Henry IV, King 48, 137
Henry, Prince (son of James I) 88
Henry V, King 51, 61, 79, 130, 132
  Blackheath 138
  Richmond Palace 143
  Syon House 144
Henry VI, King 75, 130
Henry VII, King 51, 54, 61, 64, 84, 86, 138, 152
  Richmond Palace 143
  Windsor Castle 152
Henry VIII, King 30, 32, 34, 44, 67, 85, 129
  and Anne Boleyn 52, 64, 75, 132, 155
  divorce from Katherine of Aragon 61, 66, 78
Henry, Duke of Cumberland 38
Holborn Circus 100
Horse Guards Parade 6
  Beating Retreat 19
  Changing of the Guard 44
  Trooping the Colour 6, 19, 44
Howard, Catherine 75, 144, 148
Humphrey, Duke of Gloucester 130, 132
Hyde Park 103, 112–15

Ireland Yard 66
Isabella of France (wife of Edward II) 136

James I, King 20, 22, 28, 30, 51, 52, 144
  coronation 74
  statue of 64
James II, King 23, 34, 46, 82, 96, 119, 124, 134
  as Duke of York 144
  mistresses 40, 85
James of Scotland, Prince 74–5
Jewel Tower 53, 54
John, King 66, 98, 137
  and the Magna Carta 154
John of Gaunt, Duke of Lancaster 90, 101, 137
Jones, Inigo 37, 92, 134
Jordan, Mrs (mistress of William IV) 91, 116, 142

Katherine of Aragon 61, 66, 78, 106, 132, 148
Kensington Gardens 112, 122–3
Kensington Palace 108, 121, 124–6
Kent, William 44, 86, 122, 124, 150
Kerwin, William 97

Kew
  Palace 140–1
  the Queen's Garden 140
  Royal Botanic Gardens 139, 140
  the White House 140
King's Library 108–9
King's Road 116

Lambeth Palace 128, 129
Lauderdale House 102, 110
Le Nôtre, André 30, 132
Leopold of Saxe-Coburg-Saalfeld, Prince 39, 56
Lightfoot, Hannah 81
Llywelyn ap Gruffydd, Prince of Wales 74
London Bridge 76, 78–9
London Zoo 104, 106

The Mall 29, 42–3
  State Opening of Parliament 6, 20–1
Mandarin Oriental Hyde Park Hotel 115
Marble Arch 102, 103
Marble Hill House 145
Margaret of Anjou 130
Margaret, Princess 10, 36, 51, 115
Marie Louise, Princess 38
Marlborough House 36, 39
Mary I, Queen 34, 51, 59, 60, 61, 66, 75
Mary II, Queen 34, 37, 46, 51, 67, 82, 94
Mary of Modena 134
Mary, Queen of Scots 51, 70, 119
Mary, Queen (wife of George V) 39, 82, 104, 115
Matilda, Queen (wife of Henry I) 66, 85
Matilda, Queen (wife of King Stephen) 106
Monmouth, James, duke of 83
Monument 76–7

Nash, John 23, 24, 25, 27, 56, 103
  and Regent's Park 104
National Portrait Gallery 84

Orleans House Gallery 145

Palace of Westminster 30, 52–3, 54
Pall Mall 38, 42, 91
Perrers, Alice 143
Philip, Prince, Duke of Edinburgh 10, 11, 13, 36, 51, 63, 98
Philippa of Hainault 68, 101
Prince Consort Lodge 129

Queen Elizabeth Gate 114
Queen Square 107
Queen Street 81
Queenhithe 66
Queen's Chapel 37
Queen's Gallery 23
Queen's Walk 32

Ranger's House 138
Regent's Park 97, 104-5
    London Zoo 104, 106
Richard II, King 51, 60, 74, 136
    and Richmond Palace 143
Richard III, King 51, 75, 84
Richmond Palace 139, 143
Richmond Park 142
Rotherhithe 137
Rotton Row 115
Royal Albert Hall 120
Royal Botanic Gardens, Kew 139,
    140
Royal Exchange 72, 100
Royal Gun Salutes 19
Royal Maundy Service 18, 19
Royal Mews 27, 86
Royal Observatory, Greenwich 132,
    133
Runnymede 154

St Anne's Church 81
St Bartholomew-the-Great church
    59, 60
St Bartholomew's Hospital 58, 60
St Bride's Church 80, 98
St Dunstan-in-the-West church 97
St George's Church 107
St Giles-in-the-Fields 85
St James's Church 82
St James's Palace 30, 32, 34–5, 36,
    82, 91
St James's Park 28, 30–1, 34, 42

St James's Square 40
St John's, Smith Square 55
St Katharine's Church 106
St Lawrence Jewry 67
St Martin-in-the-Fields 86, 88
St Mary Abbots Church 127
St Mary le Strand church 96
St Mary-le-Bow church 68
St Paul's Cathedral 56, 61–3, 64
St Paul's Church Covent Garden 87
Sarah, Duchess of Marlborough 39
Savoy Chapel 90
Scott, George Gilbert 121, 127
Sedley, Catherine 40, 85
the Serpentine (Hyde Park) 112
Seymour, Edward, Duke of Somerset
    92, 96, 144
Seymour, Jane 63, 148
Simpson, Wallis 104–5
Smithfield Market 60
Soho Square 83
Somerset House 80, 92–4, 96
Sophia Matilda, Princess 138
Spencer House 33
State Opening of Parliament 6, 19,
    20–1, 27, 52
Stephen, King 74, 106
Stone, Nicholas 72
Stuart, James 'Athenian' 33, 130
Syon House 144

Temple Bar 64–5
Temple Church 95
Theatre Royal, Drury Lane 91
Tower of London 48, 56, 73–5
Trafalgar Square 27, 86, 103
Trooping the Colour 6, 19, 44
Tyler, Wat 60

Vanbrugh, Sir John 122, 130
Victoria and Albert Museum 119

Victoria, Queen 81, 140
    Albert Memorial 121
    assassination attempts on 23
    Diamond Jubilee 63
    and the Great Exhibition 113
    Royal Victorian Order 90
    Victoria and Albert Museum 119
Victoria, Duchess of Kent (mother of
    Queen Victoria) 36, 126, 140
Villiers, Barbara, Lady Castlemaine
    150
Villiers, George, Duke of Buckingham
    99

Waterloo Place 41
Westminster Abbey 48–51, 101
    burials 51
    coronations 48, 51
    royal weddings 51
    Stone of Scone 51
William I, King (the Conqueror) 48,
    52, 136
    and the Tower of London 73–4
    and Windsor Castle 152
William II (William Rufus) 52, 61
    and the Tower of London 74
William III, King 37, 46, 51, 67, 94
    statue of 40
William IV, King 24, 36, 39, 79
    statue in King William Walk 132
William, Duke of Cambridge 16, 17,
    36
    christening 26
    wedding 16–17, 51, 115
William, Duke of Gloucester 38
Williamson's Tavern 67
Windsor Castle 144, 152–3
    fire (1992) 150
    Garter Day Ceremony 19, 20
    Round Tower 152
    St George's Chapel 90, 152